Complete Guide to Landscaping

Meredith® Books

Des Moines, Iowa

Getting the Most Out of Your Landscape   **4**

Elements of Your Design   **10**

Making Plans   **27**

Hardscape Design   **41**

Planning for Easy Maintenance   **58**

Designing with Plants   **68**

Plant Selection   **110**

Installing Your Landscape   **186**

GETTING THE MOST OUT OF
Your Landscape

Let your landscape change your life. This book will show you how to design the space outside your home so it's as attractive and useful as the inside. Instead of looking at landscape design as a subject full of intimidating Latin plant names, think of it as a tool that will make your yard work for you.

Your landscape will serve whatever purpose you desire, and the way you use it will help you divide it subtly into separate zones. Those divisions will allow you to achieve several goals at once. One area may be for entertainment, where friends and family gather; another will offer solitude, escape, and relaxation. You may have a play area for the kids and areas for vegetable and flower gardens as well as for storage.

Landscaping can solve day-to-day problems too. It can create privacy where there is none; cool overheated, sunlit rooms; and expand an inadequate parking area. It can also get you off the couch and out of doors—yard work and puttering in the garden are rewarding pastimes. And even if yard work is not suited to you (or vice versa), you'll find yourself wanting to spend more time in the pleasant outdoor environment you've created.

Added value

Landscaping adds value to your home. First impressions are everything, and curb appeal will be an immeasurable asset if you put your house on the market. The connection between house and yard will be immediately apparent to buyers, even though they may not be conscious of it. An attractive landscape says, "This home has been well kept and well loved." Conversely, if you're a buyer, don't overlook the potential of a plain house in a nice neighborhood. It will often prove to be a bargain. Adding landscaping that highlights architectural features and hides flaws can turn an ordinary house into a charmer.

But what about the cost? The well-planned landscape can save you money. When you consider all your options, you can choose the one that's best and build it right the first time. Planning the total environment in advance lets you implement as funds permit, without sacrificing the harmony of your design.

No matter how large or small an area you have to work with, every inch is an opportunity to create a better landscape for your home.

Surrounded by carefully chosen plantings, fencing, and other appointments, this pool suits its cozy space perfectly.

The secrets of design

Good landscaping, however, is more than an enterprise for saving money or adding value to your home. It means more than creating areas of respite and other zones arranged for use. You may hear a landscape designer say, "Let your landscape speak to you," and at first that may sound impractical. But a well-designed landscape is an expression not only of your personality but also the configurations of the land. Where you place the children's play area, for example, or the deck or garden pond should be determined not only by convenience, but also by the way they "fit" your yard. The edgings and transitions that define these spaces and the materials, contours, and plantings that express your style should fit also.

Designing your outdoor space is in many ways not much different from interior design. It is the creation of "living" rooms, with natural or constructed ceilings, walls, and floors, each with its own purpose and decor, each with its own special feeling.

Together these "rooms" make a single statement of your personality within the attributes of space.

Don't leave your design instincts at the back door, but do resist the temptation to "get right to it." You'll need a plan, and creating one begins not with a lesson in horticulture, but with a good working knowledge of the process of design. That's where this book comes in.

You will learn, step-by-step, the same procedure designers use to develop lovely and livable landscapes. You'll start first with some general information that will help you explore possibilities and set your goals. Then you'll be guided through the development of your own design, using a chapter-by-chapter evolution of a plan designed for a real landscape.

So go ahead and let your landscape speak. It can tell you things you've never dreamed of. Developing your own plan is a process, and the journey is exciting. Along the way (and when you're done), you may surprise yourself at just how well you've learned the secrets of design.

What Is Landscape Design?

Landscape design is a four-part process: research, analysis, conceptualization, and the production of working drawings. It is important to follow the steps in sequence, but it's equally important to realize that your best design will emerge from many revisions. Professional designers always rough out several concepts before choosing the best one. In this book, we'll follow their lead.

The landscape design presented throughout this book is one that was prepared by a landscape architect for a family of four. Refer to the illustrations below and in the following pages. You'll see how their plan evolved (and yours will, too) from a rough conglomeration of ideas, needs, and styles into the finished document they would need to build their dream landscape.

Design plan

The *design plan* has several elements, shown below. It starts with a *base map*, the foundation on which all other plans are built, and progresses through several stages to, finally, a *planting plan*.

The *base map* is the skeletal information used in developing other plans. It includes measurements of buildings, trees, property lines and other major features of the landscape. Other plans are often drawn on tracing paper, laid over the base plan, and drawn on regular paper.

Analyze your site

Conducting a *site analysis* is the next step. You'll examine everything from your interior design to existing outdoor conditions. The way the sun hits your yard, where trees create shade, how the surface water flows, views, and wind patterns all affect your use of the yard and will impact where you locate play, garden, and pool areas, for example. Understanding existing conditions will help you modify any areas that need improvement and make the most of natural assets.

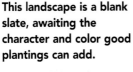

This landscape is a blank slate, awaiting the character and color good plantings can add.

THE LANDSCAPE DESIGN PROCESS

BASE MAP

You'll start by making a Base Map (pages 28–29) that represents your existing property. Measure trees and other features and draw them to scale.

SITE ANALYSIS

Next you'll conduct a Site Analysis (pages 32–33) to mark problem areas, views, access, and the assets of your landscape.

BUBBLE DIAGRAM

Bubble Diagrams (pages 34–35) let you test several schemes for the uses of your yard before you commit to where things go. They will help you examine how each area relates to the others.

CONCEPT DIAGRAM

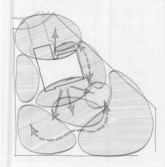

On your Concept Diagram (pages 36–37)—a sketchy drawing based on your favorite Bubble Diagram— you will begin to refine ideas and make notes about features to include in each area.

Analyze your site

Conceptualization is the third phase of design. You'll start by making *bubble diagrams*—quick outlines of areas defined by use—and you'll study how they relate to each other. And you'll play with them, change them around. The more you explore your options, the better your design will be.

The next step is a *concept diagram,* and here you'll explore ideas you sketched on your favorite bubble diagram, adding notes about what is needed to make each zone work—this time more specific.

Although it may seem like a huge leap forward, the *master plan* comes next. You've already laid the foundation for your design. You'll try several versions of each area and fit them together to create your best solution. The designations become more detailed in this stage. The hardscape area in our gracious living zone becomes "Patio" and "Deck" with an overhead arbor connected to the deck. (See page 41.) Plants are shown by general shapes and labels, not specific names. The master plan will be the foundation for detailed drawings and provide a basis for ballpark cost estimates.

Working drawings

Working drawings direct implementation, specifying materials, quantities, sizes, and locations of things you want to add to your landscape. This is where you put things in detail—enough to help you build the features yourself or to obtain bids from contractors. You may also find yourself revising your design as the realities of construction become apparent.

You'll make a *layout plan* to guide construction of hardscape, such as patios, walls, and decks. A *grading and drainage plan* will show how you will shape the land for paving and structures, for play or entertaining, and to add interest to the landscape. A *planting plan* shows quantities, spacing, and location of plants.

Even if you plan to hire a designer to prepare working drawings for you, it is important to understand the guiding principles of design outlined in the following chapters. Design the landscape of your dreams. This book shows you how.

The backyard deck on this project property lacks privacy and the aesthetic support of strategic plantings.

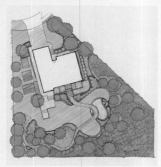

MASTER PLAN

On your Master Plan (pages 38–39) you'll figure out approximate shapes and locations for planting beds and lawn areas, as well as decks, walkways, parking areas, and other hardscape features.

LAYOUT PLAN

A Layout Plan (pages 56–57) is the next step. You'll trace hardscape elements from your Master Plan, including measurements to scale. You can still refine your design at this point.

GRADING PLAN

The changes needed to shape your land to accommodate your new design features—in a detailed Grading and Drainage Plan (pages 194–195).

PLANTING PLAN

On your Planting Plan (pages 108–109) you'll draw in bed lines that show the separation between lawn and planting areas. Then you'll decide where trees go and how to fill planting areas with shrubs, groundcover, and seasonal color.

Landscape Essentials

The rugged stone and lively shrubs make the most of a hillside landscaping challenge.

When it comes to landscaping, use the whole world as your palette. Take a look around you. Study the contours of your land. Look at other landscapes; watch how trees and shrubs make "living" rooms. Make note of materials that appeal to you, the kind of walkways you find attractive. Get to know the plants that thrive in your region, and consider amenities such as fountains, pools, and benches. Ask other gardeners about things you like. The research you do now will help you make decisions when you prepare your plans on paper.

Natural elements

Earth, sky, water, and fire are all elements you may have taken for granted, but each of them can have an effect on your landscape.

The earth itself has a huge influence on design. Landscaping a mountain site, for example, is different from landscaping on the plains. Not only is the terrain of one steep and the other flat, but each has a different soil, and that affects which plants are grown. Rock, stone and boulders are elements of

the earth and can contribute to your landscape.

It's important, of course, that you work with the natural characteristics of your site, but that doesn't mean you can't shape it to suit your needs. Grading can yield gently rolling, tranquil hills or level lawns for active children. Steep slopes can be left wooded or neatly planted with ground cover.

Sky is often "overlooked" because it's always there. But the sky can change your landscape. A broad horizon, for example, makes a spectacular view—you may want to remove trees to make the most of such a vista. On the other hand, a heavily wooded site with only glimpses of the sky can create a sheltered feeling. And on a large, flat, treeless site, the sky may seem overwhelming.

Water can work wonders. Still water is a natural mirror; swimming pools are fun. Moving water adds both sound and motion; like liquid music, a waterfall or fountain can make your landscape a world unto itself.

You may never have thought of fire as an aspect of design. But fire is light, and the play of sunlight and shade will influence the location of play and entertainment areas—as well as what and where you plant. Fire and light can lure you into the landscape when you might otherwise stay indoors. A safe fire (in a fire pit or outdoor fireplace) can warm you in chilly weather, and well-planned lighting can bring you outdoors after dark.

Wildlife—fish, birds, and other animals—may become a part of the landscape, too, especially if your site is near a woods or you add a garden pool to your plans.

Hardscape and touches of style

Hardscape refers to elements that are constructed—decks, arbors, patios, walkways, steps, driveways, planters, walls, and fences. Hardscape materials offer abundant choices that can influence not only landscape construction but also its beauty and its mood.

A pond offers a reflection of the architecture and a natural woodside setting—doubling the visual pleasure.

Loose gravel or river rock, crushed stone or brick, and decomposed granite give surfaces a soft look. Solid materials such as stone, brick, concrete, asphalt, and wood produce a harder, more definite appearance.

The way you use a material will also have a lot to do with the style it yields. For example, irregular stone appears natural and informal; cut stone lends a formal air. Brick mortared in a slab has a regular, permanent look—quite different from the informality of brick laid in sand. Concrete may be left white or may be tinted or its surface patterned. Asphalt is nearly black when new but fades to a weathered gray. Wood has its own appeal, a natural choice for decks and boardwalks.

Don't limit your look at hardscape to the horizontal. All of these materials may be used vertically, as well. You may want to build a wall, an arbor, or a shed for utility storage. Metal has a place in the landscape, too, in trellises and arbors, gates and fences, and in railings and artwork. Rope and chain make rails or vine supports.

Fabric forms umbrellas, blinds, cushions, and awnings—even tents.

Then there are style touches—a garden pond or fountain, a stream with waterfalls, objects such as benches and sculpture, architectural relics, swings, wind chimes, and other items that express your personal style.

Plantings

Plants, of course, are integral to all landscape styles. Trees, shrubs, ground covers, vines, lawns, perennials, and annuals make your choices nearly endless. Plants add color and texture to the landscape and can establish the lines that define your style—in bed lines that curve across your yard or in grids that grow in geometric configurations. Plants can add privacy, frame entrances or views, and make structures look at home. Plants add scale too. A two-story home, for example, may dwarf a person standing beside it, but add a tree or other element of intermediate height, and the proportions feel more human.

When you're planning for plants, add to your research some knowledge of your climate and the conditions in your yard. Every site has limitations, and yours is no

exception; but if you know them, you will choose plants that will thrive in your landscape. Limitations, after all, are only opportunities for design.

A gazebo nestled among a variety of ornamental grasses offers an inviting retreat.

You'll find further information on plants and the other elements of design as you read through the following pages. But be sure you read the entire book before you start making plans on paper. Landscape design, although sequential, is also cyclical. It's a process of revision and refinement; the more you know about each aspect and its relationship to all the others, the more exciting the process will be and the better your design.

The dramatic arch of the low stone wall in this intimate landscape draws the eye on a tour of the lush plantings.

ELEMENTS OF
Your Design

Form follows function is the slogan of good design. Although aesthetics are important in design development, your landscape must be practical as well as pretty. For example, your cobblestone front-door walkway may be beautiful, but if it's too difficult to walk on, your guests may tend to come to the back door. Likewise, a quiet retreat that lacks seating won't get much use. On the other hand, if you locate your outdoor dining area just outside your kitchen door—and make it comfortable—it may prove to be the most popular spot of your home.

A writer's studio looks out on a patio and pond.

From the picket fencing to the walkway crowded with roses to the colors of the house, this landscape expresses a warm and friendly personality.

The low-growing succulents and oversize mounds of ornamental grass perfectly punctuate this modern southwestern landscape.

Design for real living

Let your needs dictate your plans. Then meet those needs with solutions that are both practical and attractive. Adequate, easy parking, for example, is a common goal. But don't stop there; your parking area can be attractive too. Surround your turnaround with a retaining wall, add in fill soil behind it, and plant weeping shrubs that will spill over the top.

Pave a level parking surface with decorative gravel or crushed stone instead of an impermeable material. This is a solution that blends parking with the landscape and may solve drainage problems too. Then with a few small, ornamental trees, separate your new parking area from the entry to your home.

Begin looking at your landscape for all the everyday problems you've never had a chance to solve. They are opportunities for design. For example, are you constantly moving the car to get the lawn mower out? Consider a storage shed to keep the often used landscape equipment and supplies where you can get to them when you need them. Dress it up with trellises and vines to incorporate it into your landscape. A pathway worn in the lawn means there probably should have been a gravel walk or other hardscape path there in the first place.

Now is the time to start thinking about specific areas you want to include in your landscape—that open space for the kids to play, the sunny spot for raising vegetables, and the place for entertaining friends and family. You don't need to make a list now—that can come later. But now is the time to look at the potential of your landscape with an eye toward making it fit your lifestyle.

SMART YARDS

If you choose the right plant for the right place in your yard, you won't end up spending time and resources coaxing it to grow. For example, stop trying to grow grass where it doesn't want to grow. Make plans to fill that bare spot with a shrub-and-groundcover bed or replace it with paving. The idea is to plan ahead to get the most out of your planted landscape. Study plants so you will choose the right ones for the right effect and purpose—and then plant them in conditions where they will thrive. Any effort you expend now in research will pay off in time and money saved later.

Outdoor Comfort

Outdoor comfort should be a priority when you design the exterior of your home. But face it—the great outdoors can sometimes be too hot, too cold, too windy, too wet, and too full of tiny flying things that bite. Don't let nature chase you indoors. There is a whole, big bag of design tricks you can employ to make your outdoor living areas comfortable and inviting.

Planning for sun and shade

Watch how the sun crosses your landscape. Plan to protect western exposures in hot climates and northern exposures in regions that are cold. If your yard will host the neighborhood touch-football league or small-fry soccer, orient the playing fields on a north-south axis to keep the sun out of the players' eyes. Shade can have both a positive and negative impact on the livability of your landscape. It's cool and inviting, but if there's too much of it, it can seem dim and dreary.

Dappled shade will give you the best of both worlds. The honey locust is a classic tree for dappled shade. Its open leaves and branches let in just the right amount of sunlight. Locate shade trees so they cast a shadow on favorite areas when the sun is directly overhead. Trees planted to the east

If they aren't situated in locations to which you have easy, natural access, you won't use the amenities you might like to introduce to your landscape. Porchside seating (above) is a natural; a bench swing draws you into the privacy of this garden escape (right).

An aquatic enthusiast enlists a hot tub for relaxation and a pond and fountain for the soothing sight and sound of water.

STRATEGIC PLANTING FOR COMFORT

Plants can block harsh winds and reduce noise and nighttime glare. Tall, sturdy evergreens along the northwestern edge of your property can knock down bitter winds. Strategically planted trees or shrubs can cut off the glare of headlights shining into windows at night. Combine plants with solid walls for sound barriers. They do double duty—walls block sound and foliage absorbs it.

of your home will reduce the heat of morning sun; trees along the west will cool it in the afternoon. Deciduous species (they lose their leaves during dormancy) will give you summer shade; but when they're leafless, they will let in the warming winter rays. Balance shade with sunny zones for interest and practicality.

Air and water movement

Increase the air circulation across your yard and eliminate stagnant water and you'll do more to reduce the biting insect population than any bug zapper. Consider mounting an exterior ceiling fan to a pergola or a porch to do the bug shooing for you. Latticework with vines offers privacy without blocking breezes.

If you have a water feature in your landscape, water movement will also reduce mosquito breeding. Install a submersible pump; they're sold in kits and are the easiest way to keep the water moving. Remove anything that collects rainwater from your yard; don't have a birdbath unless you're committed to tossing out the water in the basin every few days and replacing it with fresh water. Finally, consider screening a section of your deck or patio.

There is an abundance of sun and shade available in this backyard landscape, as well as a pleasing mix of stone and wood, planted beds and containers.

Privacy

Your home's interior has shared spaces and private spaces, and so should your landscape. Landscape architects frequently rank establishing privacy as a top priority in landscaping projects. That's because they know you're more likely to use your yard in a variety of ways if you don't feel you're on display.

Plan for privacy, and start plants growing where you need them right away. Building fences or walls early on makes it easier to move on to other projects, such as flowerbeds, without incurring construction damage at a later date. Then you can plant around those structures and soften the stark look of new construction.

As you evaluate your privacy needs, consider all possible solutions. Fencing will fix some situations, but plants will work best in others. A fence or hedge along your property line is one solution, but it may not be the best. Carefully placed natural buffers (trees or shrubs) can solve two dilemmas at once: They can screen individual personal areas of your yard and can give them definition at the same time. You can shape your separate garden spaces without feeling too confined by the features that define.

Privacy comes naturally to this outdoor dining area thanks to the backdrop of shrubs and vines that climb the pergola overhead.

SECURITY MATTERS

Privacy and security are not the same thing. A solid fence will make your yard private, but a thief may roam about undetected. Combine solid and see-through fencing for privacy that doesn't sacrifice security. Lights triggered by motion sensors will also intimidate intruders.

The right plant in the right place also enhances security. Correctly selected foundation shrubs will stay below window height with a minimum of pruning. Conversely, plants whose mature height obscures windows and doors can shield break-ins from view. Consider adding thorny or sharp-leafed shrubs beneath first-floor windows to deter intruders. Avoid planting low-limbed trees near your home; they can serve as natural ladders to the upper floors.

Mature trees and plentiful shrubbery allow for an intimate dining area in this urban oasis.

Don't limit your considerations of privacy to merely blocking neighbors' views. Dividing your landscape into outdoor rooms means that you will want to establish a hierarchy of privacy within your landscape similar to your home interior. Just as your bedroom is more private than your living room, your garden will have spaces that are intimate or for alone time and spaces that are more communal.

Planting for privacy

Plants, depending on your selection, can give you either seasonal or year-round privacy. If it's unbroken privacy you need, educate yourself about evergreens. In the plant world, they do the best job of providing continuous screening. Because evergreens such as holly and conifers shed and replace their foliage a little at a time instead of losing them all at once in autumn, they retain plenty of view-blocking greenery even in winter.

Vines are also great for adding privacy. Because they grow up and over (trellises and walls, for example), vines are like living cloaks. Plant a fast-growing annual or tropical vine together with a slower-growing species. You'll get a quick screen that in time will be replaced with one that is permanent.

Total privacy is not always needed, of course. You can achieve degrees of

privacy by mixing deciduous plants in with evergreens. Or, omit the evergreens entirely.

Sometimes the form of a plant is enough to establish a sense of separation between you and other spaces. For example, the trunks and limbs of river birch or aspen provide a feeling of enclosure even when their leaves drop for winter.

Fencing

Different kinds of fences address privacy needs in different ways. Tall wooden fences and solid walls offer the most immediate forms of total privacy. You may need tall fences to screen a courtyard, but shorter fencing will be more appropriate for other areas. For example, in the front yard—usually the most public section of the landscape—waist-high picket fences work well. They define the space but allow for a friendly openness. Open metal fencing can likewise add a decorative touch without completely blocking all views.

Though fences provide quick solutions, they don't grow. But plants do. Combine the two to meet both long- and short-term needs. Wire fencing, though unattractive, will immediately keep children and pets from straying; shrubs, vines, and trees will grow to make them pretty.

A high stucco wall gives both visual privacy and a measure of security to this setting. At the same time, it also gives it a courtyard effect.

Waist-high fencing allows you to define space without inhibiting views.

Outdoor Living

Make the most of your property—bring the activities of the indoors into the outdoors. Don't limit your landscape to a mere collection of plants and other decorations. Your landscape plan can offer you a place for play, a relaxation area, an exercise zone, or fun spots for gathering with friends and family. Think about what you and your family would like to do outside and plan your space to meet these needs. In design circles this step is known as user analysis, and it's only one tool that you can use to tailor the outdoors to better meet your needs.

Connecting indoor and outdoor spaces

Consider the relationship you will be creating between interior and exterior spaces. Design your landscape so that the view through interior windows looks out on garden space instead of dull or unattractive sights. Pleasant views will encourage you to keep the curtains open, letting in more natural light. Interior views that look out on the landscape will also keep the walls from closing in around you, especially in a smaller home.

That limited indoor space can feel more open when the outdoor space is properly designed. Make the transition from indoors to outdoors less abrupt with a design that will move your living space to the outdoors. Stepping through a wide doorway out onto a generous patio "expands" the floor space inside. Consider replacing a narrow stoop with a deck or an inviting porch. If you don't have the space or budget to build an area large enough to throw a party, a landing big enough for a bench and a few planted pots will do nicely for a smaller gathering. It also provides a pleasant spot to enjoy a cup of coffee on a pretty morning—not to mention creating a handy area to park muddy boots or wet umbrellas.

A deck or patio is one of the most efficient ways to expand the amount of your home's usable space for dining or entertaining.

ALL ABOUT FLOW

You may find that simple changes to the interior of your house will improve its indoor/outdoor connection. Sketch the floor plan of your house and label each room. Show the location of doors and windows. Examine the flow of family traffic and how people move in and out of your house. Mark these routes with arrows. Then rearrange the furniture to open views to the outdoors. Create uncluttered paths to doors for easy access to the outdoor landscape.

The entry garden on the page opposite helps visitors transition from the front landscape to the front door. Morning coffee, right, is savored in this comfortable outdoor sunroom.

Beautiful Space

The green swath of lawn lends elegance to this small formal yard.

In nature beautiful space just happens. But when you add a house and hardscape, the native beauty changes. With a knowledge of design elements (the building blocks) and principles (the methods for manipulating them), you'll be able to create space that unifies your needs with natural beauty.

Building on natural beauty

Color, texture, line, and form are the four main elements of design—these are the building blocks.

COLOR is the easiest element to identify but can be the hardest to use well. Because color expresses emotion, it's easy to use too much. The predominant color in your landscape will, of course, be green, and shades of green and hardscape will act as the background for most of your design. Carefully plan your placement of accent color—the fun stuff—against this background so the accents don't get lost or misapplied.

For example, brightly blooming zinnias accent a wall of ivy or a gated garden view. Those same zinnias planted in a garden will not stand out with others in the bed; and if planted at the base of a telephone pole, they call attention to an unattractive feature.

Color impact varies also with its quantity. Dense patches command your view; thin lines are distracting. Limiting colors to a few or sprinkling a single color throughout a mixture of hues creates a unified composition and avoids competing accents.

TEXTURE refers to tactile qualities. Fine-textured plants have many small leaflets, needles, or twigs. Coarse-textured plants have fewer and broader leaves. Pea gravel produces fine-textured surfaces; stones are considered coarse. Fine and coarse textures juxtaposed throughout the landscape add contrasting interest. A smooth, gray stone set in a bed of narrow-leaved mondo grass *(Ophiopogon japonica)* creates a pleasing textural accent in a composition whose colors are unremarkable. Use textural contrasts, like their color counterparts, sparingly for best results.

LINE describes visual paths in a composition. Tree trunks contribute vertical lines. Level ground establishes the horizontal. Lines can be curved (separating sinuous planting beds from paving) or straight (setting off angular walkways from the lawn). You don't have to limit your design to only one type; but when you combine types, let one kind dominate. For example, a landscape with curved bed lines may successfully include a square patio, but the curved bed lines are dominant to straight lines and right angles.

FORM is, simply, shape. The form of a plant—upright, pendulous, pyramidal, or spreading—describes its growth habit, and like the other elements, form lends itself to complement and contrast. For example, plants with pendulous forms, such as weeping willow *(Salix babylonica),* often

The bed of purple and red flowers, the warm brick walkway, and the formal style of the weathered bench create a winning combination of shapes and colors.

look wonderful alongside garden ponds. The vertical branches contrast with the horizontal plane of water.

Composing the landscape

Though many parts make up the whole, your design will be more successful if you view it and design it with the following principles—not as a collection of single elements, but as a harmonious composition.

UNITY ties things together, and repetition, rhythm, and sequence are the tools you'll use to create it. Repeating an element—color, texture, line, or form—is an easy way to give a scene a unifying theme. The same brick paving in both a patio and a path unites the hardscape with repeated color and shape. Repetition can be rhythmic or random. Rhythmic patterns are regular and create a sense of expectation—finials spaced evenly on fence post tops, for example. A random scattering of white blossoms throughout your flower beds unifies them informally. Sequence conveys movement from one stage to another. Your landscape style may begin with formal design near the house and become less formal at the end of your yard. Unity is maintained by the gradual progression of styles.

BALANCE in a landscape is what makes things look and feel comfortable. Balance can be symmetrical (straight lines, right angles, and mirror-image arrangements) or asymmetrical (curved lines, irregular shapes, and casual composition). If it's symmetry you want (it's almost always formal), repeat an element in even-numbered groupings. For asymmetrical design, plan odd-numbered groupings and use dissimilar items for balance. For example, a single, large tree can balance a bed of numerous and varied small shrubs.

ACCENT is the spice of design. Any element can become an accent if it contrasts with its surroundings. Accents may be as small as a blossom or as large as a bright red footbridge. But remember to place them where you want to draw attention—they are often best placed against a neutral background. The front door is a good place to start. So is the far end of a walkway; your guests will follow

it to see what's there. Think in terms of multiple accents—contrasts of both color and texture, for example—to add interest to your landscape. Sprinkle them with care, though, so they won't compete, confuse, or cause scenic overkill.

Brilliantly colored flowers stand out against a brightly painted structure.

The shaped shrubs midground speak to the formal lines of the greenhouse in the background.

Style

S tyle is the presentation of design. Landscape design may assume all sorts of different styles but can be broadly categorized as either formal or informal. Examine landscapes that appeal to you and try to distinguish among styles so you'll know what you like. Different styles may be appropriate for different areas of your landscape. For example, you may choose a formal style for your front yard and a more relaxed approach for the backyard.

The formal

Formal designs use visual cues to create a sense of expectation, much in the same way the sight of a tuxedo signals an elegant event. In landscape design, symmetry is one such cue, and matched pairs are one way of establishing symmetry.

Pairs instantly add a formal touch. A pair of urns, for example, will lend a stately air to your front steps. A pair of plants frames whatever is beyond it. Two of the same item become an instantly recognizable unit, even if the items are not placed side by side.

Even-numbered groupings create this same effect. The pattern of expectation is regular, orderly, and at rest. Geometric shapes—clearly defined circles, squares, rectangles, singly or in combinations— also establish formality. To create formality in your own plan, consider introducing these shapes in arches, paving patterns, fences, and bed designs.

SENSE OF PLACE

Make your landscape design seem at home in its site, rather than imposed upon it. Geographic regions have a great influence on style, and using materials indigenous to your region helps your landscape fit in with its surroundings. Borrowing styles from other areas can add flavor and accent to your design, but maintain a sense of balance when incorporating elements from other regions. Borrow things that you like; but unless your goal is to replicate a foreign environment, take care to preserve a natural, authentic sense of place.

Manicured beds and lawn, planted pedestals, cut-stone patio and walkways give the impression of an estate garden.

Informal doesn't mean unintentional. The rough stone steps, rustic twig bench, and carefree profusion of flowers are quite purposefully designed to work together.

The informal

Informal design strives for the unexpected and creates a casual yet balanced mood. Odd-numbered groupings—perhaps a cluster of three ornamental shrubs growing in a groundcover bed—keep the design dynamic. Consider adding triangles to your design. Three trees planted at different points on an invisible triangle along a walkway provide canopies without the formality of even-numbered rows. This trick works for any odd-numbered plant groupings as well, and repetition of elements in informal design schemes doesn't have to follow a regular pattern.

Complements, contrasts, and combinations

The architecture of a home often influences landscape style. An imposing federalist house with stately columns may be complemented by a formal landscape design. A quaint cottage may be the perfect setting for curving paths bordered by informally mixed plantings. However, the style of the house does not have to dictate what is expressed in the landscape. In fact, a contrasting style on the grounds can soften the dominant presence of the

architecture, but the landscape design overall must be clearly formal or informal. Don't settle for something in between: The resulting ambiguity will look like a mistake.

That's not to say that formal and informal designs cannot contain elements of their opposites. There's nothing quite like rounding a bend to discover a tidy pocket of something orderly and formal growing neatly within a naturalistic landscape. Mixed styles require planning, however. For example, formal walkways combined with informal beds can be charming. The trick to succeeding with any cross of styles is to know what you're after—and to be careful to transition smoothly between styles.

Study photographs of gardens that appeal to you to see what style is just right. Then you can apply the elements and principles of design in the style you find appropriate.

A patio chessboard adds whimsy to a sculpted landscape.

Planting for the Seasons

A Japanese maple commands the landscape stage in autumn.

White hydrangea and magenta azalea and allium light up the early summer garden.

Flowering quince and forsythia announce spring with colorful fanfare.

Winter frosts the leaves of a *helleborus argutifolius.*

Each season brings its own distinct beauty to the landscape. Plan ahead to use color, form, and texture as seasonal highlights in your landscape.

Color is an easy way to enhance your landscape throughout the season. Flowers put on the most obvious seasonal show. Spring is just the beginning; summer and fall boast blossoms too. In warmer climates a winter garden can be just as colorful as any spring display. Fruits are also natural decorations. Many berries ripen in fall and winter, and their clusters brighten snowy scenes. Seedpods and other fruit add color interest throughout the year.

Don't forget the leaves—foliage color has a huge impact on landscape design. Variegated foliage (with more than one color on each leaf) ranges across the spectrum. You'll find plants with leaves and needles ranging from white to yellow to nearly blue and endless shades in between.

Form and texture come into their own when plants are dormant. Winter landscape is like a black and white photo; shapes and tactile qualities dominate. Bark, trunks, and branches take on sculptural qualities, especially when coated with ice or snow.

Try combining evergreen and deciduous plants for a year-round show. The dark foliage and pleasing shapes of evergreens provides the perfect complement to color during warm seasons and shows off the form of leafless plants in winter. Evergreens shouldn't just do background duty. Plant them for year-round beauty.

Instant Beauty

It's a great idea to have large, shady trees along a landscape border in your design, but trees take years to mature. Meanwhile, little saplings are not attractive. It is possible, however, to get things growing and still plant for the future. For example, plant paper birches in front of beeches on a border. The bark of the birches will be immediately beautiful and provide the right companionship for the slower-growing beeches. You'll have focal points for now and for the future.

River birch is a fast-growing tree that can provide shade and vertical definition while you wait for slower-growing hardwoods. Red maple is also quick for shade. Many small ornamental trees such as cherries and crape myrtles can make a big difference in just a few growing seasons. Or plant ornamental shrubs in front of a grove of saplings. The shrubs will attract your attention until the trees claim their place.

Vines and flowers can quickly change a part of the landscape with a profusion of color and texture. For instance, ivies and climbing roses can dress up a landscape in a hurry. Most vines can grow at double or triple the rate of other woody plants, giving gardens quick appeal while new trees and shrubs are getting started. It doesn't take years and years to grow flowers.

Plant some perennials in your garden. In just one season, you can have a blanket of blossoms.

Planting big, mature trees is another way to give your landscape a new look right

Load up hanging planters and patio pots with bright blooming annuals for immediate gratification.

Vigorous vines like Virginia creeper make quick work of covering a bare wall or fence.

away. Tree spades can dig large specimens that have been root-pruned in advance. Big trees can cost a lot, as you pay plenty for the size of the plant and equipment and labor to move it. If you can't afford big trees, don't worry—plant a small one. Time and patience will prove that all trees of the same species end up approximately the same size at maturity, regardless of their size when planted.

River birch grow swiftly and can provide shade and vertical interest while you wait for slower-growing trees to mature.

Brainstorming Your Design

Nothing could be more basic and functional than the walkway leading to your front door, but decorative stone and colorful pattern make something simple something special.

What you want

Make a list of 10 to 15 things you've always wanted in your landscape—regardless of budget concerns. Let your imagination run wild at this point. Now is the time to jot down all of those things you've seen in books and magazines that you would love to have in your yard. Don't judge your choices as you're making this list, just allow your ideas to flow.

List major elements of style (such as a formal gated entryway into your yard) and things you want for decoration (a waterfall or a sundial). When you're finished, rank them in the order of their importance to you. For example, if you've always wanted a reflecting pool like your grandmother had, that might be higher on the list than an herb garden.

Get everyone in the family involved. Ask family members to produce their own lists and to rank them also. Then combine all the lists into a single list. You may see items that are similar on the different lists, such as a specific area to play games or a patio for cookouts. These items go to the top of the list and the remaining items are ranked in order of importance to the family.

A good landscape lets you express your style and meets your needs through the skillful use of materials, shapes, color, and plantings.

Now it's time to do some serious thinking—to transform the results of all your research and ideas into the steps that will make the landscape work for you.

You'll need to make several lists, first a list of the things you've always wanted in your landscape. Second, you'll make a list of those things you really need in your landscape. You'll combine the two lists, refine them, and finally draw up a master list of components for your design plan.

What you need

Now make your needs list—those things that are necessary to you in your landscape. For example, perhaps you need more parking or to camouflage an air-conditioning unit. Don't forget to consider indoor needs too. You may need additional privacy at one window or more natural light from another. Rank your needs as you did your wishes. Have everyone in the family make a similar needs list and combine them all into a single list, ranking the items in order of importance.

Next, compare the two lists. Are any of your wants and needs similar? Your want list may contain a stone patio, and that will meet the need you listed for "entertainment area." Match as many items on the two lists as possible and put stars by them.

Now look at what's left on the two lists (items that don't have stars). There are probably plenty of needs such as garbage can storage that aren't included on your want list, and vice versa. Are there any wants you would sacrifice in order to meet needs? If there's something you really want that doesn't meet a specific need, keep that idea on the list anyway. You can try to find a way to make it fit into your landscape, or you can omit it later. Eliminate those things everyone agrees are least important. Then combine the surviving wants and needs and rank them by consensus. The resulting list will be the foundation for your budget decisions and will guide you as you begin to put your plans on paper.

Making choices

Take a hard look at the components of your design plan. Chances are the combined items on your list exceed your budget, but there may be ways to modify your ideas to include as much as you can in the landscape.

Though you can't obtain accurate cost estimates until you produce a master plan, look for money-saving ideas now. Take "sitting area with outdoor fan," for example. If your budget can't stretch to include an outdoor porch with a ceiling fan, can you settle for a sitting area in the yard underneath a shady tree? If any such major installation is beyond your budget right now but it's important to you, go ahead and plan its future location. You may be able to build it later on.

Use your list as a guide—you probably won't actually implement every item. Some things on your list won't be appropriate to your site. Others will be perfect. Be objective. Refer to your list when you need help making decisions as you begin to create your landscape plan.

Comfort, convenience, and easy-going style are key in this patio landscape.

Designing on paper enables you to examine the relationships between different areas of your yard without belaboring the details that come later in the process, such as choosing materials and plants for your landscape.

Making Plans

Just as homes are built from detailed house plans, a successful landscape is just as dependent on a carefully executed, written landscape plan.

What you've learned so far has already gotten you started in the landscape design process. Now for the fun part: You're going to learn how to "think on paper." You'll start making your own plan by tracing a base map of your property. Then you'll plan the use of your existing spaces by producing overlay drawings known as bubble diagrams. Next, you'll expand your favorite bubble diagram to create a concept diagram, which forms the basis for your master landscape plan.

Testing your possibilities on paper

Revision is a natural part of the design process. Capturing your ideas on paper makes it easy to consider all the possibilities while you can still easily change your mind. If you aren't an accomplished artist, don't worry; there's no need to produce a pretty plan. Scribble, erase, and cross things out as much as you like. Nothing is set in stone; that's why you design on paper before you start setting the stones!

Until you can view your site and its major features, such as your house and driveway, it is impossible to decide what should go where and how much room you have to work with. To find this information, you'll begin by making a base map that accurately represents your property. You can use the plot plan that you received in the closing documents when you bought your home, but you'll need to enlarge it. (See page 28.)

Plot plans are normally small drawings that fit on a letter-size sheet of paper. They are drawn to scale, meaning that an inch equals a certain number of feet. The scale of the plan tells you how to read its dimensions. For example, the notation 1" = 10' means that every inch on your plan represents 10 feet in "real life." Your plan may be drawn at 20 scale (1" = 20'), 30 scale, etc. The scale you are working with will be noted on the plan.

The word "scale" also refers to a special kind of ruler called an engineer's scale. Learning how to use an engineer's scale will allow you to accurately represent landscape features on paper. You'll also be able to determine how many plants will fit in a certain area of your yard. And, because you'll have a good idea of quantities needed, you can figure out approximately how much your landscape will cost before you buy the first plant.

You'll also be able to determine the workability of other features you are considering, such as patios, swimming pools, and walkways, and alter your plan as needed.

PLANNING TOOLS

These can be found at any art supply store:
- Engineer's scale
- Roll of tracing paper
- 2 circle templates, ranging from ¼" to 3½" in diameter
- Thick and thin black felt-tipped pens
- Pencils and an eraser

READING AN ENGINEER'S SCALE

The easiest way to read your plan dimensions accurately is with an engineer's scale. This is a triangular ruler that has inches divided into different increments, each representing a different length. For example, on the side of the scale that is marked 10, an inch is divided into 10 equal parts. Each part is equivalent to 1 foot. Half an inch equals 5 feet, 2 inches equal 20 feet, and so on. Use this side if your drawing is labeled 1" = 10'. Use other sides of the ruler to measure plans drawn at other scales

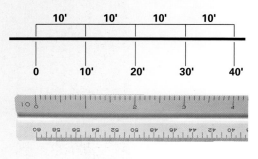

SCALE: 1" = 10'

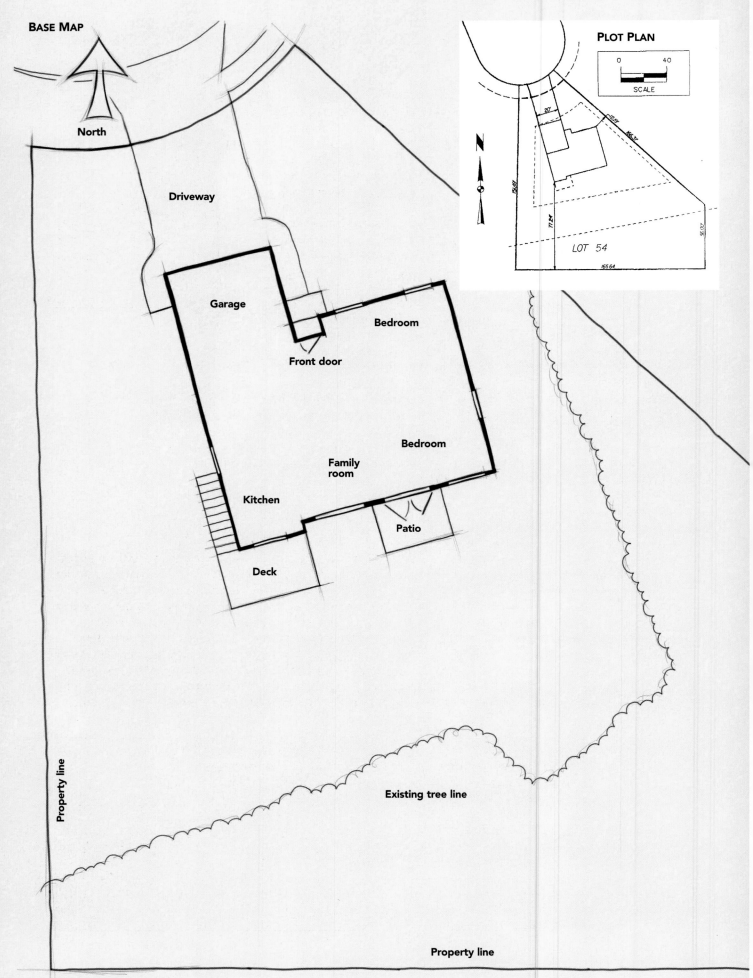

BASE MAP

North

Driveway

Garage

Front door

Bedroom

Bedroom

Family room

Kitchen

Patio

Deck

Property line

Existing tree line

Property line

PLOT PLAN

SCALE

0   40

LOT 54

Develop a Base Map

Mapping your property is the first step in designing a landscape plan. A base map will show property lines, existing structures, paving, and trees; anything that is going to remain the way it is will be represented on your base plan. You'll also indicate on your base map any existing trees you plan to remove. This base plan will be the foundation for other traced drawings you'll develop in later stages of the design.

Start with the plot plan prepared by a surveyor when you purchased your home. This is usually on notebook-size paper—too small for sketching ideas. Take your plot plan to a reprographics store for enlarging. Here's what to do:

1. Take an engineer's scale with you. Make a same-size photocopy of your plot plan, preserving your original. Draw a dark 1-inch-long line in the center of your photocopy. Look at the scale of your plot plan. If one inch equals 30 feet, label your line 30 feet. If the scale of your plan is 1"= 40', label your line 40 feet. This line is necessary to check the accuracy of your enlargement.

2. Circle the drawing of your property, excluding the title and all excess space. The circled portion is the image area.

3. Ask the store to make an enlargement for you. To save money, explain that you need only the image area enlarged to fit on a 24×36-inch sheet of paper. Stress that the enlargement must be to scale. It's generally best to request 1"=10' scale.

4. Ask that the copy be made on bond paper; vellum costs more and isn't necessary for this project. Explain that it's okay if the enlargement is on several separate sheets of paper, as long as the image overlaps. You can tape pages together and trace a composite later.

5. Check the scale of your enlargement before leaving the shop. The 1-inch line you drew on your photocopy is now longer on your enlargement, but dimensions should still be proportional. Turn your engineer's scale to the side that matches the scale you requested. Measure your enlarged line. It should reflect the same dimension you labeled earlier. If your original drawing was at a 40 scale, your 1-inch line represented 40 feet. On the reproduction at 10 scale, the line you drew should now be 4 inches long, but it still represents 40 feet. You now have a larger drawing, but all the proportions are the same. Take your enlargement home and add the measurements of existing features. This is your base plan.

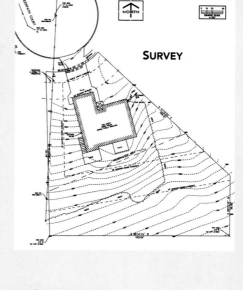

SURVEY

MAPPING TREES

Show existing plantings such as trees on your base map. Use a tape measure to measure items from a fixed point shown on your plot plan. Always measure in two directions to confirm approximate locations. Use your engineer's scale to replicate these dimensions on your plan. Use a circle template to draw a circle that represents the tree. Label circles if you know tree names; if not, describe with simple notes such as "nice shade tree," "damaged tree," or "young tree." Note whether the tree keeps its leaves in winter or loses them to help you map out them and note that too.

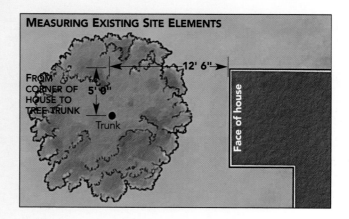

MEASURING EXISTING SITE ELEMENTS

FROM CORNER OF HOUSE TO TREE TRUNK   5' 9"   12' 6"

Trunk

Face of house

Know Your Assets and Problems

This view from the front door is flat, plain, and focused only on neighboring houses.

It's time to look at your property as if you were visiting for the first time. You're going to determine the existing advantages and shortcomings. This is the first step in creating your site analysis.

Take notes of site assets and problems from front yard to back. Translate all of these observations to a "problems and assets list." Include all areas of the property-side yard too. (See the sample list on page 31.) This list will form the basis of your site analysis.

A fresh look

Start with a look from the road to see the first impression your property makes. Work your way up the driveway and then to the front door. Is it clear which door guests should enter? Is the walk to that door comfortable, convenient, and inviting or dull, colorless, and narrow? Then pay attention to the route your family takes into the house. Your landscape should welcome the people who live there each day as well.

Take pictures

Next, take pictures of your yard. The camera is less forgiving than your own eyes. It's easy for you to overlook things you see every day; you'll be surprised how much the photos call attention to unsightly details. It's also easier to think objectively when studying photographs.

Stand across the street and take panoramic shots of your front yard. Hold the camera at the same level while clicking shots and overlap them slightly. Be sure to include the house in the photos. Tape the developed pictures together to form a composite view of what your home looks like to neighbors and passersby. You may be surprised to discover that there's a clear view from the street right into your living room. Or you may have never noticed how unattractive your garbage cans are. Sometimes making cosmetic improvements is as easy as removing that pile of scrap lumber you've come to ignore.

Take pictures of other areas of the yard too. Pay attention to views seen from windows and exterior sitting areas. Photograph existing features as well as the areas you see as problems. Most design professionals use this technique to analyze the site and design the best solutions. It is helpful to be able to glance at a photograph of trees in your yard when working on your plans. All those dots you carefully plotted on your base map will be more useful if you have a handy visual reminder of the real thing.

Photos will help you evaluate the features of your home. Perhaps you'll see your porch is an architectural asset, but the side of your garage is nothing more than a blank, windowless wall. This information will help you design a landscape that will play up good features and minimize flaws.

Paths and access

As you study the photographs, consider access to and from your house. Do interior and exterior spaces relate? For instance, does your living room open onto an outdoor entertaining area? Is there a fresh-air dining spot close to the kitchen? Now look at routes through your landscape. Are there areas of your yard that you never visit because they are hard to reach? Is it easy to get from the front yard to the back? Are there paths leading to nowhere? Are walkways wide enough to walk two abreast? Include this information in your inventory.

The existing deck offers a nice rear view of the woods, but the view to the side looks onto the neighbors' home. More privacy is needed.

Don't forget your assets

Don't get so discouraged with the problems of your yard that you overlook its potential. Note good views, attractive plants, healthy lawn areas, spots with established privacy, level places, slopes, and areas of sun and shade in morning and afternoon. Be sure to list good features of your house, too, such as attractive windows, convenient exterior doors, chimneys, and pretty trim or rails.

Your inventory will prove valuable as you translate the flaws and opportunities of your landscape to your site analysis. This analysis is the next step in developing your plan, and it will guide you through the evolution of design ideas. Use the sample list below as a guide.

Site analysis will help identify problems, such as bad drainage, steep stairs, and toxic weeds.

PROBLEMS AND ASSETS LIST

Area of Yard	Problems	Assets
Front yard	Easy to pass by house, nothing distinctive about first impression Lack of color Front door seems to recede Needs foundation planting No trees—house seems too tall Run-on lawn	Healthy lawn Level yard Bay window Angled lot sets house away from neighbors (not in a row) Sunny Tidy new home has fresh look
Western side yard	Slope makes it difficult to go around house Access to deck steps through lawn, no hard surface No destination—no reason to visit the side yard No separation from neighbor's yard Lack of vertical interest; no trees and few windows on side of house	Healthy lawn Access to deck Spacious Sunny
Backyard	Underside of tall deck dominates yard Minimal sitting area Lacks interest near house—no plants except lawn No destinations—no reason to leave existing patio or deck Poison ivy in woods limits exploring Mowing a slope No privacy on western side	Excellent view: beautiful woods along back of property with good natural vegetation Existing wildlife feeding station French doors open onto existing patio Pretty view from deck off of kitchen Healthy lawn Interesting topography: level by house, sloping down to lawn and woods Privacy along three sides (north, south, and east) Southern exposure allows winter sun while house blocks winter winds No glare—do not have to look into sun to view woods Pleasantly sunny, with some shadows cast by woods Native wildflowers along edge of woods Pleasant sound of breeze through trees
Eastern side yard	Inconvenient to walk around house Excess lawn—mowing an area that isn't used	Private Plenty of room

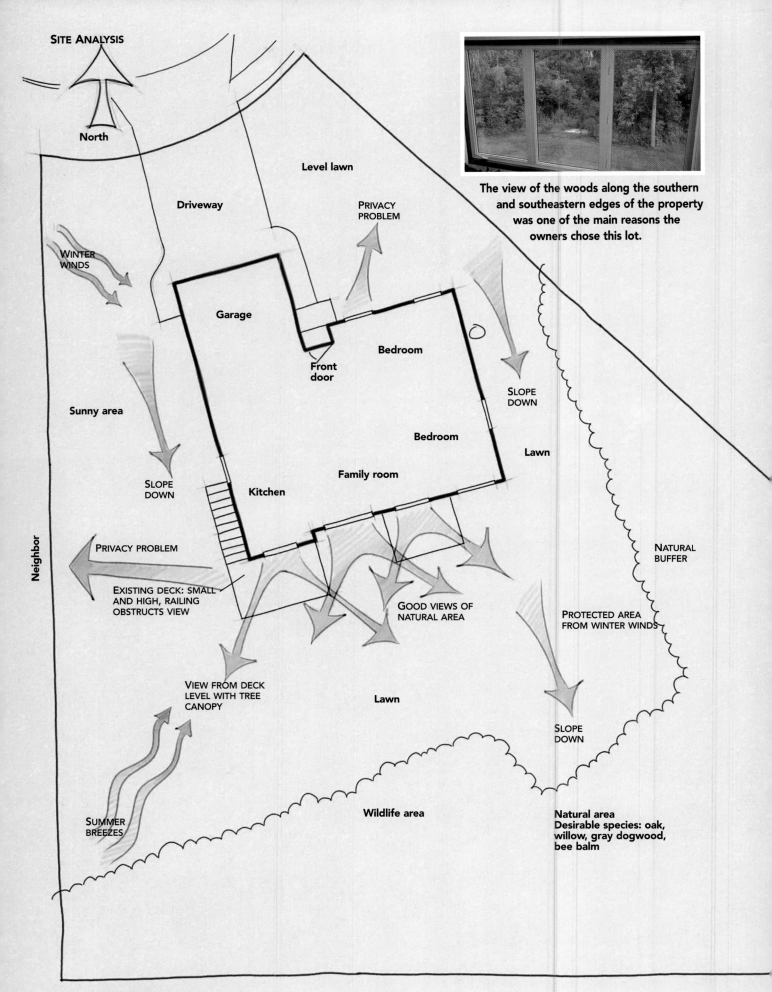

SITE ANALYSIS

North

Driveway

Level lawn

PRIVACY PROBLEM

WINTER WINDS

Garage

Bedroom

Front door

Sunny area

SLOPE DOWN

Bedroom

SLOPE DOWN

Lawn

Family room

Kitchen

PRIVACY PROBLEM

NATURAL BUFFER

Neighbor

EXISTING DECK: SMALL AND HIGH, RAILING OBSTRUCTS VIEW

GOOD VIEWS OF NATURAL AREA

PROTECTED AREA FROM WINTER WINDS

VIEW FROM DECK LEVEL WITH TREE CANOPY

SLOPE DOWN

Lawn

SUMMER BREEZES

Wildlife area

Natural area
Desirable species: oak, willow, gray dogwood, bee balm

The view of the woods along the southern and southeastern edges of the property was one of the main reasons the owners chose this lot.

Analyze Your Site

Completing the inventory of assets and problems will get you thinking about the condition of your existing landscape. Now you can transfer those thoughts to your plan to make a graphic representation of what is good and bad about your yard. This makes it easier to see what you need to consider when designing your new landscape plan.

Spread out your base map and unroll enough tracing paper to cover it. Trace existing items—property lines, the outline of your house, existing paving, structures, and trees—from your base map. This duplicate will become your site analysis. (Always keep a clean version of your base map.) Refer to our sample site analysis for examples and transfer items from the inventory to this map. Put labels on the approximate location of each item or condition. Use arrows to indicate patterns of access, views, and slopes, labeling each. After you've gone through your notes, take your plan outside and see if you missed anything. Add any new observations to the site analysis by writing right on the page.

Now take a look at what you've created. For the first time you have an emerging picture of what your yard looks like. Having a drawing of your site lets you examine your property from a bird's-eye view.

Look at the relationship between spaces. Is your parking area near the door you use most often? You may realize that you have incompatible zones of use side by side. For example, the area right outside the master bedroom is probably not the best place for a dog run. Can you see garbage cans when you sit on your patio or deck? Then you may need to move your utility area. What kind of view do you see from your front door?

Add additional notes, circles, and arrows as needed to show how existing zones of the house and yard work together or clash. Your yard may be completely lacking any definition of zones and may form, instead, a single, run-on space. Note that as well.

Without distinctive landscaping, the garage and driveway are the dominant features of this home.

Not only is the view from this window unappealing, but the easy view in from the outside creates a privacy issue that landscaping can help solve.

No continuity exists between the front and back yards. Instead the walkway drops off abruptly.

Sketch it Out

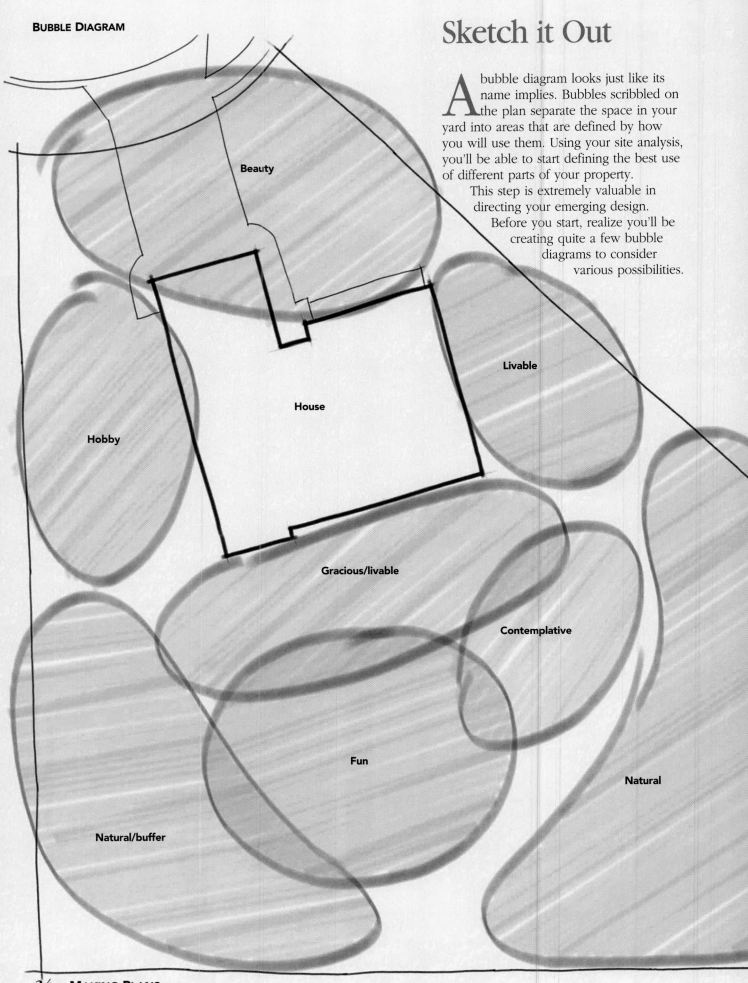

A bubble diagram looks just like its name implies. Bubbles scribbled on the plan separate the space in your yard into areas that are defined by how you will use them. Using your site analysis, you'll be able to start defining the best use of different parts of your property.

This step is extremely valuable in directing your emerging design.

Before you start, realize you'll be creating quite a few bubble diagrams to consider various possibilities.

Beauty

Livable

Hobby

House

Gracious/livable

Contemplative

Fun

Natural

Natural/buffer

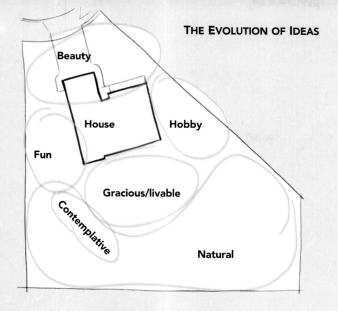

Lay tracing paper over your base map and again quickly trace the basic information (property lines, house, driveway, existing decks, patios, or walkways).

Pin your site analysis on a wall nearby so it will be a handy reference. You will find that some conditions of your property dictate that a zone be used in a specific way. Other areas will be changed to accommodate your ideas. For example, for this project, the wooded area was preserved as a natural zone. But the area immediately adjacent to the back of the house was picked as a spot to be developed for gracious living. Slide your site analysis beneath your bubble diagram to get a better idea of how your proposed uses match assets (or will solve problems) in your landscape.

Let the ideas flow

Relax and expect to use a lot of tracing paper. That's the best way to draw bubble diagrams. Draw as quickly as you think. Remember, the purpose of this step is to examine relationships between proposed zones of use with each other and with existing conditions. Careful drawing isn't necessary: It takes longer, slowing down the freedom of thought and the evolution of ideas. Besides, nice drawings are hard to discard. Don't limit yourself to a particular plan just because you spent a long time drawing it. Draw bubbles that are loose and abstract, not shaped like a deck or a pool or a flower bed, and keep searching for the best solution.

Divide your entire site into zones. There's no hard and fast rule about what goes where, so allow yourself to experiment. Each bubble represents an area of the exterior space. Areas are defined by use, not by future content.

For example, don't try to figure out exactly where to put a patio at this stage; decide where the best place is for an entertaining area. You may end up deciding the best, most practical spot for entertaining is an area that is too steep for a patio. So your ultimate solution may be a deck not a patio, but if you'd spent all your time looking for patio spots, you might not have considered this solution.

Evaluate each drawing in terms of how well each use relates to each other and to the site. For instance, your more public areas, such as entertaining and fun areas, can be next to each other and work well together. More private areas, such as contemplative areas, work better near a buffered area where it will be quieter. Look at how your zones work with the site as well. For example, by locating the contemplative area on the edge of the woods in the sample bubble diagram, the designer borrows from the site's natural beauty but still locates it within view of the house.

Rearrange bubbles to try various schemes. Evaluate your diagrams by examining how the proposed zones of use relate to your home. An early bubble diagram (above left) for the sample project placed the Contemplative area too close to the neighbors; a later diagram (above right) discovered a better location, facing the widest existing natural area. The Hobby zone was also relocated to the sunny side of the house for better fruit- and vegetable-growing conditions. The Fun area was moved from the side yard on an earlier plan to the backyard so it would take advantage of an open lawn area and relate better to the entertaining (Gracious) area. The final, fine-tuned bubble diagram is on the page opposite.

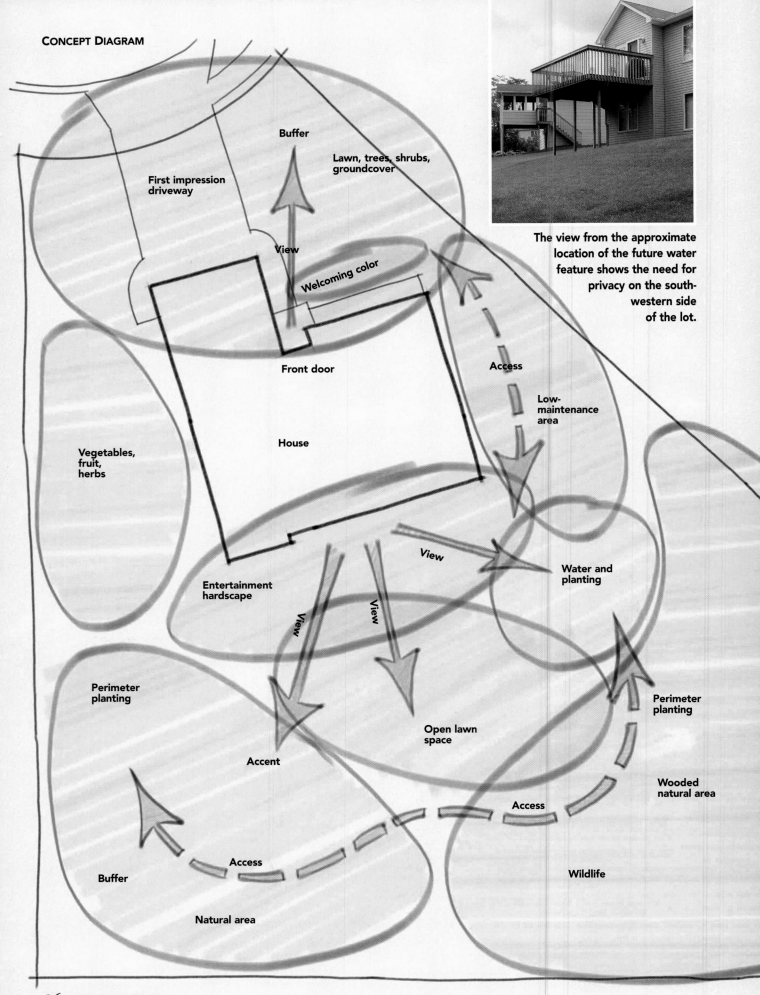

Buffer

Lawn, trees, shrubs, groundcover

First impression driveway

View

Welcoming color

The view from the approximate location of the future water feature shows the need for privacy on the southwestern side of the lot.

Front door

Access

Low-maintenance area

House

Vegetables, fruit, herbs

View

Water and planting

Entertainment hardscape

View

View

Perimeter planting

Perimeter planting

Open lawn space

Accent

Wooded natural area

Access

Access

Buffer

Wildlife

Natural area

Define Your Concepts

I t's time to add another layer of detail to your plan—this time with a concept diagram. First, choose your favorite bubble diagram. Now that you've figured out what zones you want the exterior space divided into (and what purpose each area should serve), you can start applying design ideas to your spatial scheme.

It's important to continue thinking generally. For example, you may know you want to include both hardscape and planting in your entertainment area; note that on the appropriate bubble. Jot simple notes on your concept diagram to develop similar ideas for each of your proposed zones of use.

Connect your bubbles with arrows to show where you think traffic will naturally flow, where walkways should be built, and what views need to be considered. Do your bubbles satisfy these needs? If not, you may need to rearrange them again. Remember, there's a lot of tracing paper on a roll. Use what it takes. Keep trying until you get a set of spaces you like and some rough ideas about how to fill those spaces.

Now it's time to explore the options you have to fill the space within each area. The concept design has solidified your intentions for each space around the yard, but there are still decisions to be made about the actual content.

For instance, if you've labeled an area on your concept diagram as contemplative, consider what features may work within that zone. It may be as simple as a place to sit. Now is the time to "try on for size" a bunch of different scenarios so you can see which will work best for your purposes. On our project, the designer decided to add a water feature in the contemplative area for its reflective and soothing qualities. By locating the contemplative area on the edge of the woods, we are borrowing from the site's natural beauty but still locating it within view of the house. Water in this location will also attract wildlife. In this case, a pond is the water feature. What has been done is to transform what began as a bubble scribbled on a sheet of paper into a workable plan for the creation of a peaceful sanctuary.

During this stage, take the time to explore your options by trying out a variety of possibilities. Take into consideration your lifestyle, your budget, and your original program plan and you may just find the perfect combinations to fit your needs.

The healthy, level lawn is a plus. All it needs is trees, shrubs, and seasonal color to brighten and soften this entrance area.

The expanse of bare wall is an aesthetic challenge, while the lack of connection between the front drive and rear deck is a practical one.

Create a Master Plan

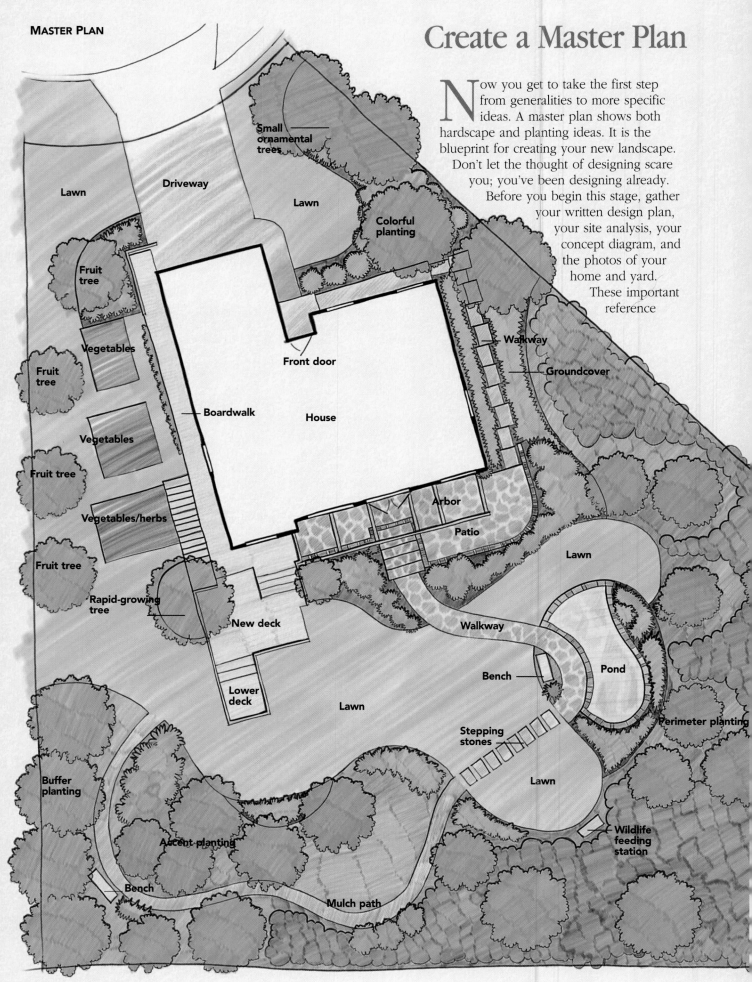

Now you get to take the first step from generalities to more specific ideas. A master plan shows both hardscape and planting ideas. It is the blueprint for creating your new landscape. Don't let the thought of designing scare you; you've been designing already. Before you begin this stage, gather your written design plan, your site analysis, your concept diagram, and the photos of your home and yard.

These important reference

Lawn

Driveway

Small ornamental trees

Lawn

Colorful planting

Fruit tree

Vegetables

Fruit tree

Vegetables

Fruit tree

Vegetables/herbs

Fruit tree

Rapid-growing tree

Boardwalk

Front door

House

Walkway

Groundcover

Arbor

Patio

Lawn

Walkway

New deck

Bench

Pond

Lower deck

Lawn

Stepping stones

Perimeter planting

Lawn

Buffer planting

Accent planting

Wildlife feeding station

Bench

Mulch path

tools will guide you in the decision-making process. Producing a master plan combines what you've learned so far to produce a whole plan. You've already done a lot of legwork on your design and probably have some definite ideas about how to use the elements and principles of design to help you solve problems.

Lay your concept diagram over your site analysis and place a clean sheet of tracing paper on top of both. The combined layers of information give you a clear idea of what problems you need to solve (that blank, windowless garage wall), what assets you should highlight (frame a pretty window with plants), how you should divide the space into zones of use, and how these zones relate to one another. To get started, choose a zone delineated by a bubble on your concept diagram.

Hardscape first

Start by figuring out hardscape solutions. The underlying layers of information will help you choose locations and shapes for patios, decks, parking areas, landings, water features, and walkways. Use your engineer's scale to sketch your ideas. Plan your projects around trees you want to keep. Label trees that must be removed with an "×" in a small circle.

Examine the site analysis notes that apply to each area. Sketch out rough ideas for filling the space on your plan, as if you were in an airplane above your property looking down. Think about solutions that both meet your needs and fulfill your wants.

If you think you want a deck, don't draw careful deck plans. Instead, take the ideas you came up with while developing the concept diagram and go through a trial-and-error process to come up with the best solution. Play with the different shapes and placements until

Natural area

you find an option that works for you. Always take time to look at the big picture, double-checking the relationships between proposed solutions. You may find that you'd prefer to have a deck as a private retreat outside your bedroom and revert to your original patio idea for entertaining. Let your mind work though the possibilities as you plan out your ideas.

Bed lines and planting areas

After you have a sketched your favorite hardscape ideas, figure out your bed lines. Wrap planting beds around hardscape items to frame them, but leave some access to grassy areas. Remember, your bed lines shape the lawn as well as planting areas. You may choose smooth, flowing curves or geometric lines. (See page 19.) Use your engineer's scale every now and then to check the width of planting beds. It's easy to get carried away and sketch 20-foot-wide beds that will require too many plants. Keep things workable.

Trees are next. Scribble rough circles to indicate where you want to add trees. Look at your site analysis and check the arrows that indicate views you don't want to block, areas that need privacy, and areas that need shade. Consider existing trees that you're going to keep (shown on your base map) before drawing in new ones.

Use your photographs as design tools so you can sketch existing planting areas and designate the plants you want to keep. Indicate new plantings to take the place of ones you'll remove.

It's also a good idea to roughly label the floor plan of your house so you can examine the indoor/outdoor relationships. You may remember that you wanted to plant a buffer or build a fence to create more interior privacy. Make sure your hardscape ideas relate well to nearby rooms in your house.

Trace your favorite hardscape solutions and planting schemes to form a composite. This is your master landscape plan. Even if you only implement one part of your new landscape at a time, you'll end up with a unified design.

Producing a perfect drawing isn't your goal. Sketches are opportunities to explore ideas; shown here are a few trial schemes for the pond shape.

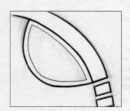

In this garden, hardscape in the form of the pergola not only makes a welcoming entryway, it also provides an ideal vantage point to view the beautiful landscaping.

Hardscape Design

Anything that isn't soil or planting is considered part of your hardscape. The hardscape elements of your landscape can be broken down into four basic categories—flooring, enclosure, overhead, and aesthetic and/or active.

Flooring hardscapes are elements that provide a base for an outdoor "floor" area. These hardscapes include items such as driveways, walkways, paths, decks, and patios. Enclosed space hardscapes, such as fences or stone walls, offer a feeling of privacy by marking boundaries. "Ceiling" hardscapes designate an outdoor area with an overhead element. Arbors, pergolas, and gazebos are all examples of ceiling hardscapes. Lastly, some hardscapes serve as either an aesthetic or an active part of the landscape. Fountains,

decorative containers, reflecting ponds and sundials are all garden amenities, or aesthetic hardscapes. Swimming pools and deck or patio furniture are examples of hardscapes that are actively used in the landscape.

Hardscapes should serve a functional purpose in a landscape. They may provide shade, privacy, mark a boundary, or serve as focal points in the yard. It's important to take the time to plan your hardscapes so they work within the area and don't take attention away from the whole landscape.

Once you've incorporated your hardscapes into your master plan, you'll need layout plans to build them. But first it's a good idea to consider some of the things that can affect their installation.

Your choice of hardscape materials is endless, from stone to wood to gravel and brick, and all the many varieties of each. Mixing materials is one way to create a layered and distinctive look. Here a paved drive gives way to a short gravel front walk, bordered by planted beds and a lattice-style fence.

A curving stone and gravel path punctuates this informal garden setting perfectly.

Paving

Think of paving as the floor for outdoor rooms and hallways. The term paving describes any surface that is not planted and is suitable for walking or driving. Driveways, parking areas, walkways, sport courts, and patios are just a few examples of hardscape paving.

Paving materials vary greatly and can be broadly categorized as impermeable and permeable. Impermeable surfaces—asphalt, concrete, and brick or stone mortared to concrete slabs—are firm enough to shed storm water. These surfaces lend an air of permanence and formality.

Carefully plan and design the areas that will be paved with impermeable surfaces since these materials are usually used in permanent hardscapes. You'll be looking at these areas for a long time, so have a solid plan in place that will provide you with many years of use and satisfaction.

You will usually need to hire a contractor to pave areas with impermeable materials, since the subsurface requires preparation to prevent cracking. First of all, the area will need to be carefully graded to prevent water from pooling in areas—especially near the foundation of the house. Poured-in-place concrete also requires forms to hold it in place until it has cured, and a contractor can set and remove the forms properly. Precast concrete pieces such as stepping stones are already hardened and ready for placement, but the area still needs to be graded correctly to keep the material from shifting.

Permeable surfaces provide a firmer surface than the ground alone but still allow water to penetrate. They give your landscape a more informal tone than an impermeable surface. Gravel and mulch are common examples of permeable materials. If you're looking for a way to create a different look to these hardscapes, the size and color of gravel stone can make the difference. Larger stones are less formal while the smaller the stone, the dressier the appearance. Dark stones tend to make the prettiest pathways, but a light color is a nice contrast to the surroundings.

If you're interested in a "middle ground," consider stone, brick, or pavers set in a sand or gravel course; they have a stronger presence than gravel or mulch alone. Sand-set bricks tend to shift over the years, making a surface uneven, so they may need to be reset over time. Moss and plants may grow in pockets that occur between the stones, creating a whole different look to the hardscape as time passes. Impermeable paving materials in sand or gravel beds need to be contained with steel, stone, brick, or wood edging to keep the materials out of plantings and create a definitive border to the hardscape.

Paving is a great way to transition from one space to another. For example, irregularly shaped stones set in a loose gravel path may lead to a patio made of the same stones mortared to a slab. A rectangular inset of cut stones centered in the patio acts much like an exterior area rug, lending subtle identity and a touch of formality to a sitting area. Different shapes of interlocking cement blocks, cut stone, or patterns made with bricks can create different effects that will highlight the hardscape. Examine your plan for areas that will be paved and consider different materials to achieve the look you want.

It's important to know what you can do yourself and when it's time to call a contractor. A brick-on-sand patio project or a gravel path lined with brick or stone is within the skill of many homeowners. It's best to hire a contractor for larger jobs such as paved driveways or patios to be sure the job is done right. If you're going to do it yourself, projects with straight line are easier than those with curves. Also,

This stone-in-concrete snail-patterned paving is the star of this courtyard garden.

SPECIALTY CONCRETE

Adding concrete to your landscape doesn't mean you have to settle for the same old blinding white pavement. Integral color mixes added to concrete before pouring can create a range of hues. Most start off dark and fade to lighter shades, so choose a tone darker than what you ultimately want. Existing concrete can be stained with a chemical product that etches the surface for a pleasingly mottled look. Adding shells or decorative stone into the wet mix and hosing an unset surface to expose aggregates gives concrete an interesting texture. Closed-mold stamps used on the surface of wet concrete can create amazing patterns that suggest cobblestones, bricks, or rocks.

projects with dimensions that divide into an even number of bricks or blocks are easier than those that require anything to be cut to fit. Always work out the pattern on paper before you begin to be sure you've got the right amount of materials and can handle the job yourself.

Cost factors

The price of paving depends on the availability of materials and labor necessary for installation. Anything that requires intensive craftsmanship will cost more than a simple surface. Is the project in a difficult-to-reach backyard? Accessibility to your project area also affects the price, as does the amount of site preparation needed.

Geography makes a difference too. What materials are most available in your area? For instance, brick in south Florida may cost more than other places; the lack of local clay for making masonry means shipping costs are an added expense. On the other hand, native stone may be readily available in your area. By choosing materials native to your area, you'll not only save money, but you'll also ensure that your design will achieve a look appropriate to your region.

Getting rough bids

Because your master plan is drawn to scale, you can measure the paved areas and calculate square footage. Obtain rough bids from several contractors to see if your plans are affordable. You may need to reduce the amount of paving or select materials that are less expensive. After you prepare a layout plan, you'll be able to determine all your costs more precisely.

A warm terra-cotta color brings this southwestern cut-concrete patio to life.

The elegant wood of the garage door works well with a cobble-style drive.

Brick is a favorite material for adding rich color and pattern to your landscape.

Layers of decking on this Asian-inspired backyard patio create a variety of areas for use.

Decks

There's nothing quite as versatile as a deck. You can add outdoor living space adjacent to any floor of your house, over slopes and ravines, nestled in the trees, or right at ground level. A deck can make the most of views, summer breezes, and winter sunshine. Like paving, decks and boardwalks form the floors of outdoor rooms and passageways. But unlike paving, decks give you the option of building above ground and grading is rarely necessary.

Location

Access, comfort, and privacy are all important factors in deck design. If you have trouble getting to your deck, you'll rarely use it. Your deck is a destination; study the best ways to access it. A deck can be a natural extension of the house—

sliding glass doors left open to the deck will extend the indoor space to the outside. If you use a grill on your deck, an entry close to the kitchen makes the whole process easier.

In addition to having good access, you should feel comfortable on your deck. If you feel that you are on display to the neighborhood or the location of the deck is too hot or cold, you won't enjoy it much. If another space in the landscape isn't optimal for easy deck access, you may need new planting for increased privacy or shade. A wall of latticework or a deck umbrella can make all the difference and shield you both from view and the hot sun. Double-check your concept diagram for the optimum location and make any planting or other adjustments necessary to make your deck a comfortable place.

Consider how you will use your deck. Make sure the shape and size shown on your master plan meets your needs. A small, cozy deck can be perfect for an intimate spot just off the master bedroom; a place for outdoor entertaining may require more room. Both the size and the location of the deck should reflect your lifestyle so you'll use the deck to its fullest.

Features and costs

Storage is a valuable feature. A deck beside a kitchen garden may include storage for garden tools and harvest baskets; a deck that doubles as a landing for the front or back door is an ideal spot for hooks and shelves. Built-in benches and planters make a deck more useful and result in a few less things to store in the shed.

Think about what kind of handy features you can add to increase the use and enjoyment of your deck even further. You can plant for added features such as lighting, overhead fans, exterior outlets, and outdoor cook tops and sinks in the beginning of the process, even if they are added later.

It's often a good idea to add a focal point in the yard that aligns with the main view from the deck; mark this spot on your master plan. Strategically placed decorative benches, sundials, or bird feeders enhance the view. A view of a fountain or other water feature can also be a lovely addition to a relaxing afternoon on the deck.

Generally decks are one of the most affordable hardscape options. Redwood, cedar, and pressure-treated pine are usual materials; check with local suppliers to see which is the best value in your region. You can build a deck yourself or hire a carpenter to do the work for you. It may pay to have a carpenter handle more

elaborate decks, but if it's a straightforward design, there's a good chance you can do it yourself.

Use your engineer's scale to make adjustments in your master landscape plan now. Later you'll produce an accurately dimensioned drawing called a layout plan based on the footprint of the deck you design now. It's important to have the initial layout and size correctly displayed on your master plan so you can design any other things that need to go with it before you nail a single board.

Stairs lead to a decked dining area enveloped in shrubs to make the most of a steep and narrow landscape.

Arbors

Arbors represent doorways and ceilings in the outdoor world. Compare your master plan to your concept diagram. Do you need more delineation between zones of use? An arbor may be just the thing you need to suggest a passageway from one area of your yard to another. Would you like to highlight a portion of the yard and set it apart from other areas? An arbor can mark a special place in the yard and frame whatever is behind it.

Adding an arbor to your garden can also give it presence and style. Add an arbor where you want to mark an entrance into the garden or link garden rooms. An arbor adds structure to the landscape, balancing the softer lines and billowing forms of plants. It also adds a vertical element, making the scene more than just beds of flowers at ground level.

A simple two-post structure is perfect for framing the entry into your garden. Larger arbors with multiple posts can make big spaces feel comfortable. Most interior ceilings are 8 to 9 feet high; bringing that height outside with an overhead structure can make large exterior spaces seem people-sized. As a rule of thumb, include beams or rafters within those heights and the proportions will feel comfortable.

By studying the angle of the fiercest rays the area receives, you can slant rafters to

Here an open pergola overhead creates a connection between house and garden.

This traditional arbor acts as a welcoming gateway between garden spaces.

BUYING AN ARBOR

Smaller arbors are available at garden centers, from catalogs, or online. Most of these arbors are partially assembled so all you have to do is attach the sides to the top and you've got your arbor all ready to put in place. If you'd like to be more hands-on, you can certainly design your own arbor and build it. If making design plans isn't your forte, buy just the arbor plan itself, then choose your own materials for its construction.

block bright sun. If you'd like more shade than just the rafters will provide, train sun-loving vines to grow up the arbor to help block out more of the sun. You may need only a few rafters if the purpose of the arbor is to define space. The sight of the structure within the yard signals that the area designated is special.

Design for style

Arbor construction varies with design intent. Curved arbors contribute a romantic quality to the garden; white arches covered with climbing roses establish the cottage style. Repeating the bottom half of the arch along the top of a gate completes the circle. Known as moon gates, these arbor-gate combinations frame porthole views of the area beyond them. Position a focal point so that it can be seen while looking through the circle; this point of interest doesn't have to be centered like a target. Consider setting it slightly to one side to balance the geometric shape of the moon gate. A curving path, leading invitingly to some unseen destination, is another good view to frame.

Rectilinear arbors without curves make a different statement in your landscape. Consider repeating the peak of your rooftop or the horizontal line of your fence top. Whether the style becomes formal or informal depends largely upon the materials and colors you use. Dressed and painted lumber suggests a formal presence. Rough cedar posts lend a rustic air. You can also combine stone or brick pillars with wood or iron to form a gateway planted with trailing vines. Design an arbor to reflect your personal style and to complement the architecture of your home.

This classic curved arbor is a gentle invitation to explore the garden beyond.

A pergola helps define the space and use of this outdoor room.

Walls and Fences

A low mortared stone wall gives neat definition to a sloping landscape.

Your master plan and your site analysis have helped you see where you need to add buffers for privacy or to define space. Now it's time to decide whether you need a wall or a fence.

Design with walls

The solid form of most walls lends a sense of permanence. Age a new landscape by building a wall with old materials; it will seem to have always been there. Planting vines to creep over it marries a wall to the garden. Tall walls can appear imposing, adding a hint of exclusiveness or creating an air of mystery by piquing curiosity about what is out of view. Walls taller than eye-level can seem forbidding and unfriendly when built next to a sidewalk with no planting between. What kind of wall you build will depend on what affect you are trying to achieve.

Walls and fences claim a corner of earth for your own. You can build walls to create outdoor rooms, to limit access, define space, and to direct the flow of foot traffic. Fences can give you privacy, as well as keep people and pets either in or out of the yard.

Walls don't have to be tall; they can be less than a foot high. A low line of stacked stones makes an effective area divider; a short wall topped with a picket fence makes a clearly defined boundary that doesn't obscure views. The line the wall follows influences the style of your

The circular opening in this otherwise traditional brick wall frames a view that's pretty as a picture.

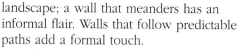

Here the lattice fencing lends privacy, while the lower fence edges the drive and porch.

This 7-foot-high stockade fence gives maximum privacy and provides support for a variety of clematis.

landscape; a wall that meanders has an informal flair. Walls that follow predictable paths add a formal touch.

Walls may be made of stone, brick, adobe, concrete, stucco, or any combination of materials. The type of material you use can make a design statement as well. A solid brick wall makes an area feel secluded. An unmortared stone wall is perfect for a cottage or rustic look.

Building larger walls can get expensive. To cut costs, you can construct walls of concrete block and cover the face with a decorative veneer. When planning to build a wall, you must take legal restrictions into consideration. Remember that walls need footings, which may extend beyond its width on both sides—make sure you've planned enough room.

A weathered country picket fence, planted effusively with roses and perennials, adds charm to the landscape.

Fencing with a flair

Fences offer even more style variations than walls. Waist-high picket fences add cottage charm and define space without seeming unfriendly. Tall privacy fences screen unwanted views or create privacy. Rustic fences can suggest a cabin or countryside setting. Fences may be made of wood, wire, metal, or a plastic material that resembles real wood. Choose one or combine materials to get the look and level of maintenance you want. Decide whether you want to completely block views or merely add a sense of separation from surrounding areas.

Remember, you don't have to use one type of wall or fence around your entire property. Consider repeating materials to create unity, but vary heights to serve a host of purposes.

The scalloping curve to this fencing makes for a gentle definition of space while not interrupting the view.

LIVING FENCES

You can combine fences or walls with hedges for a different kind of boundary. Build corners and segments of fencing and plant shrubs in between. Thorny plants make an effective barrier; flowering plants add a decorative touch. Depending on the density and eventual height of the shrubs used, you can achieve a range of effects, from a high enclosure surrounding an estate to a charming hedge fronting a bungalow.

Water Features

The stone coping, irregular shape, dark bottom, and abundant water plants give this pond a natural feel.

Ponds and waterfalls

Garden ponds are popular ways to bring water to the landscape. The sight of water has a cooling effect in summer. A dark bottom enhances the reflective qualities; that's why pond liners are usually black.

Ponds can be naturalistic or elegant and formal. If a natural pond is your goal, use an irregular shape and obscure liner edges with stones, wood, or plants. For a formal look, build a raised geometric coping. Add water plants to mimic a natural pond.

Splashes, gurgles, and falling water make a garden come to life. Waterfalls can be built from kits with pumps that return the water from a pool to the top for an ongoing flow. Waterfalls look best when integrated into the landscape. A pile of wet rocks in the center of the yard isn't as naturally striking as stones set on a slope that's lush with ferns and iris. Pay attention to what's behind your waterfall; screen distractions so your water feature will stand out.

Fountains add splash

Fountains offer a chance to incorporate water in your landscape without the expense or space of a large pool. A wall-mounted fountain adds sparkle to the sight and music to the air. Small bubblers can add movement to garden ponds. Fountains flowing into pools can be made of anything from ornate cast iron to broken pottery. Use your imagination to discover how everyday materials—urns, galvanized feeding troughs, watering cans—can help create a water feature.

For adults there are two main types of water features: water you look at and water you get into. Children frequently and willfully fail to make the distinction. Make any water feature both pretty enough to admire and safe enough for everyone to enjoy.

Study your master plan and site analysis to see where you may want to add the sound of water to mask outside noises and enhance privacy. Look for spots that need focal points too. Some water features, such as garden ponds, can add a contemplative quality to your landscape. Other options—splashing fountains or swimming pools—can add activity to an area. Design the water feature to match the use of the area.

SAFE WATER FEATURES

Always consult local building codes for safety and liability information before adding any outdoor water feature. Fencing, wiring, lighting, and water depth may all be subject to local regulations. Work with an electrician to connect your pump to its power source for either a swimming pool or a pond; include a ground fault circuit interrupter in all water features.

Poolside beauty

A swimming pool doesn't have to be a big blue hole in your landscape. Consider it a large water feature that will complement the space when not in use. Any pool can be pretty enough for any landscape, even if you have no plans to swim. Add a stone patio with an arbor and lush plantings, and it becomes a focal point for even the most formal gathering. The sound of gently splashing water makes the pool even more inviting; consider building small jets into the side of a swimming pool to turn a plain wall into a row of arching spouts. Or direct a flow of recirculating water over a pool lip and down into a hidden trough for a poolside waterfall.

The location of your swimming pool plays a part in its appeal too. Don't plop it in the center of the back lawn where it

dominates. Tuck it along one side, connect it to your bedroom with a deck, curve it around existing plants; list as many options as you can before planning where to excavate. You'll also want to allow room for pool equipment, and you'll want to screen it from view.

Is a swimming pool what you really want? If swimming laps isn't what you had in mind, perhaps a spa would make better use of your space and resources. Install an in-ground spa or build a raised deck that can attractively house a prefabricated model.

Good design and excellent materials can make a swimming pool an important feature in your landscape, not just a place to swim.

A small water feature like this modern birdbath with lotus and water lily makes a subtle accent.

PLANTS, FISH, FILTERS, AND PUMPS

Plants for ponds must be chosen carefully. Hardy water lilies will fare better in most climates than tropical varieties. Set water lilies and other water-loving plants such as umbrella plant (Cyperus alternifolius) in containers on shallow shelves built into the sides of your pond. Avoid puncturing pond liners or basins when you install plants. Iris, rushes, and ferns are good choices to plant beyond the pond's edge.

Fish add color and movement to the water. Always purchase fish from a reputable source and never free exotic fish in local waterways, where they may become invasive. Include water plants in your pond so fish can hide from predators. Fish are cold-blooded and can survive

the winter outdoors if the surface of the water is not allowed to freeze solid, depriving them of oxygen.

Filters help keep ponds clean but may not be necessary in a properly balanced ecosystem—some carefully designed systems rely on the roots of water plants to naturally filter pond water.

Pumps are either remote or submersible. Most garden ponds utilize small submersible pumps that sit on the pond bottom. Pumps keep water recirculating, which helps the pond stay healthy. Pump sizes are dependent upon the desired flow and the height water will have to ascend to a waterfall. Many pond kits come complete with properly sized pumps.

This fountain brings energy, sound, and movement to the backyard.

Garden Amenities

A landscape is as much fun to decorate as a house. You should, of course, include ornamental items as a part of your design. But too much stuff can result in cluttered chaos. Use the design principles—balance, unity, and accent— to make your decorations striking.

A wooden bench positioned against a weathered brick wall backdrop and framed by a pair of obelisks make a peaceful, traditional impression.

Balance, unity, and accent

You can achieve balance in different ways. For example, a symmetrical grouping of hand-thrown pots will divide itself neatly into identical halves. For an asymmetrical arrangement, group small pots beside a big one.

Balance is also a matter of relating a piece to the space around it. If a lion's head fountain is too small in relation to its surrounding wall, the fountain will get lost. You could choose to buy a larger fountain, but what if you particularly want to use the small one? Train a plant to grow flat against the wall—a technique known as espalier— to provide an intermediate matte to balance the object with its setting. Then the fountain no longer appears out of scale.

Understanding different unifying techniques can give you new ideas. Alternating the same large and small terra-cotta pots on the ledge is an example of rhythm. Stagger the pots from largest to smallest—that's sequence. For design with repetition, use the terra-cotta color elsewhere in the scene by echoing the hue in the stain on an arbor.

Place accent items where the composition needs pizzazz. Don't always aim for eye level; unexpected accents placed high or low keep a design dynamic. Rusted relics, architectural fragments, salvaged items, and antique tools find new life as garden accessories. Keep in mind that it is the position of an article that makes it an accent. Contrast the color, texture, line, or form of an item with its setting to make it noticeable.

A bright Mexican tile can add a colorful accent where you need one, but where not needed, it could be an unwanted distraction. A layer of coarse-textured river rock can serve as a foreground to a planting bed, but too much rock could upset the balance of texture.

A little something extra

Furniture is an amenity that's also functional. Even a landscape designed for a lot of family activity needs a place for repose. No matter how lovely your courtyard may be, if there isn't a comfortable and convenient place to sit, you probably won't spend time there. There are benches and table-and-chair sets of all styles to choose from, but don't stop there. Swings, rocking chairs, and hammocks also offer rest, and they introduce a relaxing form of movement.

Vertical structures offer all sorts of design solutions. Arbors (see pages 46-47) serve as doorways and suggest a division of space. A gazebo can add a distinct focal point to an outdoor room and make the landscape usable in wet weather by providing a dry, comfortable place to sit and watch rain fall. Storage sheds can do

A trelliswork screen gives this corner intimacy and definition, as well as a bit of privacy.

more than keep clutter out of sight; properly positioned, a shed can increase privacy by blocking views.

Paint doesn't need to be limited to interior walls. Color can help camouflage utilitarian items such as meters and irrigation risers. Black is often the best; it tends to recede. Muted shades of olive green and brown are effective, too, but avoid bright greens. Artificial colors stand out among natural greenery and may ambush your camouflage attempts.

Bright paint colors can add eye-catching accents. Furniture and fences are easy canvases for brushing on color. Picket fences are traditionally painted white to make them more noticeable. But if your fence is intended to serve as a background for your composition, a dark or neutral paint or stain may be a better choice.

Movement of all sorts adds interest to the landscape. Incorporating water is an excellent way to keep a space from becoming static and dull; swimming fish and falling water add motion. (See pages 50–51.) Wind chimes, weather vanes, and some sculptures react to breezes flowing through an area. Wildlife can add movement that comes and goes; feeders and houses combined with habitat and food-source plants will attract birds to your landscape. Plants attractive to butterfly larvae and nectar-bearing flowers will entice butterflies as well as hummingbirds to grace your yard.

Plan ahead

Most garden amenities should be planned in advance. You may decide to widen a pathway to provide a solid surface to house a bench. Sculpture and interesting plant forms may need night lighting for maximum enjoyment. Moving water requires a power source. You'll address all of these considerations during this part of the planning stage. Later, after your new landscape has become reality, you can add a few additional accessories as finishing touches to your outdoor rooms.

This rustic shed is perfect for its country setting.

SHEDS IN THE LANDSCAPE

Before you add a shed, decide whether you want to highlight it as a feature or downplay its appearance. Bright paint, flowers, weather vanes, and hanging relics make sheds stand out. Dark, neutral paints and stains, evergreen plantings, and less prominent placement can make your shed subordinate to the rest of your landscape.

Ingenious design allows for storage beneath layered plantings.

Materials Comparison

As you choose materials for the hardscape elements in your design, compare their suitability and cost. The materials listed below are often used in hardscape construction; the charts provide comparisons of costs, maintenance needs, life expectancy, and the skill level required for installation. These ratings are approximate, and some factors, such as cost and life expectancy, will vary between regions.

WALLS

Walls are most commonly built of masonry but also can be lattice structures or made from other materials. For comparisons on wooden materials, see the chart below for fences and arbors. All walls need regular maintenance to preserve their beauty and increase their lifespan.

The main enemies of masonry work are water and ice. Regular maintenance revolves around keeping these invaders out. When choosing a stone material, ask your supplier which types are readily available locally. You'll also want to gather information about maintenance schedules and sealants. The chart below lists several things you should consider when choosing materials and ranks them on a scale of 1 (least or shortest) to 5 (most or longest).

Type	Cost	Maintenance	Life	Skill Level Required
Concrete block with veneer				
Brick face	4	1	5	5
Irregular stone face	4	1	5	5
Cut stone face	5	1	5	5
Interlocking units	3	1	5	4
Dry-stacked stone wall	2	3	4	3

FENCES AND ARBORS

Several choices of fencing material are available. Each retailer may represent different manufacturers, so spend some time visiting lumberyards and home centers before making your decision. Ask to see brochures from the different manufacturers; they're packed with information about materials available as well as tips for installation and maintenance. You should weigh cost, appearance, and maintenance qualities in making your decision. Determine if beauty or barrier is more important to you. Chain link and stockade fencing are the most secure but the least attractive. Conversely, picket and split rail models are beautiful, but they aren't very effective at keeping animals or people in—or out—of your yard. The chart below lists several things you should consider when choosing materials and ranks them on a scale of 1 (least or shortest) to 5 (most or longest).

Type	Cost	Maintenance	Life	Security	Skill Level Required
Chain link	4	1	5	5	4
Picket (prefabricated sections)					
Cedar	4	3	3	2	2
Pressure-treated pine	3	3	4	2	2
Stockade (prefabricated sections)					
Pressure-treated pine	2	5	4	5	4
Cedar	2	3	2	5	4
Redwood	5	1	5	5	4
Split rail					
Oak	2	1	3	1	1
Cedar	2	1	4	1	1
Woven					
Pine	3	5	2	3–5	5
Cedar	5	3	4	3–5	5
Lattice	1	3	1	1–2	2

PAVING

The materials used for paving range from simple stepping stones to manufactured stone composite pavers; prices vary greatly. As with walls, using local natural material is often the least expensive option and may tie in nicely with existing walls, or stone or brickwork on your house. Flagstone and shale are common choices but can be slippery on slopes. Pavers are quickly becoming the material of choice because of their durability, beauty, and low cost. In all cases, the life of the paving system you use will be determined most by the degree to which you properly prepare the area in which the stones are laid. The chart below lists several things you should consider when choosing materials and ranks them on a scale of 1 (least or shortest) to 5 (most or longest).

Type	Cost	Maintenance	Life	Skill Level Required
Stepping stones (local stone, shale, or limestone)	2	1	5	3
Stone mortared to a slab	5	2	5	5
Brick				
In sand	3	3	4	4
Mortared to a slab	5	1	5	5
Interlocking pavers	3	1	5	4
Concrete				
Natural	2	1	5	4
Tinted				
Integral color	3	1	5	4
Stained	3	1	5	4
Stamped	4	1	5	5
Asphalt	2	2	4	5
Decomposed granite/pea gravel	1	4	2	1
Mulch	1	4	2	1

DECKS

Solid wood products, such as redwood, cedar, and pressure-treated lumber, have been the choice of deck experts for many years—but that is changing. More varieties of composite materials are being offered every year. Composite materials may be wood byproducts (wood chips or flakes), wood and plastic combinations, or 100 percent plastic (often recycled). These materials have an extremely long life, due to their rot and insect resistance. You may need to use lumber for the supports and joists, however, because composites are usually not strong enough to support the weight of deck structures. The chart below lists several things you should consider when choosing materials and ranks them on a scale of 1 (least or shortest) to 5 (most or longest).

Type	Cost	Maintenance	Life	Skill Level Required
Redwood	5	3	3	3
Cedar	4	3	2	3
Pressure-treated pine	2	3	4	3
Composite wood	3	1	5	3

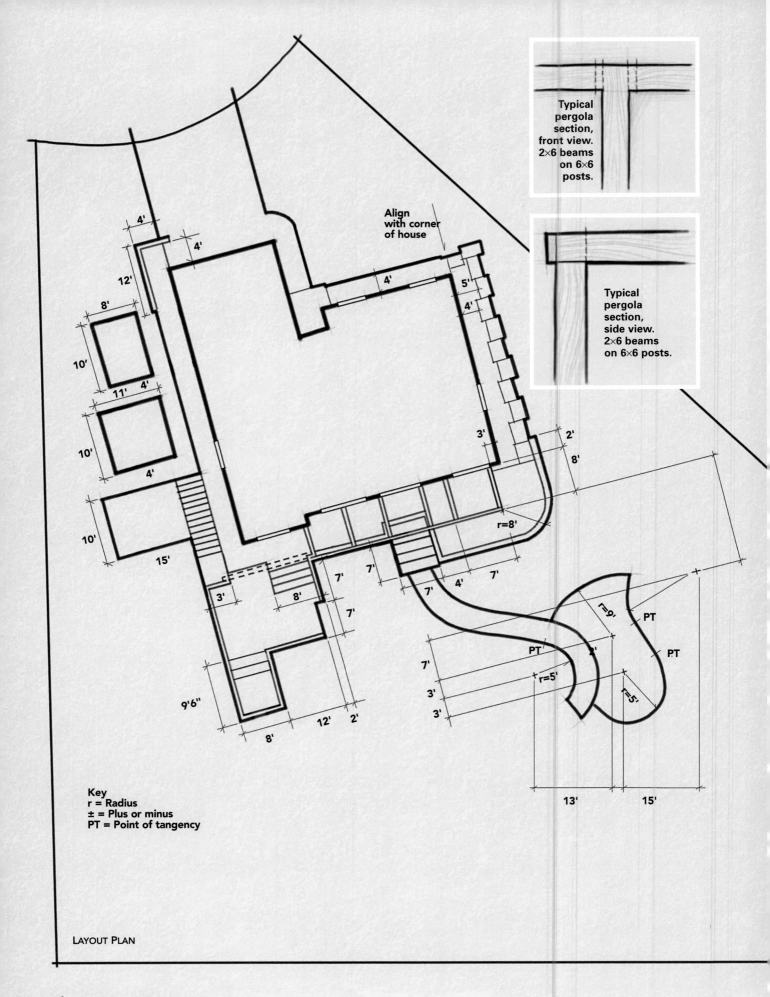

Typical pergola section, front view. 2×6 beams on 6×6 posts.

Typical pergola section, side view. 2×6 beams on 6×6 posts.

Align with corner of house

4'
4'
12'
8'
10'
11' 4'
10'
4'
10'
15'
3'
8'
9'6"
8'
12' 2'

4'
4'
5'
4'
3' 2'
8'
r=8'
7' 7'
7'
7' 4' 7'
7'
7'
3'
3'
r=9'
2'
PT
PT
r=5'
r=5'
PT
PT
13' 15'

Key
r = Radius
± = Plus or minus
PT = Point of tangency

LAYOUT PLAN

Create a Layout Plan

A layout plan shows the outline of new hardscape items, such as decks, patios, walkways, and arbors. The layout plan is the first of the action plans that allow your vision to actually happen. Don't worry if you don't have any drafting skills. Your master plan, tracing paper, engineer's scale, and a couple of pencils, felt-tip pens, and a good eraser are all you need.

Trace the outline of proposed hardscape items and existing features with a felt-tip pen. Don't show proposed plants or existing plants you plan to remove; do include major existing plants (such as trees and large shrubs) that you plan to keep. Your new hardscape features need to conform to what is already there so you don't have to cut down valuable trees.

Dimension lines

Next, draw dimension lines in pencil, bracketed on each end (each looks like

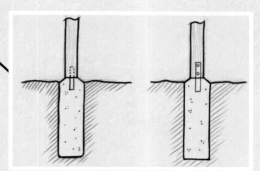

Deck post and footing detail. 4×4 posts set on preformed piers with metal post anchors.

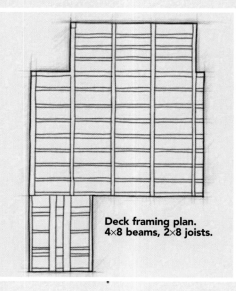

Deck framing plan. 4×8 beams, 2×8 joists.

an elongated "H"), with the measurement in the center. Draw dimension lines to show how far new items will be from existing features. Next, use your engineer's scale to measure the distances indicated by your dimension lines. Use the layout plan at left for reference.

Critical and adjustable measurements

When measuring, focus on one new feature at a time. Some dimensions will be more critical than others. For example, if you plan a deck designed around an existing tree, the deck must be correctly sized to fit.

Other dimensions can be adjusted to make the more critical dimensions work. Label these measurements with a plus-or-minus (±) sign. For example, the length of the deck from the tree to the house is less critical. Placing the plus-or-minus symbol in front of this measurement indicates that the deck must reach from the tree to the house, but the exact length is subject to adjustment. This technique conveys your desires to the contractor. If you show the length of the deck from house to tree at exactly 24 feet, you may come home to find that your tree has been cut down in order to make room for the deck.

Consider uses

Consider how you will use your new landscape. If you are going to place an umbrella table with chairs on a proposed patio, set up the actual furniture and measure the space required. If your patio is not a dead-end destination, people will walk across it to get from one place to another; you'll need to allow room for the furniture area off to one side to access a walkway.

Make changes

Don't be afraid to adjust your design as needed to fit your site and your needs. A layout plan is a great chance to refine your design and improve your ideas. Preparing a layout plan is part of the ongoing design process; by combining your dreams with reality, the layout plan allows you to come up with creative solutions you will enjoy long after they are implemented.

PLANNING FOR
Easy Maintenance

If there is a single common thread among all successful gardens, it is the availability of consistent moisture. Deciding how water will be delivered to your landscape is one of the most important elements of your maintenance plan.

Watering

Make watering easy on yourself; don't haul hoses. At a minimum, locate bibs on every side of the house and mount reels for separate hoses at each location.

Although quantity is important, consistency is almost as essential. If roots are allowed to dry out in between waterings, they are not as efficient at absorbing water the next time. Water regularly, preferably in the morning. Watering in the morning gives plants the moisture they need to face the heat of the day. It also helps prevent fungal growth that may occur on foliage and mulch left damp overnight. The amount of water needed by plants in your landscape will determine how often you will need to water.

A typical lawn and shrub planting may require 1 inch of water per week, but vegetable and flower gardens that are packed with plants all competing for the same moisture may need up to 1½ inches per week. Some properties have a high water table that keeps the soil regularly moist; those with sandy soil may require more frequent and generous waterings to compensate for the rapid runoff. Needs vary in different regions of the country too; check with

Water deeply occasionally rather than shallow and often. It's better for the plants.

Timers attached to spigots make watering automatic; a soaker hose waters plants evenly and deeply.

your county cooperative extension to get specific recommendations for your area.

It's better to provide a greater quantity of water three times a week than a little bit every day. Greater quantities will soak in deeper and encourage deep root growth. Smaller quantities only keep the first few inches of the topsoil damp, encouraging shallow root growth.

Consider conservation

Water conservation should be a concern of gardeners everywhere. Use whatever amount of water you need to keep gardens healthy and growing, but look for ways to conserve. Overhead watering loses more than 15 percent to evaporation. Whenever possible, use soaker hoses that deliver water directly to the soil and to plant roots. Soaker hoses are black, porous hoses made from recycled rubber and polyethylene. They have numerous tiny pores through which water weeps. You can design your own system with "T" and elbow fittings. Lay the soaker hoses 2 feet apart through vegetable, rose, and flower gardens and around shrubs and trees. Cover the hoses with mulch for greater efficiency.

Soaker problems

Soaker hose systems have a few problems, but their remedies are easy. Fix periodic breaks or splits with a coupler and hose clamps. Prevent clogging with filters. Perhaps the worst problem is the potential for waste when water is not shut off. A forgotten sprinkler is hard to overlook, but soaker hoses can run unnoticed for quite a while.

Two simple cures can solve this problem. The first is a common kitchen timer which you can set to ring at the end of your watering period. The second is an automatic timer that attaches between the hose and water source. Several models are available; some are driven by the water pressure going through the timer. More sophisticated, more accurate models are battery-powered. Some can be programmed

TWENTY DROUGHT-TOLERANT PLANTS

LAWN GRASSES

Buffalograss
(*Buchloe dactyloides*)
Blue gramagrass
(*Bouteloua gracilis*)
Fairway crested wheatgrass
(*Agropyron cristatum*
'Ephraim')
Hard fescue
(*Festuca longifolia*
'Scaldis')
Canada bluegrass
(*Poa compressa* 'Cannon'
or 'Rubens')

TREES

Boxelder maple
(*Acer negundo*)
Scotch pine
(*Pinus sylvestris*)
Common hackberry
(*Celtis occidentalis*)
Green ash
(*Fraxinus pennsylvanica*)
Black Hill spruce
(*Picea glauca var. densata*)
Colorado spruce
(*Picea pungens*)
Ponderosa pine
(*Pinus ponderosa*)
Bur oak
(*Quercus macrocarpa*)

SHRUBS

Artemisia
(*Artemisia* spp.)
Siberian pea-shrub
(*Caragana arborescens*)
Silverberry
(*Elaeagnus commutata*)
Alpine currant
(*Ribes alpinum*)
Buffaloberry
(*Shepherdia argentea*)
Threelobe spirea
(*Spiraea trilobata*)
Soapwood
(*Yucca glauca*)

to turn the water on and off on specified days of the week, as well as certain times of the day—the water-conservation answer for the gardener who must be away from home.

Irrigation systems

Irrigation systems are the best—and, of course, the most expensive—option for watering. Some systems are homeowner do-it-yourself projects; intricate systems, however, may call for professional installation. You'll want to include a timing device to regulate the system throughout the week. Get one that can be set for early morning watering; that's when the water pressure is highest. Some systems have an override feature that prevents it from watering when it rains.

Irrigation systems can be custom designed with different sizes and types of sprinkler heads strategically placed in specific parts of your landscape. Such design delivers large amounts of water to large areas such as lawns but smaller amounts at ground level for planting beds.

Drought-resistant plants save the day in areas that are arid or have water restrictions.

Healthy Soil

Mulch is attractive and also helps retain moisture and reduce weeds.

Before you begin your maintenance plan, get to know your soil and become familiar with steps you can take to maintain its health.

Mulching

Your maintenance plan should designate the mulching system you will use in your new landscape. Mulching is the practice of covering the surface of the soil with organic or inorganic material after all the planting is done. Organic mulches include wood chips, bark, grain hulls, mounds of hay, dried grass clippings, or pine needles (called pine straw in the South). Inorganic mulches, such as black plastic or layers of newspaper, can be covered with white marble chips or gravel.

Inorganic mulches last longer but can be problematic. Gravel migrates into lawns and onto walkways and drives. Those lovely marble chips look dirty after a while. Plastic breaks down and is reduced to a thousand plastic chips.

Organic mulches are preferable, but need to be renewed more often. They improve the soil, with the help of earthworms. As the mulch degrades, the earthworms consume it. They deposit digested material in the form of castings deep in the soil where it will do the most good. If the soil around your foundation plantings is hard and dry, organic mulch will attract the worms, and they will repair and enrich the soil in only a few months.

WHY MULCH? Mulch makes plants look nice. Mulch laid around trees, foundation shrubs, and garden plantings is like a frame on a picture; it makes the planting appear finished.

Applied around vertical elements, such as trees or poles, mulches make mowing easier.

Mulches help control weeds. They don't insure you'll have a weed-free garden, but the few that do come up will stand out against the mulch and will pull more easily.

Mulch also reduces the amount of evaporation from the soil. With well-mulched soil, you'll use less water.

Finally, organic mulching recycles products that might go into a landfill but instead become valuable landscape assets.

HOW MUCH MULCH? Two to three inches of organic mulch is sufficient. You will need to top it off every year or two as it degrades. If you are using mulch to stop erosion on a hillside and you don't have immediate plans to plant there, spreading 6 or more inches will

GOOD MULCHES

Many different organic materials make good mulch. It is important to see what is readily available in your area to cut costs and make it easier to replenish beds annually. Ground pine bark is preferable to large nuggets, which float and may wash away during a heavy downpour. Many nurseries are carrying shredded melaleuca as a substitute for shredded cypress to avoid cutting down native cypress stands. Pine straw and hay work well. Fine pebbles can do the job and help solve drainage problems, but they won't add organic matter to the soil.

Don't use grass clippings from the lawn as mulch for your plants. The chemicals added to the lawn from fertilizers are still in the clippings and the concentrations are not good for landscape plants and trees. The grass clippings may be added to a compost pile, as the chemicals break down and are dispersed throughout the compost.

The following are all good organic mulches:

Redwood (small bark)
Mushroom compost
Rotted manures
Straw
Shredded tree leaves
Pine needles
Composted sawdust
Home compost
Pine straw
Rice hulls
Ground corn cobs

inhibit erosion and dramatically improve the soil.

Some gardeners think the best combination is black plastic under organic mulch, but this, too, has disadvantages. The plastic remains intact longer because it is protected by the mulch on top. But the organic material can't enter the soil and improve it. Porous weed fabric, made of a nylon weave, is a better option than plastic, but be aware that weeds will grow on top of the fabric after it ages a year or two.

Fertilizers

Your earlier plans called for soil evaluation; now your maintenance plan should determine the type of fertilizers you will use. Soils often contain many of the trace minerals and nutrients that plants need to grow, but you may need to add nitrogen, phosphorous, and potassium (N, P, and K on fertilizer labels). Fertilizers contain one or more of these elements in a variety of percentages. The numbers on all fertilizer labels list the percentages of these three elements for that particular formulation. For example, a fertilizer rated as 5-10-5 contains 5 percent nitrogen, 10 percent phosphorous, and 5 percent potassium.

As a general rule, use high nitrogen fertilizers, such as a 10-6-4, for plants grown for their foliage (hedges and shade and evergreen trees) and high phosphorous fertilizers for plants grown for flowers, fruits, and vegetables. The most common fertilizers on the market are the water-soluble variety. These are mixed with water before application and can be used on landscape plants effectively. Always apply fertilizers according to label directions. More is not better! The amount recommended is the maximum you should apply. This is especially true of nitrogen. Too much nitrogen can burn and even kill plants.

Using compost

Don't overlook the opportunity to plan for a backyard composting center in your new landscape. Compost is the best soil amendment available to gardeners. No other single substance improves the texture, water retention, and drainage qualities of your soil better than compost. Compost, however, is relatively low in nutrients. Most compost measures at about 1-1-1 or less, so you'll still need to add fertilizer for the added nutrients.

Dig compost at least 12 inches deep into vegetable and annual flower gardens in the spring, fall, and in between crops. Top-dress perennial beds and trees and shrubs with compost. Then cover it with mulch.

Soil testing

Soil can be tested for its nutrient content as well as for its pH. The pH of a soil is a measure of its acidity or alkalinity. Soil pH is important because it affects the ability of plants to gather nutrients from the soil. Here's how to test your own. Gather a group of four to six tablespoon-size samples of soil from the lawn (at a depth of 4 to 6 inches), another group from the vegetable garden, and so forth. Mix each group in separate brown paper bags and allow to dry. Test the soil with a good quality pH test kit (available at garden centers and hardware stores), or send them to a soil-testing laboratory, and correct the soil according to the test results.

Your plants are only as good as the soil in which you plant them. Test your soil and amend it as necessary to give your plants the best chance to thrive.

MAKE YOUR OWN COMPOST

Anything that is organic was once alive and will compost naturally. The goal is to do it with the least amount of smell and mess, and to avoid attracting vermin and neighborhood animals. Buy a system or construct a container that allows you to turn the material, add to it, and easily harvest it when it's done. The container you construct may be as simple as a snow fence or chicken wire bin; purchased systems can be as elaborate as a three-bin, pressure-treated wood structure with galvanized wire sides. As you add to the mixture, pay attention to the balance between the fresh green vegetation and kitchen scraps, which account for most of the nitrogen, and the dried leaves, which account for most of the carbon. If your pile develops a foul smell, it needs more carbon. If it doesn't generate heat, it needs more nitrogen.

Mowing, Pruning, and Weeding

Mowing, pruning, and weeding are regular chores for every landscape. If you're a gardener who doesn't like these chores, the simplest solution for you is to plant less lawn and fewer plants that need pruning and use mulch to deter weeds. But even if you enjoy the work, thoughtful design can make it easier.

Examine your plan. Consider the following ways of reducing mowing chores. One of the biggest favors you can do for yourself is to make sure lawn areas are relatively level and wide enough to be mowed easily.

Steep slopes and narrow grass strips are a headache. Plant banks and hillsides with groundcover and shrubs; do the same in shady areas or where tree roots make mowing difficult. Or create terraces with retaining walls (make sure access from one to another is easy with a mower). If your bed lines make strips that are less than a mower width, widen the grassy areas.

Grass that grows next to walls, fences, and trees is difficult to mow. So is lawn around stepping stones. Save time with design—add a mow strip at the foot of walls, mulch the base of trees, and recess stepping stones. To make mowing easier next to planting beds, cut V-trenches between lawns and garden areas.

Finally, think twice before clearing natural areas. Add trees or shrubs instead of creating large spaces you'll need to mow forever or incorporate more planting beds into the landscape instead of open grass.

Keep pruning to a minimum by putting the right plant in the right place. Although it's important to know how tall and how wide a plant will grow, it's equally important to know what form it will assume. Choose plants that meet your design intentions so you won't have to

CHOOSING PRUNING TOOLS

When choosing a pruning tool, consider the size of the branches you will be cutting. Long-handled loppers are necessary for cutting anything as large as your index finger. Use hand pruners for smaller stems and a pruning saw for branches that are ¾ inch in diameter or larger. Using the right tool will make clean cuts. Jagged cuts can encourage insect entry and damage.

Purchase quality pruning tools. The difference between the inexpensive and the more expensive tools lies in more than just the price. Quality loppers, hand pruners and pruning saws will last longer and hold a sharper edge. Quality pruning tools pay off in the long run— both for your wallet and for the plants.

prune all the time to keep them in shape. Allowing a plant to grow in its natural form significantly reduces your maintenance efforts. Other than occasionally trimming stray branches, you won't have to prune. Plan ahead so the form and size of naturally shaped plants will fit into your landscape.

Space plants far enough from paved areas to allow room for growth without crowding. Also keep your pruning on a schedule that conforms to the needs of the plant; a little done at the right time will save you a lot of effort later.

Maintaining healthy plants

The most important step to maintaining healthy plants is to research the conditions in which they thrive. Plants have specific preferences for where they like to grow, and choosing the right plant for the right place will go a long way toward reducing its care.

Although it's not possible to create a specific environment for each plant, you can plan their locations now so you will grow them in the places they'll do best.

Locate plants that require full sun in areas receiving at least six to eight hours of sunlight a day (partial sun is defined as about four hours daily; shade means less than two hours of direct sun daily). In wet areas of the property, use plants that thrive when their feet are wet.

Make plant maintenance easier on yourself. Consider building raised beds—even waist-high with supporting walls; they will save both time and reduce the toll that bending and stooping takes. And even if you don't raise your planting beds, consider their width and the space between them. Where possible, design your beds so you can reach the middle from both sides for plant-care chores and weeding. And plan to leave room between foundation plantings and the house for access.

Good air circulation is a must for preventing plant disease; plan your planting, especially that for trees, to allow enough space for airflow. Proper and timely pruning of roses and vines will keep the interior of the plants open and reduce conditions favoring disease. (Planning won't replace the need for inspection and intervention,

MAINTENANCE SCHEDULE FOR PLANTS

Lightly prune spring-blooming shrubs after bloom.

"Drastically" prune (more than one-third of plant) spring bloomers before new growth begins in late winter.

Prune summer bloomers during dormancy.

Deadhead spent flowers throughout the season.

Remove foliage of perennial flowers only after it turns yellow or brown.

Fertilize perennials at planting and when they first appear in the spring.

Fertilize annuals (including vegetables) when planting and throughout the season.

Apply pesticides as needed.

so check your plants regularly and take appropriate steps to control any pests.)

Controlling weeds is one of the best ways to keep plants healthy. Weeds consume water and nutrients that desirable plants need. Pulling, cultivation, and tilling are all time-tested methods, but mulch is the greatest timesaver of them all. A thick mulch cover reduces weed growth, makes pulling them easier, and helps retain moisture. Plan to use a preemergence herbicide to prevent germination of annual weeds such as crabgrass.

Regular mowing to remove no more than one-third of the length of the grass is the key to keeping your lawn trim and healthy.

Shaped shrubs can be beautiful but require regular attention to keep their form tidy.

Backstage Essentials

Don't forget to plan areas for all the action that will take place behind the scenes. A well-maintained landscape requires tools and activities that require a designated space. The challenge is to allow for that space without detracting from your landscape.

Storing tools and equipment requires space. Make a list of all the things you'll need to store. A lawn mower, spreader, gardening tools and gear, patio furniture, pool equipment, toys, and outdoor game equipment are just some of the things that might be on your list. A central, organized place to store all of your things is essential to help you maintain your landscape easily.

The range of options for storage can go from a beautiful garden shed with a potting table to an equipment shed to a portion of the garage or a simple outdoor storage container that sits next to the house. Whatever you choose, be sure it genuinely fits your needs. For instance, you may choose to designate a part of the garage for storing your lawn mower. Ideally you'll be able to open the garage door and wheel out your mower whenever you need it. Realistically, unless you organize your garage carefully, you may find yourself having to move the car, push out some bikes and haul out the garbage cans just to get to the mower.

You may find that mixing a couple of different storage options meets your needs better than just one. You can purchase an inexpensive outdoor storage container to hold all the pool equipment and store all the yard tools and supplies in the shed. That way you won't be fighting with the pool hoses to get to a shovel.

Simple shelving and colorful climbing vines turn this brick wall into an inviting work area.

Also consider designating an area for a work space. Having a place to sharpen your tools, mix fertilizer or fill the lawn mower with gas will make your maintenance chores easier. Ideally a work space should be near your storage area so you can get to what you need, but it also needs to be in an area where you can work without damaging your plants or lawn. An accidental spill of fertilizer or gasoline onto the lawn can be avoided with a properly designated work space.

If you're going to have a compost pile, plan for that also. You'll want it in an area that's easily accessible, yet far enough from the house and deck or patio so the smell won't interfere with your indoor or outdoor activities. The kind of container you choose for your compost plays an important part in your plan. If space in your landscape is limited, consider a solid compost center to contain the odor. If you have a large yard, a chicken wire enclosure tucked in the corner of the yard may be just fine.

BASIC TOOLS FOR THE WELL-STOCKED TOOL SHED

Long-handled spade
Short-handled spade
Square-nosed shovel
Garden fork
Narrow trowel
Wide trowel
Hoe
Lubricating oil
Leaf rake
Iron rake
Scissors-type
   pruning shears
Loppers
Pruning saw
Bow saw
Lawn spreader
Lawn mower
String trimmer
Linseed oil (for
   wooden handles)
Sharpening file
Long-handled
   trimming saw
Garden shoes or boots
Gloves
Chemical masks

Watering implements need to be conveniently located.

Landscape tools and equipment

The right tools and equipment can make the difference between hard work and rewarding chores. Buy the best tools and equipment you can afford and take care of them. In many cases, they will last a lifetime and become old friends.

■ The first step to taking care of your equipment is to have a proper place to store them. A utility shed is ideal for this purpose. Arrange hangers on the wall and bring in drawers and boxes so every tool has its place. Designate spaces for larger equipment (like mowers and spreaders) that will make them easy to access. This will encourage you and the kids to put everything away when you're done.

■ Keep all instruction manuals and warranty information in a designated drawer. This will be a great asset when you have to replace the string on your weed whacker or mix oil and gas for the chain saw for the first time in a while. In addition to garden tools, keep repair tools organized and handy. A set of socket wrenches, pliers, screwdrivers, and files are a must. Stock your shed with oil, grease, general lubricants, and boiled linseed oil.

■ Rub the wooden handles of tools and wheelbarrows with a rag soaked in linseed oil to preserve the wood. Clean any soil and dirt from shovels, rakes, and other tools, and oil the metal parts. Sharpen not only pruning shears and clippers, but also shovels and hoes.

TOOL STORAGE

Yard tools are an investment worth taking care of. Storing your tools properly will dramatically increase their life. Hang tools out of the weather to keep them dry and handy. A pegboard rack or specialty tool hangers can do the trick. You're more likely to get to work if you can quickly find what you need. Hanging tools is also a good way to keep them out of the reach of children.

Maintain your tools regularly to keep them in good shape. Sharpen your tools, such as pruners, shears and the mower blades, to help make your maintenance routine more effective. Dull tools require too much pressure to work and can leave plants damaged. Sharpen mower blades, too, for clean cuts with no stray sprigs left standing tall. Always clean tools before you store them to help make them last longer.

HOW TO STORE AND CARE FOR CHEMICALS

Whether you use natural pest controls and fertilizers or the synthesized variety, all sprays, dusts, and granules are chemical compounds. As such, they are subject to chemical change and breakdown of key components. These changes are caused by age, temperature, moisture, and sunlight. Freezing almost always damages pesticides and liquid fertilizers. Storage in garden sheds over the winter in cold climates will render them useless. Dry fertilizers, on the other hand, have a very long life if kept dry. Keep all garden chemicals locked up. Ironically many organic pesticides are as toxic as are their synthesized cousins.

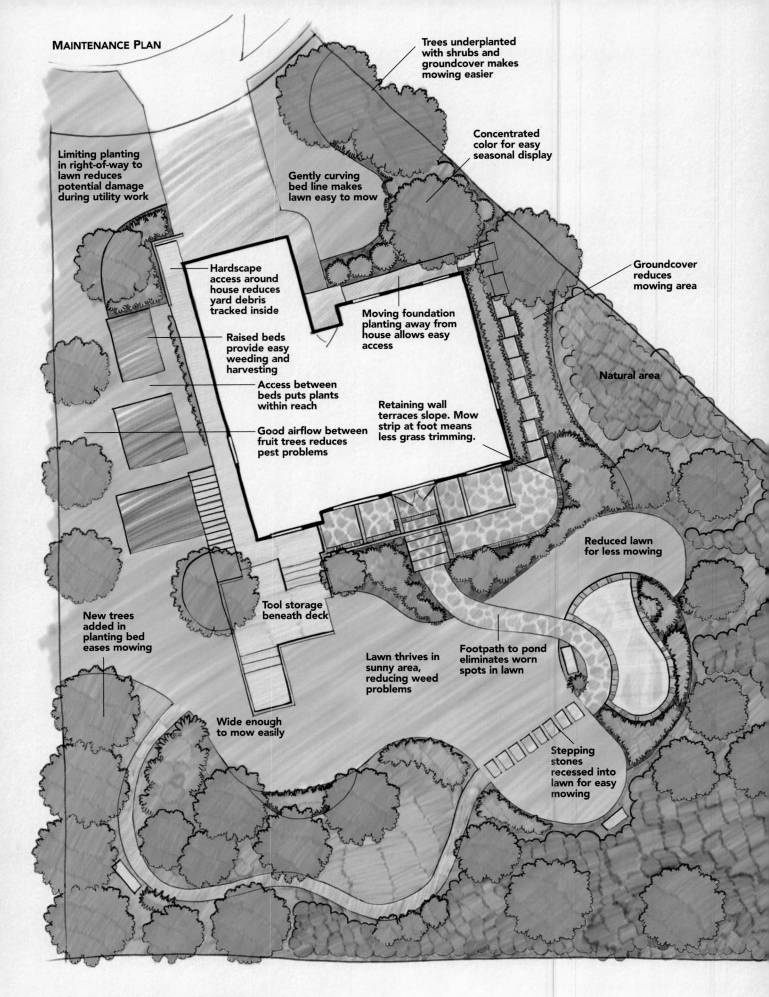

Trees underplanted with shrubs and groundcover makes mowing easier

Concentrated color for easy seasonal display

Limiting planting in right-of-way to lawn reduces potential damage during utility work

Gently curving bed line makes lawn easy to mow

Groundcover reduces mowing area

Hardscape access around house reduces yard debris tracked inside

Moving foundation planting away from house allows easy access

Natural area

Raised beds provide easy weeding and harvesting

Access between beds puts plants within reach

Retaining wall terraces slope. Mow strip at foot means less grass trimming.

Good airflow between fruit trees reduces pest problems

Reduced lawn for less mowing

New trees added in planting bed eases mowing

Tool storage beneath deck

Footpath to pond eliminates worn spots in lawn

Lawn thrives in sunny area, reducing weed problems

Stepping stones recessed into lawn for easy mowing

Wide enough to mow easily

Creating a Maintenance Plan

Maintenance is the part of landscaping you may not want to think about. After all, planting flowers is more fun than pulling weeds. But it pays to consider maintenance before you install your new landscape. Prepare a maintenance plan similar to this one to identify improvements you can implement now to make your life easier later.

■ Take into consideration the forms of maintenance discussed in this chapter: watering, mulching, fertilizing, composting, mowing, pruning, treating plants for disease or pests, weeding, and storing and caring for tools. Your maintenance plan should address all of these areas and consider their interaction.

■ Planting smart will eliminate many maintenance problems. Raising vegetable and flower beds makes planting, weeding, and harvesting easier with less bending. Groundcover planted in difficult-to-mow areas can reduce your yard work time for years to come.

■ Careful selection of mulch will reduce time spent weeding. Applying preemergence herbicide at the right times will help too.

■ Place foundation plantings away from the house for easy access behind them (for a hose bib and for general pruning and fertilizing).

■ Well-planned storage access will reduce steps and frustration later.

■ Careful placement of trees can reduce pest problems.

■ Install hose bibs on all sides of the house with separate hoses available to each; use hose reels for quick retraction.

■ This is also the time to consider traffic flow; the access you provide in your landscape can create maintenance problems or solve them. Inadequate circulation routes through your yard will result in worn paths through lawns and shortcuts taken through beds. Make sure any walkways follow logical routes. Create pathways everywhere you travel often, such as to the trash area, the pond, and the utility area. Masonry or gravel pathways cut down on the amount of dirt tracked into the house.

■ Widen the intersection of walkways to form landings, especially when connecting to other paved areas such as driveways, parking courts, patios, and streets. Landings form transitions from larger paved areas to smaller ones and prevent people from cutting across the corners of planting beds. Landings also provide places for people to pause in the landscape as they greet one another or say good-bye; providing a paved surface for this purpose makes your landscape welcoming.

Carefully planning how you will take care of your landscape is the key to enjoying the outdoor areas of your property as much as the indoors.

Groundcover or low, spreading shrubs are often the best strategy for planting under trees, where grass often struggles to grow.

Preserving natural area means less yard to maintain

A brick mow strip at the base of a wall makes mowing easier.

Designing with Plants

On your master plan you've shown, in a general way, how trees, planting beds, and lawn areas will fit in your new landscape. Now you need more detail—for this, you need a planting plan. As you draw it, you may find you need to alter the bed shapes and tree locations on your master plan, but that's just part of the process of refinement. Your planting plan is also the place you'll add a layer showing shrubs, vines, groundcovers, and seasonal color. You'll select specific plants and figure quantities on this plan too.

Remember, you haven't solved all your problems yet, so refer to your concept diagram and site analysis to remind yourself of the design problems you want plants to solve. Look for situations where you can apply the following design fundamentals.

Introduce exciting accents

Accent is interest achieved through contrast. When the color, texture, line,

or form of a plant differs noticeably from the qualities of its setting, the plant stands out. But too many plants competing for attention will destroy the unity of your design. Some accents—flowers, fruit, bark, and forms—will be seasonal; their contrasts will vary at different times of the year.

A colorful bed of mixed petunias makes for an eye-catching corner.

A formal hedge-edged bed is the centerpiece of the yard.

Clematis 'Nelly Moser' puts on a welcoming display at the threshold.

Create focal points

Focal points are fun to add. Nearly anything can be the center of attention. Plants, artwork, gates, and water features make lovely garden highlights. Placement is the key.

A rustic willow arbor frames a path.

If your focal point is freestanding, such as a sundial or a small ornamental tree, make sure the background is sufficiently neutral to showcase it. If it's an existing item that you want to spotlight, design the surrounding space to show it off. Aligning new views with existing features will bring energy to the look of your landscape.

Use framing techniques

Framing is another way to play up the best aspects of your home and yard—both new and existing elements. Consider strategic plant arrangements that frame pretty views, decorative items, and architectural elements. Designers frequently employ framing to call attention to garden entries and to add irresistible allure to the areas beyond them. You can use this technique yourself; first identify the proposed item or area of attention and the angle from which it will be viewed (the sight line). Then position plants so they make a clear path along the sight line. Remember, a sight line can originate from within your home as a view through a window or door to a garden focal point.

Golden arborvitae (*Thuja orientalis* 'Aurea Nana'), in a mixed border with lupine and iris accents, forms an effective and visually appealing screen.

Plant for screening

Screening with dense plant groupings is an easy way to block unsightly views and add privacy. These living walls can give an area a sense of intimacy and can also help reduce noise and mitigate harsh winds or glare.

For privacy, plant evergreens or deciduous plants or a combination of the two. Decide which views you need to block to give either interior or exterior rooms (or both) privacy. Next, determine how much privacy you want—total and continuous or partial and seasonal? A single tree may be all you need. Evergreen shrubs are good for total year-round barriers. Consider screens as backdrops for other plants or accent items.

Delineate your space

Plants are also great for giving shape to areas. Design your planting to help create the zones that you identified on your concept diagram. (See page 36.) Formal hedges, informal shrub groupings, groves of trees, or a single tree properly placed can define space.

Plants do not have to be taller than eye-level to shape space. Even a minor barrier makes one area of the landscape distinct from another. Think about the inside of your home. Walls are the most obvious space dividers, but a waist-high bar may

EVERGREEN OR DECIDUOUS?

Is the plant you are considering evergreen or deciduous? Find out before you buy. Evergreen plants do not shed their leaves in a single season and provide year-round greenery. Deciduous plants may be leafless for months. Both types of plants add value to your landscape, but make sure you know what to expect, especially when choosing plants for screening views.

The well ordered brick walks and symmetrical accents and plantings make a strong formal statement.

The phlox, daylilies, and more combine pleasantly in this informal border mix.

define the kitchen, and furniture groupings may establish zones of conversation within the living room. Plants of varying heights can play similar roles in your outdoor rooms.

Planting design with style

Once you've decided what function your plantings will serve—screening, focal, or accents, for example—you need to consider what type of landscape style you'll use and which plants are most suitable for your style. Generally, landscape style can be broken down into formal and informal or a combination of both.

The formal style is characterized by symmetrical and geometric designs. These landscapes are symmetrically balanced so that the layout on one side of the axis mirrors the opposite side. Geometric shapes, straight lines, and even numbers of elements are all characteristics of a formal design.

Informal landscapes are asymmetrical and more naturalistic. They require considerable skill to create because without proper planning, they can end up a chaotic collection of plants. If you draw a line down the center of an informal plan, both sides are different but carry similar weight and interest. Irregular shapes, uneven numbers, and contrasting forms are all elements of informal style.

Combining both styles may be a way to satisfy the need to highlight the architecture and lend an unexpected element to the landscape. You may choose to design more formal plantings closer to the house, yet create a more naturalistic landscape further away. You can mix and match to suit your tastes by contrasting formal elements, such as rigidly clipped boxwood, among more natural forms, such as a loose grove of gingko trees.

The landscape style is often dictated by the style of the house, so the plantings are congruous with the architecture and the setting. A suburban center-hall colonial may lend itself to a symmetrical approach that highlights the architectural qualities of the house, whereas a restored farmhouse at the edge of the woods brings to mind a more naturalistic setting.

The crape myrtle (*Lagerstroemia indica*) is one of the best bang-for-your-buck trees to plant in a small landscape. It's beautiful in bloom and it does the work of a much larger shade tree when properly placed.

Trees

Like other plants, properly placed trees can be used to solve design problems in your landscape. They can become accents, add privacy, define zones of use, make an area seem more intimate, provide shade, and contribute vertical definition. Like no other plant, trees can prevent the landscape (especially new-home lots) from looking flat and static.

Trees also keep us comfortable. They shade us in the summer, act as windbreaks, clean pollutants from the air, and buffer noise. Not all trees provide the same benefits, of course, but plant the right tree in the right location and you can create a comfortable place for outdoor living; reduce your heating and cooling costs; enjoy clean, fresh air; and have a beautiful garden as well.

Deflect wind

You can reduce your annual heating bill by up to 20 percent if you plant a windbreak on the windward side of your house to deflect prevailing winter winds. Evergreen trees, with low-growing branches and dense winter foliage, are the best choice.

Cool and clean the air

Trees are efficient at cooling the air. Working somewhat like an evaporative air-conditioner, a tree pumps water vapor from its leaves (a process called transpiration), and the air cools as the moisture evaporates. This is why it feels cool and fresh under a tree even on a hot day.

Like living filters, trees are nature's purifiers. Through openings (stomates) in their leaves, trees absorb pollutants. Each leaf dissolves sulfur and nitrogen, breaks down ozone, and metabolizes other compounds so the tree can use them. After processing all the chemicals, trees give off water and oxygen. Trees also physically remove particles like soot and dust from the atmosphere. The particles stick to leaves and are washed away by rain.

Reduce noise

Though it's a quality often overlooked, trees have an impressive ability to muffle noise. Their leaves and small branches act as baffles, absorbing and deflecting sound. You'll get maximum noise protection from a tree with dense leaves, not an open, lacy-leaved variety. A combination of evergreens, deciduous trees, and dense shrubs is the best sound-absorption solution.

This row of flowering crabapples, tulips, and zig-zag fence make for a friendly divide.

Improve soil

Even below the ground, trees are doing beneficial things for the landscape. Tree roots anchor the tree in the ground and soak up water and nutrients from the soil. They support an underground universe of beneficial insects and microorganisms. These, in turn, keep all the soil around them healthy and teeming with life.

Choosing trees

Design should influence your choices. For each location on your master plan, list the characteristics of the ideal tree. For example, a tree for the center of an entry courtyard should be relatively small when mature, have noninvasive roots that won't buckle paving, have accent qualities at least part of the year, and remain attractive even when not in peak color. When listing characteristics to match your design needs, note what won't work as well. For example, you won't want damaging roots near concrete, messy fruit near sitting or parking areas, or tall trees beneath power lines or eaves.

By writing descriptions, it will be easy to pick the right one for the right spot. You'll also want to choose trees that thrive in your climate zone, and you'll need to know something about their cultural characteristics too—which trees grow in sun or shade and which trees require good drainage or boggy soil. Even if you don't know anything about plants, you can get the information you need from local nurseries or extension agents.

If you can't afford to do anything else, plant trees. You will get more long-term value from even a tiny, young tree than you will from a flat of annuals. A house sitting on its lot is just a house, but a house nestled within trees is a home.

WHERE TO PLANT A TREE FOR MAXIMUM SHADE

Both deciduous trees (those that lose their leaves each year) and evergreens (those which keep their leaves) provide shade. But you'll get maximum shade in the summer and maximum winter sun from a tall deciduous tree with a broad canopy of dense leaves. The temperature beneath a leafy tree can be 8°F cooler than in the open, and this cooling can be passed on to the inside of your house. By reducing the hot sun against your house, your cooling bills are reduced as well. For the most effective shading, place trees on the southwest, west, or northwest sides of the area or building to be shaded. These are the sides where the hot afternoon sun strikes in summer. The sun is highest in the early afternoon, so plant the tallest trees on the southwest side. Three well-placed shade trees can reduce your cooling costs by 35 percent.

The mighty oaks *(Quercus)* are the long-lived workhorses of the American landscape, giving maximum shade and support for wildlife.

Trees: Shaping Your Space

Trees are the bones of any design; they shape spaces and add structure like nothing else. Your first step toward a great garden is analyzing your space; your second step is defining it.

Enclose

To unify an open area, first enclose it. Think of it as putting up walls. A large, open lawn becomes a welcoming space when bordered by trees. The classic choice for this is evergreens, which have the added plus of working year-round, but you can use a mixed border or even a staggered grove of trees to get the same effect with less of a solid feeling.

Once you've created the larger space, break it up into smaller spaces—into outdoor rooms. These smaller rooms invite visitors to sit and stay awhile. They create private spaces within your landscape. Make the walls of the rooms as solid or as light as you want, and in and around these rooms, plant shade trees for a roof or a ceiling.

Cause movement

Trees are crucial to guiding traffic within and among these rooms. They can welcome people into the backyard, announce the entrance to a garden room, or tie the house and yard together.

In a larger sense, trees create corridors and avenues within the garden. These can be formal or informal, dense or airy, but they will guide movement, so take advantage of this. Use them to show off special plantings or favorite areas.

Create dramatic views

The corridors and rooms you've created to this point are natural settings for your favorite garden views. If you're especially proud of a particular tree, design a room around it or with a great view of it. Elegant columnar trees can show off a favorite vista as well as any picture frame. Use your most spectacular trees at the end of corridors and they will draw attention. And don't forget the views from your house; plan your more dramatic plantings with an eye toward the view from the house.

Expand

If your space begins to feel cramped, there are ways to expand it. Prune lower leaves of trees to make a space under the canopy of a tree and create a room without walls. Use perspective; with larger trees planted close and smaller ones farther away, the space will feel larger than it is. Or treat the garden as an expansion of the house and it will make the house seem that much larger.

Flowering okame cherry trees (*Prunus okame*) gently frame a curving walkway.

A black locust 'Frisia' (*Robinia pseudoacacia*) will grow quickly to provide shade, fragrant spring blooms, and a focal point for this small house and yard.

1. Define Boundaries
Enclosure can be as solid as a dense wall of evergreens or as suggestive as a single tree. Trees in staggered groves contain space while retaining openness.

2. Block Views
Trees can protect your privacy and screen unsightly views. Such screens are usually walls of thick foliage.

3. Develop Corridors
The trunks and foliage mass of trees direct traffic and connect garden rooms together. Passageways can be wide and sweeping or narrow and intimate. They can be straight and direct or meandering and full of mystery.

4. Set Focal Points
A tree with an unusual sculptural frame or seasonal color draws the eye like a magnet. Tall, narrow trees attract attention from a distance like exclamation points. Up close, such columnar trees direct the gaze skyward. Use focal points with care; too many can simply confuse.

5. Enclose Intimate Rooms
Large properties can be made more intimate by dividing space into rooms. The connections between rooms become points of interest, and they encourage movement and exploration.

6. Establish Gateways
The trunks of trees establish gateways and portals between different parts of the yard. Areas between garden room and corridor, between the house and the yard, and between the private backyard and the public front yard are all places for special treatment.

7. Spread Canopies Overhead
A canopy overhead not only protects from hot sun and rain, it provides its own sense of enclosure and intimacy—a garden room without walls.

8. Extend the Indoors Out
Trees arching over both house and yard create transitional spaces that extend indoor rooms out into the yard.

9. Frame Views
As with a painting, looking through a frame sets off a view and magnifies its effect. A view out a window can be enhanced with a frame as simple as a single tree trunk to one side.

10. Expand Sense of Space
Placing large, overscale trees up close and smaller trees farther away increases the sense of depth and distance.

Trees: Composing a Landscape

The golden rain tree (*Koelreuteria paniculata*) is a lovely rounded tree with lush yellow blooms in summer.

A weeping Higan cherry tree underplanted with daffodils makes a distinctive impression with shape and color.

Trees provide the basic structure and mass of the landscape. And the shapes of the trees are vitally important to this. When seen from a distance, such as from the street, the mass and skyline of the trees in your yard give your landscape weight and form. Rounded and spreading trees provide a horizontal mass that extends the house outward, while the vertical mass of columnar and pyramidal trees extends your house upwards.

Overhead, the leafy canopy of spreading trees frames the view below it; the verticality of columnar trees lifts up the view almost like a tall window. Repeating these forms intensifies the effect and varying them creates a dynamic, changing impression.

At eye level, tree trunks can frame a view, extend the vertical lines of the house into the landscape, or send the eye through the mysterious depths of a grove. When repeated, these trunks establish rhythms, calming if repeated uniformly and more dynamic if interspersed with different shapes. Showy trees, or trees with unusual form, especially interrupt such a rhythmic path and should be used sparingly.

The shapes of trees

Classifying the myriad shapes and sizes of trees into a few general forms helps us to combine trees in a landscape that is unified and pleasing to the eye.

Rounded and oval trees offer a regular shape that is ideal for a formal statement in rows and grids. Use them to create an effective corridor flanking a drive or street. Planted alone in an open yard, they tend to achieve their most perfect, regular form. But in groups of three or more, their tops create a billowing mass of foliage that's pleasing from a distance.

Spreading trees provide a horizontal reach that is very useful for continuing the horizontal lines of the house out into the landscape. These are the trees to choose when you are looking for a canopy over a patio or sitting area. Their overarching branches are perfect to establish a powerful frame for a favorite view.

Pyramidal trees have crowns that taper toward the sky; when seen from a distance, they tend to lift the eye upward. They can be cone-shape evergreens, such as spruce and fir, or deciduous trees. Pyramidal greenspire lindens or scarlet oaks are as well suited for street tree plantings as for dramatic contrast behind rounded and spreading trees.

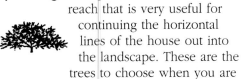

CHECKLIST FOR CHOOSING TREES FOR YOUR DESIGN

Here are the characteristics you should use in evaluating trees for your planting plan:

- Purpose of tree within your design
- Mature size (height and spread)
- Rate of growth
- Evergreen or deciduous
- Seasonal interest
- Form
- Cultural requirements
- Availability and expense
- Negative characteristics to avoid

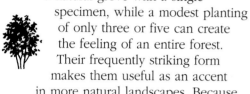

Columnar or fastigiate trees have a narrow, vertical form. They make dramatic sentinels that attract attention from a distance and lift the eye upward like an arrow pointed to the sky. Their narrow diameter makes them a favorite for planting in colonnades, as screens and windbreaks, and creating garden rooms with walls of foliage.

Multiple-trunk trees lend the effect of a natural grove with a single specimen, while a modest planting of only three or five can create the feeling of an entire forest. Their frequently striking form makes them useful as an accent in more natural landscapes. Because they tend to arch out, they are often used at the corner of a house to soften its lines.

Weeping trees are the ideal accent to command attention in an important spot and are fitting and effective next to water. A weeping cherry, for example, is a spectacular living sculpture. It makes a beautiful adornment for a pool or other small water feature.

GOOD TREES FOR SMALL SPACES

Amur maple
  (*Acer tataricum ginnala*)
Japanese maple
  (*Acer palmatum*)
Lemon bottlebrush
  (*Callistemon citrinus*)
Eastern redbud
  (*Cercis Canadensis*)
Flowering dogwood
  (*Cornus florida*)
Carolina silverbell
  (*Halesia tetraptera*)
Goldenchain tree
  (*Laburnum ×watereri*)
Flowering crabapple
  (*Malus* 'Adirondack,' 'David' *M. Sargentii*)
Amanogawa Japanese flowering cherry
  (*Prunus serrulata* 'Amanogawa')
Okame cherry
  (*Prunus* 'Okame')
Kwanzan cherry
  (*Prunus* 'Sekiyama')
Japanese tree lilac
  (*Syringa reticulata* 'Ivory Silk')

The Japanese red maple is a classic specimen tree for small spaces, offering a delicate shape and brilliant foliage throughout the growing season.

TEN BEST WEEPING TREES

Cutleaf Japanese maple
  (*Acer palmatum* dissectum)
Weeping Katsura tree
  (*Cercidiphyllum japonicum* 'Pendula')
Weeping European beech
  (*Fagus sylvatica* 'Pendula')
Red Jade crabapple
  (*Malus* 'Red Jade')
Weeping Serbian spruce
  (*Picea omorika* 'Pendula')
Weeping Yoshino cherry
  (*Prunus ×yedoensis* 'Shidare-yoshino')
Weeping Higan cherry
  (*Prunus subhirtella* 'Pendula')
Weeping willow
  (*Salix babylonica*)
Weeping Japanese snowbell
  (*Styrax japonicus* 'Pendula' ('Carillon'))
Weeping Canadian hemlock
  (*Tsuga canadensis* 'Sargentii')

TEN BEST COLUMNAR TREES

Columnar red maple
  (*Acer rubrum* 'Columnare')
Goldspire sugar maple
  (*Acer saccharum* 'Goldspire')
Columnar European hornbeam
  (*Carpinus betulus* 'Columnaris')
Columnar European beech
  (*Fagus sylvatica* 'Fastigiata')
Gingko or maidenhair tree 'Princeton Sentry'
  (*Gingko biloba* 'Princeton Sentry')
Crabapple 'Centurion,' 'Sentinel,' 'Red Baron'
  (*Malus* 'Centurion,' 'Sentinel,' or 'Red Baron')
Columnar Sargent cherry
  (*Prunus sargentii* 'Columnaris,' 'Spire')
Amanogawa Japanese flowering cherry
  (*Prunus serrulata* 'Amanogawa')
Callery pear 'Capital' or 'Chanticleer'
  (*Pyrus calleryana* 'Capital' or 'Chanticleer')
Bald cypress 'Shawnee Brave'
  (*Taxodium distichum* 'Shawnee Brave')

A small specimen tree nestled in a richly planted island bed makes for quick accent in a newly landscaped yard.

Trees: Planting Strategies

Your tree planting strategy should be planned according to both the use of the tree and how long it will take the tree to mature enough to accomplish your goals. For instance, if you need a row of trees to enclose a part of the yard, you've got plenty of options to choose from. If time is of the essence, your choices become more limited. To many gardeners, waiting for trees to grow is frustrating. You may be patient, but still not want to wait 30 years for a tree to give you the gift of shade. Fortunately, there are several remedies.

TEMPORARY TREES give the fastest effect for your money. Many will seem to spring up overnight, filling space very quickly. That's the good news. The bad news is that almost all of these trees have problems—they are weak-wooded, throw lots of litter, or have numerous pests. If you try one of these, be aware of its problems and be prepared to deal with the cost of having it removed (which can be expensive).

The river birch (*Betula nigra*) is a fast-growing, distinctive tree that works well alone or in groups.

GROVES AND GROUPS of small trees can create a fast, strong effect. You should use only trees which do this in nature (others will not grow properly), such as birches. You can even combine fast growers with slower growers that are shade tolerant; over time the slower trees will replace the faster ones. This option is not without its dangers, though. The top growth of trees planted in groups adjusts to its situation; that is, it grows differently than if the tree was freestanding. So, if you thin the group later, the upper part of the trees will look odd. Also, as mentioned before, the expense of removing trees later is not to be taken lightly.

MATURE TREES are the fastest option. What could go wrong with buying an already mature tree? Plenty. Besides being very expensive, mature trees also don't take planting shock very well, and they run the risk of dying in the process. And even if they do survive, it might take them a few years to get back to a healthy growing state. In those few years, smaller trees might have already caught up to them.

The best solution borrows from all of these strategies. First, pick the highest quality, medium-to-fast growing trees that fit your needs and wants. Then give them the best site for their needs and follow up with the best care you can give. Plant them carefully, tend them regularly, and pay attention to them year-round. Watch for pests and signs of disease, water them correctly and deeply, and mulch their root zone. This way, you get a quality tree, and more than likely, a good, fast effect in your landscape.

SMALL TREES are great if you have all the time in the world for them to grow. Buy the best trees you can and give them the best possible care. When kept pest free and disease free, sited correctly, watered regularly, and mulched properly, many trees will respond with faster-than-average growth. With such care, a good slow-growth-rate tree will grow at its best rate. Taking care of your tree from the beginning is the most effective way to guarantee its success.

FASTEST GROWING TREES

Box elder
 (*Acer negundo*)
Silver maple
 (*Acer saccharinum*)
European black alder
 (*Alnus glutinosa*)
Leyland cypress
 (×*Cupressocyparis leylandii*)
Royal paulownia
 (*Paulownia tomentosa*)
White poplar
 (*Populus alba*)
Lombardy poplar
 (*Populus nigra* 'Italica')
Willows
 (*Salix* spp.)
Green Giant arbovitae
 (*Thuja* 'Green Giant')

MEDIUM TO FAST GROWING TREES

Red maple
 (*Acer rubrum*)
Heritage river birch
 (*Betula nigra* 'Heritage')
Green ash
 (*Fraxinus pennsylvanica*)
Thornless honey locust
 (*Gleditsia triacanthos* var. *inermis*)
London plane tree
 (*Plantanus* ×*acerifolia*)
Pin oak
 (*Quercus palustris*)
Northern red oak
 (*Quercus rubra*)
Coast redwood
 (*Sequoia sempervirens*)
Bald cypress
 (*Taxodium distichum*)
Chinese elm
 (*Ulmus parvifolia*)

Planting somewhat mature evergreens, such as Albertina spruce (*Picea glauca* var. *Albertina conica*), is one of the best, most economical ways to get immediate gratification in your landscape.

Shrubs and Hedges

Shrubs are the garden's backbone, bringing beauty, comfort, and pleasure to the landscape by adding structure to the outdoors. Before purchasing another plant for the garden, invest in shrubs. They offer years of low-maintenance satisfaction, often at a minimal price. Shrubs change how you feel about being outside. They can create a sense of privacy and psychological comfort—by hiding unsightly views—and physical comfort by altering wind, light, and noise pollution.

What shrubs do for the landscape

Shrubs are one of the most versatile plants you can use in your landscape. They can help you control the wind in your yard by creating a windbreak to divert harsh winter winds or to channel a soft summer breeze. Shrubs create shade to manage light, glare, and reflection levels in the garden. They can slow erosion in problem areas such as slopes, where soil, grass, and flowers wash away, and hold the bank in place. Well-placed shrubs can prevent the hot summer sun from entering the house or allow winter sunlight to brighten and warm the house. Shrubs hide the source of street noises, making your time at home and in the garden more peaceful and relaxing. Densely branched shrubs form the essence of privacy and screen unwanted views from your landscape. Shrubs help to direct people and animals where you want them to go, forming either real or perceived barriers to activity.

A shrub with unusual, showy properties can easily become the focus of an entire landscape design. Shrubs delineate space. Like walls in a building, they create spaces for outdoor living, as well as ease the shift between constructed and natural environments. More than any other garden plant, shrubs can establish the ambience of the landscape, emphasizing either a formal or informal style with different types and placements of plants. Shrubs set the stage. A mass of dark green shrubs accentuates and shows off a sculpture or a colorful bed of flowers. The fruit of many shrubs attracts birds and other wildlife in winter. And some ornamental shrubs (such as blueberry) produce tasty fruit too.

Consider them for accents too. Many shrubs flower and fruit at different times of the year and are good seasonal show-offs. Shrubs range in size from dwarf and pygmy selections to plants the size of small trees, so there's a shrub for any place in the landscape.

Rhododendron and azalea in a mix of colors and shapes are the basis of this dramatic shrub border.

A profusion of pink rhododendron is a showstopper each spring.

Plan for shrubs

When you're preparing your planting plan, compare your site analysis with your master plan. You probably haven't solved all the problems yet, so consider shrubs in places where you want to add privacy or improve the view of your home from the street.

Foundation planting refers to plants set near the base of a house. They hide foundations and marry the architecture with the land. Shrubs are perfect for foundation plantings. To be effective, however, foundation plantings should be more than mere rows of shrubs. Consider filling beds in tiers or layers to give shape to the landscape and to provide a transition from the vertical form of the house to the horizontal lawn. Shrubs are effective in such mass plantings, and you can complement them with small trees, vines, perennials, groundcovers, and annuals.

The most common mistake made with foundation planting is underestimating mature sizes. If a shrub will require lots of pruning in the future to prevent it from blocking a window or crowding a walkway, then it is not the right choice for that location. Know how high and wide a shrub will grow before planting it. And resist the temptation to plant shrubs too closely together; you'll avoid future maintenance headaches.

As you did for trees, list the qualities your shrubs should have to meet the needs you've shown on your master plan. Research which shrubs thrive in your climate and conditions of your landscape, then choose the right shrub for your specific needs.

WHAT MAKES A HEDGE

Simply put, a hedge is a living wall formed by a row of closely planted shrubs. Hedges can serve many purposes, such as directing traffic, providing a screen or barrier, reducing wind, and buffering noise. They can delineate areas in the garden or provide shelter and food for wildlife. Unlike a path that may merely suggest where people should walk, a hedge creates a clear route that isn't easily broken through. A densely planted hedge can create a fine wind barrier, screen off an area, or reduce noise as well as any solid fence. Considering that some hedges can last for hundreds of years, it could be cheaper in the long run to plant a hedge instead of a fence.

A carefully clipped hybrid yew (*Taxus* × *medea* 'Hicksii') makes an effective privacy hedge.

Shrubs: Shaping Your Space

Shrubs enclose a small patch of lawn and picnic table, creating an informal outdoor dining room.

Space is the basic element of the landscape, and its successful organization is fundamental to creating a usable, liveable, and beautiful place around your home. For example, rows of hedges, spread widely apart, can be beautiful in and of themselves, but it is the perfectly proportioned space, or void, in between them that can make a landscape sing. Compare the space formed by widely spaced hedges to the very different narrow corridor formed by closer hedge rows, where the confined space makes the eye race to its destination.

A lawn path cuts a curving swath through mixed beds of shrubs and perennials.

Learn to see your landscape as a series of spaces rather than a collection of objects and plants. Shrubs, of course, are a fundamental tool for shaping the space around you. At their most basic, shrubs can mark boundaries, delineating, for instance, your property lines. Walls of shrubs can enclose the garden into rooms, much as the walls in your home do, with gateways and paths for entrances and connecting corridors. Both short and tall hedges can frame the view, as well as move people and even cars along pathways.

HOW TO INCREASE THE SENSE OF SPACE

The color, size, line, form, texture, and placement of shrubs affect the perception of space in the garden. For example, you can increase perceived space dramatically by forcing the perspective from a single viewpoint. Thus, for a viewer standing at one end of an allée (a landscape term meaning a straight, linear passage), parallel hedges or shrub borders of similar consistent height gradually recede into the distance. To speed up the perceived recession, thereby increasing the sense of distance and depth, slope the tops of the shrubs so they are taller in the foreground and shorter in the distance. Decreasing the actual width of the passage as it moves into the distance accentuates the forced perspective.

Color is another way to tease the eye into perceiving greater distance. In general, the darker and cooler the colors, the more they appear to recede; whereas bright, warm colors tend to stand out. Therefore, dark bluish green foliage would retreat into the background when contrasted with leaves of clear yellow-green. Placing shrubs with showy chartreuse foliage at the far end of a hedge or border actually serves to decrease that planting's visual depth.

Likewise, coarse-textured plants dominate fine textures in the landscape. Shrubs of fine to medium-fine texture, such as box or privet (that are densely covered with short-stemmed small leaves), make a smooth, neutral statement and work especially well in hedges or backgrounds. Conversely, coarse-textured shrubs with large leaves on long stems accentuate moving patterns of light and dark, thus drawing attention to a planting and reducing the perceived size of the area. Interesting plants with bold sculptural shapes appear closer to the viewer than smooth clipped hedges or uniform shrub plantings that quickly disappear into the background.

Plant size also affects the perception of space. For instance, surrounding a small garden with tall hedges or filling it with jumbo shrubs, flowers, and trees quickly shrinks the space. On the other hand, choosing dwarf shrubs and small flowering trees can lend a small garden a sense of spaciousness, proportion, and proper scale.

1. Screen Out Eyesores
A shrub border of evergreens makes an effective screen for a neighbor's unsightly play equipment, while a hedge masks a utility area.

2. Create a Sense of Privacy
A living screen can be a harmonious addition. Virtually any shrub can be used to create privacy if it is sited appropriately.

3. Enclose Your Spaces
Use shrubs to create garden "rooms" or surprise elements in the landscape. Block open views for additional interest in the landscape.

4. Direct Movement
Use a planting of mixed shrubs to not only direct the eye within the garden landscape, but to also direct the flow of foot traffic.

5. Frame a View
Create an enticing view of the trees, shrubs, or ornament beyond by carefully siting shrubs to make the most of the entire garden.

6. Create Corridors
A mixed hedge of shrubs and perennials flanks a wooden pergola, creating a pleasant pathway between elements in the landscape.

7. Enlarge the Sense of Space
Using shrubs to squeeze space into a corridor increases the sense of expansion in the garden room beyond.

8. Attract Attention
A specimen may be a single shrub at a visual focal point or in an area where you like to sit and appreciate the plant's color and shape.

Shrubs: Foundation Plantings

Foundation plantings appear in front of many American homes. This uniquely American landscape feature started as a cover-up for the tall, lattice-covered foundations constructed under the fashionable front porches of big Victorian abodes. Yet even as the Victorian style passed into history, these voguish plantings continued to crop up where foundations were low and there was no need for them.

With careful consideration, you can create an effective foundation planting.

Such a planting will disguise and lend visual stability to a tall foundation and also can soften the corners of a house and tie it into the surrounding landscape. Some foundation plantings enhance the style of a house. A symmetrical pattern reinforces the regularity of a foursquare colonial home, while an asymmetrically balanced planting is in keeping with a prairie-style house. A well-designed planting focuses attention on the front door, the focal point of most homes.

SIZE AND PROPORTION is the key to a successful foundation planting. Large shrubs often look best with a tall house of two or more stories, while smaller shrubs complement the lines of a one-story dwelling.

Find out the mature size of a shrub before buying it. Choose shrubs not for how they look in the nursery but for their mature size. Too many houses have windows, doors, and front steps darkened by formerly shrub-size conifers grown into giant trees. Try to keep the mature height of doorway plants to about one-third the distance from the ground to the eaves overhanging the walls, and corner plants under two-thirds

Barberry and spruce create striking contrast.

HORIZONTAL SHRUB FORMS

Rounded/globular
(*Buxus sempervirens*)

Mounding
(Evergreen azalea, southern indica)

Prostrate
(*Arctostaphylos uva-ursi*)

Horizontal layered
(*Viburnum plicatum* var. *tomentosum*)

Weeping
(*Tsuga canadensis* 'Pendula')

Blue spruce, hydrangea, and hosta make for an active mix against a foundation.

VERTICAL SHRUB FORMS

Pyramidal/conical
(*Taxus cuspidata*)

Columnar
(*Thuja occidentalis*)

Vase/fan-shape
(*Hamamelis ×intermedia*)

Arching/fountain
(*Spiraea ×vanhouttei*)

Oval
(*Ilex cornuta*)

These azaleas are an appropriate shape and scale for the foundation of this house.

the distance between the ground and the eaves. Corner plantings are taller because they both frame the house and create a transition to the landscape. If you have an existing overgrown foundation planting, you may be able to prune the shrubs to fit the scale of the house or you may have to remove them and start from scratch.

HORIZONTAL AND VERTICAL SHRUBS perform different but complementary visual functions. Shrubs with horizontal form hold the viewer's attention near the ground or pull the gaze downward. These shrubs create effective visual transitions from the vertical architectural lines of a house into the horizontal lines of open landscape. Vertical shrubs are effective accents and can punctuate or emphasize a planting composition. Together horizontal and vertical shrubs form a kind of visual melody, with high and low notes that engage the viewer in the landscape.

EVERGREEN AND DECIDUOUS shrubs complement each other as well. When designing a foundation planting, note that broad-leaved evergreens and conifers have a year-round presence but look best when softened by a few deciduous shrubs. Although you'll want flowering evergreen and deciduous shrubs to create a harmonious effect when they flower concurrently with other plants, don't choose them for flower color alone; flowers are at best a temporary phenomenon for many shrubs.

LOCATION is important. Place foundation plants in front of the eaves so they will receive water when it rains and in front of the snow line so they won't be crushed when snow slides off the roof. If your house is limestone or stucco and your plants are acid-loving evergreens such as hollies (*Ilex*) or rhododendrons, acidify the soil; rain may wash the residue of these materials into the ground. Finally, pay attention to safety. Overgrown shrubs near the entry give vandals or burglars an easy place to hide.

Hinoki false cypress (*Chamaecyparis obtuse* 'Hinoki') is an effective vertical foundation shrub.

Shrubs: Using in Borders

A bed of hydrangea is hedged with yew clipped like a wave.

If you can design a shrub border, you can create a garden. Shrub borders are useful for enclosing space. Not only are they an attractive way to delineate the boundaries of your property, they can turn a yard into a garden by creating privacy and limiting views. Like hedges, shrub borders form the walls of outdoor rooms. These walls can be evergreen, deciduous, or both. They can serve as a background against which flowering annuals and perennials display their charms, or they can make their own brilliant and harmonious color display.

Shrub borders are more than handsome groups of shrubs. Although a well-designed planting may create a place of visual interest or focal point in a landscape, its plants are too far apart to create the massed, wall-like effect of the shrub border. In shrub borders, mature plants typically overlap by about one-third to create a sense of depth, richness, and mass.

Similarly, a shrub border differs from an island planting. The latter is designed to be seen from all sides. It can be treated as a bold landscape mass with overlapping shrubs or as a balanced but sparser group of plants. The shrub border, on the other hand, will be seen from at most three

A mixed border of shrubs and cool-color perennials makes an elegant natural border along a stone wall.

sides. The back of it is against a fence, wall, or property line.

To create an attractive shrub border, it's necessary to understand how scale, balance, sequence, variety, emphasis, and repetition—the principles of design—affect a border's mass, line, color, and texture—the building blocks of your plan. In fact, making a shrub border is similar to playing with blocks. Some are tall and narrow, giving height and impact to a design. Some are a bit shorter and wider to create a sense of mass and bulk, while others are little cubes, spheres, and slabs. These small blocks link the main masses of the design and enhance its depth and contrast. Both ends of a well-designed shrub border will have a large shrub or a strong, well-defined group of shrubs that anchor it. In addition to choosing plants for mass, include plants for visual interest. Attractive bark, berries, branching habit, and the color and texture of leaves and flowers give seasonal character and beauty to a planting.

Shrubs in the mixed border

Mixed borders may contain small trees, shrubs, perennials, and some annuals. Perennials and annuals make excellent space fillers for newly planted, deciduous and evergreen shrub borders where the plants have not reached their mature spread. A mixed border offers variety but requires more care than an all-shrub border, since flower gardening can be labor intensive.

GROUNDCOVER SHRUBS

Bearberry
    (*Arctostaphylos uva-ursi*)
Heather
    (*Calluna vulgaris*)
Bearberry cotoneaster
    (*Cotoneaster dammeri*)
Wintercreeper
    (*Euonymus fortunei*)
Aaronsbeard
    (*Hypericum calycinum*)
Evergreen candytuft
    (*Iberis sempervirens*)
Fragrant sumac
    (*Rhus aromatica* 'Gro-low')
Lowbush blueberry
    (*Vaccinium angustifolium*)

Note the mix of heights, shapes, and color in this richly planted shrub border.

Shrubs for massing

Shrub massing implies using one kind of shrub in each bed or border. In a woodland garden, azaleas, rhododendrons, or mountain laurels (*Kalmia latifolia*) can be grouped under deciduous trees for a stunning effect. Beds made up entirely of roses in a formal garden add elegance and unity to the design, while massing small, fine-textured shrubs such as rosemary (*Rosmarinus officinalis*) or lavender (*Lavandula angustifolia*) adds textural contrast. Before planting flowering shrubs such as azaleas, determine when the plants flower and whether selections with overlapping periods of bloom will create a harmonious look.

Heather (*Calluna vulgaris*) is a versatile and varied groundcover shrub.

Vines

The leaves of this Virginia creeper (*Parthenocissus quinquefolia*), growing alongside evergreen English ivy (*Hedera helix*), will turn red in the autumn if grown in full sun.

Clematis 'Niobe' makes fine art out of an old stump.

Vines are amazing plants. In the wild they scramble over rocks and trees and wind themselves through brush and other plants. They arch over streams and sprawl through woodland meadows. They plunge from cliffs. They are the cloth of nature's landscape and take the form of things they cover. And because of their frequently rapid growth and unique ability to cloak and drape—often with showy color—vines play a host of unique roles in the garden. They are easy to grow, affordable, and forgiving of injury.

Plant vines in locations where you need privacy, shade, or vertical interest—or perhaps you need to soften a blank wall or a harsh angle. Vines also lend a sense of maturity to new structures and give an air of romance and nostalgia to whatever they cover. Flowering vines contribute color and fragrance. Like other members of the plant world, vines may be evergreen or deciduous.

An arc of Chinese wisteria (*Wisteria sinensis*) in full bloom frames a window.

QUICK SHADE FOR PAVED AREAS

Vines make great shade plants for carports, patios, and even cabanas over sitting areas. Build a simple arbor or other structure over a paved area and train a vine to climb up and provide shade. Make sure the structure is strong enough to support the weight. Plant at the edge of the paving, or if that is not possible, plant it in a large container set on the pavement. American wisteria, akebia, Carolina jessamine, hops, and silver lace do well in such situations.

Avoid vines with large flowers or fruit; they will shower debris from above. Trumpet vines, Asian wisterias, and grapes are among the messiest.

Climbing roses and clematis twine about a rustic cedar arbor.

A vine's method of climbing is important to know because it determines the kind of structure you can grow it on. Twiners, like morning glory and wisteria, wrap their stems around supports and will grow on posts, chain link, and lattices. Vines that climb by tendrils, such as sweet pea and passionflower, reach out and curl threadlike extensions of branch or leaf around netting or the stems of shrubs. Vines that grow with clinging rootlets, such as creeping fig and climbing hydrangea, attach themselves to masonry, tree trunks, or rocks with small roots or adhesive-like pads. Climbers and sprawlers, such as rambling roses, don't climb readily by themselves but their long, arching, sprawling stems can be tied to lattice or frameworks anchored in walls or other structures, and achieve often amazing heights.

As with many other plants, vines may be annual or perennial. Annual vines live for less than a year (sometimes only a single season), but their quick growth offers "instant" color and design—and their short life span means you can change their effect from year to year. Perennials live far longer than a year and can become the fixtures that are permanent in your design. Some perennials are herbaceous; they die to the ground each winter and regrow quickly in the spring. Others, called "woody" vines, retain aboveground growth all winter. Some woody vines are evergreen; others are deciduous.

As a part of the landscape, vines offer a wonderful range of color, texture, and fragrance. They can match, complement, or contrast other plants and structures in your outdoor environment. They also can serve many functions in the landscape—moderate wind, sun, and sound; reduce erosion; attract wildlife; create an outdoor room; add height; and hide or screen areas.

Vines
(continued)

Create sun, wind, and sound screens

Vines on the west and south sides of a house can lower the temperature of the wall and reduce cooling costs inside. Plant vines directly next to your home or use arbors, lattice, or netting over the wall for training vines.

Quick shade can be obtained with a vine such as a wisteria over a patio. Plant the vine at the edge of the paving and train it over an arbor or other structure for attractive cooling in summer sitting areas.

If you would like a quieter retreat, vines (especially those with large, soft leaves) soften sounds that would otherwise bounce off hard surfaces.

Reduce erosion

Some vines grow horizontally along the ground as successfully as others scramble up trees and supports. These ground-huggers are ideal for slopes that need stabilizing. Virginia creeper, English ivy, maypops, or Confederate jasmine will cover areas quickly and thickly. They all root where stems touch the soil, so they multiply as they grow, a real advantage when the slope is very rocky and digging is difficult. They tolerate drought and

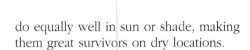
'New Dawn' roses engulf an arched trellis.

do equally well in sun or shade, making them great survivors on dry locations.

Attract wildlife

Birds will love you for your vines. Vines offer safe shelter for many species of birds and nectar for others. Vines on the house will bring birds close to your living areas, maybe within view of a window. Evergreen vines will be perches for overwintering birds at night and will provide cover during the day.

Shape outdoor rooms

What makes vines unique is their ability to form a thin and living wall, one that is quickly established, inexpensively shaped, flexible, easily modified, available in an array of colors—and never needs painting. Enclose a space with a vine-covered arbor and the area feels like a room. A vine wall gives a sense of enclosure, yet its texture is gentler than a hard-surface wall or wooden fence.

Boston ivy (*Parthenocissus tricuspidata*) is trained to frame a barn door.

Clematis in bright pink accents a house facade.

VINES FOR SCREENS

EVERGREEN VINES

English ivy *(Hedera helix)*
Persian ivy *(Hedera colchica)*
Wintercreeper *(Euonymus fortunei)*
Creeping fig *(Ficus pumila)*
Carolina jessamine
    (Gelsemium sempervirens)
Evergreen clematis
    (Clematis armandii)
Cross vine *(Bignonia capreolata)*
Confederate jasmine
    (Trachelospermum jasminoides)

RAPID GROWERS

Morning glories *(Ipomoea)*
Virginia creeper *(Parthenocissus
    quinquefolia)*
Cup-and-saucer vine *(Cobaea scandens)*
English ivy *(Hedera helix)*
Akebia *(Akebia quinata)*
Wisteria *(Wisteria)*
Dutchman's pipe
    (Aristolochia macrophylla)
Beans *(Dolichos, Phaseolus)*
Potato vine *(Solanum jasminoides)*
Moonflower *(Ipomoea alba)*
Trumpet vine *(Campsis radicans)*

An outdoor work space is defined by leafy vines and other green "walls."

Add height

Creating boundaries with vines also adds vertical design elements to an otherwise flat landscape, and they do it without "getting in the way." For example, vine-covered posts can enclose an area and keep open the view beyond. A single vine-covered structure can center the view. Repeated patterns can punctuate the openness of your garden and give it rhythm, and depending on your choice of vines, a sense of mystery or the gentle motion of the light.

Hide and screen

The beauty of using vines is that they both cover unsightly objects and become pleasant distractions. Make an eyesore a focal point with climbing roses, honeysuckle, and any of the annual vines that will produce color throughout the summer.

For example, a garden shed is extremely useful in a cluttered world, but it is rarely attractive. Drape it with poultry netting and plant English ivy for an evergreen cover. Dog pens and runs may be a necessity but are not pretty spots. Cover the fence with foliage, or better yet, with a vine that flowers. Cover a concrete block wall with a vine that clings with rootlets. Climbing hydrangea or a false climbing hydrangea will reward you with a great show of flowers each spring.

If you need to screen an unpleasant view, the solution is simple, inexpensive, and takes up almost no space. Create a quick screen with wire mesh fencing and a tendril vine. A latticework covered with hyacinth bean will be quickly covered with pink flowers and purple pods. Or transform your existing chain link fence into an attractive living wall that screens your view. Choose a vine that grows quickly, and you can enjoy that screen by summer. As screens, vines do double duty. In addition to hiding something you don't want to see, they add privacy to a garden by blocking the view from the outside. If you want less of your yard to be visible from the street, a neighbor's yard, or a commercial area, solve the problem with a screen of vines.

Distinctive architectural elements are echoed and enhanced by the profusion of Chinese wisteria.

Vines: Special Effects

Vines are more than functional. They, like no other member of the plant world, can take you on an endless journey of design. They can frame views or objects, quiet a garden setting, or bring it alive with brightness. They can be small points of interest or major backdrops for other plantings.

Frame the view

A frame guides the eye and adds a sense of mystery. Try growing Boston ivy or cross vine around a window in a masonry wall. Arch a Dutchman's pipe across the window. When it blooms, you'll have a great view of delightful, but usually overlooked, flowers.

A lone plain bench is not terribly welcoming; it's isolated and exposed. Frame or surround the sides of the bench with vines and it becomes a beautiful, comfortable, and private retreat.

A vine-covered archway makes you want to peer through it; it frames the view beyond and is a transition into the garden. A sculpture, small fountain, gazing ball, or special plant within or just beyond the arch adds depth and highlights the view.

Create focal points

An individual vine on an arch, tripod, or lattice becomes a focal point in a garden. Plant a beautiful vine on a simple stake. Cover a decorative structure with an ordinary vine. An attractive pergola or arch becomes a focal point; so do ornamental posts.

A series of vine-covered arches or tripods becomes a focal point and major element of the landscape. A series of vertical posts covered by vines forms a

VINES IN CONTAINERS

Before you plant in containers, think about the container you'll use and how the vine grows.

Permanent containers remain in place year-round. They become a fixture on a deck, balcony, or paved area, so they need to be attractive every day. Movable containers are more flexible. Winter brings other challenges. Freezing and thawing cracks and destroys most terra cotta pots, but fiberglass, wood, and concrete tolerate winter well.

Climbing vines need appropriate supports to hold them. Annual climbers are replanted each year and don't require a long-lasting structure, but perennial vines need something permanent.

A small lattice structure or netting stretched between posts or attached by hooks to a wall works well for tendril vines, such as clematis. The structure doesn't actually need to be in the container. A nearby wall or netting set up along the edge of the balcony or hard surface can provide the necessary support.

Some vines are cascaders. They help hide the container and soften its lines. Try English ivy (an evergreen that will stay colorful in the winter), sweet potato vine, wintercreeper, and climbing hydrangea.

A rich and varied palette of colors are at work here, with clematis against a deep terra-cotta wall and perennials against stone and brick paving.

Above: Hardy annual mandevilla snakes through the pickets of a rustic fence.
Right: A playful riot of clematis 'Dr. Ruppel' overtakes a lamppost.

WHIMSY

Try growing vines on unusual forms to create some whimsy in your landscape. Wire animal topiary figures (available at many garden centers and nurseries) lend themselves to a living vine animal quite nicely. Or create a faux espalier by training vines up espalier-shape forms attached to horizontal surfaces. You can also make a tepee for the kids with a vine-covered wire form. Take some chicken wire and shape it into a large cone. Set it in a sunny corner of the yard, plant some vines, and create a just-for-kids outdoor hideaway. Vines will grow on just about any outline you give them, so use your imagination and give your garden an unexpected twist.

colonnade. Use special design effects such as topiary and espalier. Cover sphagnum-moss-stuffed frames with clingers for quick topiary. Vines follow wires on walls to become architectural espaliers. Hang wires over an open space and the vine becomes a living swag.

Unify your garden

Vines are great blenders in the landscape, serving as backdrops for colorful flowers. Flowering climbers become walls of color that both adds a vertical plane to flat space and complements the bloom of other plants. After blooming, they are quiet and reflective; against their dark and textured foliage, other flowers shine.

Vines mimic fabrics in the landscape. Allow them to hang down from above and they form curtains that ripple in even the gentlest breeze. Fine-textured vines allow dappled light through their foliage, forming a semitransparent screen that encourages the eye to look beyond.

VINES FOR SMALL PLACES

Vines are perfect vertical features for small garden areas; if chosen correctly, they take up little ground space. Vines bring a touch of green or an extra flush of bloom to small gardens and balconies. They take the garden skyward, create privacy, and block unattractive views.

In apartment settings and small urban yards with no open ground in which to plant, vines are perfect in containers. Many thrive in pots and bring lush foliage and textural interest to balconies, paved areas, and decks as well.

Vines, trained on netting or fences, are only inches wide; they create

privacy without sacrificing land. If you need screening of a close neighbor's windows, an arbor or latticework covered with vines can provide it.

Kolomikta vine
(*Actinidia kolomikta*)
Climbing snapdragon
(*Asarina scandens*)
Hybrid clematis
(*Clematis*)
Climbing bleeding heart
(*Dicentra scandens*)
Hyacinth bean
(*Lablab purpureus*)
Climbing hydrangea
(*Hydrangea petiolaris*)

Sweet pea
(*Lathyrus odoratus*)
Yellow honeysuckle
(*Lonicera flava*)
Trumpet honeysuckle
(*Lonicera sempervirens*)
Scarlet runner bean
(*Phaseolus coccineus*)
Purple bell vine
(*Rhodochiton atrosanguineus*)
Climbing miniature roses
(*Rosa*)
False climbing hydrangea
(*Schizophragma hydrangeoides*)

Lawns

Large or small, urban or suburban, lawns are irreplaceable pieces of the fabric of American life. Lawns are the welcome mats to homes. They colorfully welcome visitors and neighbors and act as frames for houses.

It's difficult to imagine life without lawns. Their aesthetic value is integral to the landscape; they are design elements that provide open, horizontal space. They lead the eye (and the feet) to other aspects of the yard: trees, shrubs, flower beds, and hardscaping.

How much lawn?

Think about the practical things when planning your lawn space; for example, how you intend to use your lawn and how easy it should be to maintain. Look at the areas you've designated that will require lawn space: play areas, sports areas, entertaining, etc. Then figure out how much space you'll need for these areas. Many people don't use every square foot of their lawn for a specific purpose; it's

A simple pattern cut into a large expanse of open lawn makes a decorative statement.

NEW LAWN PLANS

The failure of many lawns is often due to their design and placement. Take a look at your existing lawn space. If any areas of your lawn are doing poorly, take a look at how they fit in the landscape. For example, it may be better to replace any worn paths in the grass with some hardscape. Where the grass has thinned from deep shade, you'd be better off installing a shade-tolerant border of shrubs, perennials, or groundcover. What it boils down to is this: Rather than forcing the lawn to grow where it can't do well, sacrifice some of it in your new plan for the good of the whole landscape.

there as part of the framework of the landscape. So factor in the fact that some areas of lawn will be mainly open space setting off the surrounding landscape.

Lawn care should be a consideration in planning how much lawn you actually

LAWN MAINTENANCE LEVELS

LOW MAINTENANCE
- Mow regularly at the maximum height for your grass species.
- Fertilize annually with a slow-release fertilizer.
- Water only when grass is severely stressed by drought.

MODERATE MAINTENANCE
- Mow at least once a week.
- Water twice a month, depending on rainfall.
- Fertilize twice annually in the North, three times in the South.
- Spot weed to prevent pernicious regrowth.
- Aerate biannually.

INTENSIVE MAINTENANCE
- Mow weekly to semiweekly.
- Water regularly, depending on rainfall.
- Fertilize monthly during the growing season.
- Use pesticides to prevent weeds, disease, and insects.
- Aerate annually.

Hedges and shaped shrubs outline the lawn of this small, formal outdoor room.

This small swath of lawn is the heart of a lushly planted backyard landscape.

want in your yard. If you don't want to spend a lot of time on your lawn, consider other uses for the space instead of grass. Perhaps you can use the space to create another planting bed or put aside part of the lawn for a bench on a stone patio set off by a vine-covered arbor. However much lawn you choose to have, be realistic in the amount of time you're going to spend taking care of it during the year.

Shape your lawn

The best thing you can do for your lawn is to give it a definite shape. When sketching ideas for your planting plan, pay close attention to the bed line— it shapes both the planting beds and the lawn areas, and that makes it a critical part of your plan.

Bed lines can follow any shape you want. Generous, flowing curves will give your landscape a natural look and soften angular lines of architecture. A square panel of lawn (or any symmetrical shape) will look more formal. Straight lines can melt into curves, or you can combine corners and curves to create unusual shapes, but try to keep it simple. The fussier your shape, the harder it will be to maintain it.

A checkerboard of moss and blue crushed-glass gravel is a bold alternative to traditional turf.

Groundcovers

Groundcovers are often inconspicuous elements of a landscape; they blend in so well that you may overlook their many uses and benefits. But these unassuming plants are the workhorses of the landscape, meeting many needs. They solve scores of design and landscape management problems, reduce maintenance requirements, and add diversity and contrast to your landscape. They furnish a transition between lofty trees and low lawns and relieve monotony in your yard as they change with the seasons. What's more, groundcovers include a wide range of plant types— evergreen to deciduous, flowering and nonflowering, creeping or upright. A groundcover plant is available for virtually any setting, need, or climate.

Underplant a tree with groundcover to make a connection with the rest of a bed, border, or lawn.

What are groundcovers?

All plants can be considered groundcovers because they all help secure and sustain soil. For our purposes, however, groundcovers are plants that exhibit low or horizontal growth habits, spread rapidly, and protect the soil from erosion. They include plants that naturally—or with minimal pruning or mowing—range in height from less than 1 inch up to 3 feet tall. Other than that, the term "groundcover" has few restrictions in this book.

Candytuft (*Iberis sempervirens*) takes enthusiastic root in rock gardens and boulder crevices.

The plants that fit these criteria include a variety of materials, from woody shrubs to herbaceous succulents to herbs to vines to ferns and grasses. Among them are plants that are specifically suited for certain growing conditions, such as wet shade, as well as plants that are adapted to a wide range of environments, such as desert climates.

The delightful thing about groundcovers is that while they are working so hard, they provide scores of design features such as color and texture, along with seasonal diversity.

Seasonal diversity

Many groundcovers change as the seasons progress, adding year-round diversity to a landscape. Their appearance alters as they bud, blossom, and produce fruit, offering ever-shifting colors and textures. Even in winter, when deciduous groundcovers lose their leaves, they often reveal

rich hues and patterns in their bark. By mixing evergreen groundcovers with deciduous ones in your setting, you can enjoy the vitality of growing plants year-round.

Color and texture

Groundcovers add color to a landscape in a variety of ways. Some have beautifully mottled or variegated leaves in shades of green, yellow, white, or red. Others have lovely blossoms and fruit that add radiant colors to your setting. Some even bring evergreen color to winter landscapes.

A solid green landscape can be monotonous, but groundcovers—even green-leaved ones—add a visual sense of grain or nap to its beauty. This nap arises from plant texture. Distinctive leaf shapes, sizes, and colors create the texture, as does the groundcover's growth habit. By mixing different leaf sizes, textures, and plant forms, you can weave a diverse living fabric into your environment.

Groundcover solutions

Use groundcovers to tie together landscape components. One way to do this is to create a transition from such taller elements as buildings, trees, and large shrubs to low-lying turf or walkways by filling the areas between them with plants that reach midway. Groundcovers camouflage bare spots, such as the shady base of a tree, or hide unattractive features in your landscape. Groundcovers offer definition to the landscape. As boundaries for flower beds, they establish a natural perimeter around these spaces and visually define the route of a walkway or path.

Groundcovers are versatile and varied, but avoid the temptation to use them so much that they compete with one another or with other plants rather than complement the setting. A few carefully selected groundcovers have greater impact than a hodgepodge of many different types of groundcovers.

Pachysandra is a versatile evergreen groundcover that easily replaces lawn where turf won't grow—or where you don't want to mow.

Creeping phlox is a dense groundcover that can fill holes and accentuate with color.

The reds of celosia, coleus, and zinnia contrast well with yellow marigold and silver ice plants.

Flower Design

Design your landscape with seasonal color in mind, and reserve strategic spots for flower beds and borders. Examine your master plan and concept diagram; look for potential accent areas and focal points and decide which views are important.

Then plant color with a purpose. Plan not only for color but for seasonal changes too. Then you can make specific choices on your planting plan.

Annuals and perennials

Annuals are colorful bedding plants that may bloom through a season or two but will die before the year is over. Perennials come back year after year. Both add sparkle to your landscape. Some plants, such as perennial daylilies, are planted for their blossoms. Others, such as hostas, are known more for their foliage. Some annuals and perennials like sun and others like shade and some plants will thrive in between, so get to know conditions in your yard before you make selections.

Think about adding flowers near the front door or at a garden entry. Surround a focal point, or plant them at the end of a path. Mix different colors and textures in layered borders for a colorful, cottage-style appearance. Plant taller plants in the back where they won't overshadow their shorter companions. Try threading a unifying color throughout your composition.

Flowers show off best when planted in conjunction with something solid and neutral. A bed of evergreen shrubs or groundcover, a wall or fence, or even the foot of a bench can provide an excellent background for flowers.

You may want to incorporate flowers, especially perennials, into the landscape as a companion for shrubs and groundcovers. Remember, perennials have a dormant season, usually winter, so make sure your composition can carry on without looking barren until perennials reappear. Evergreen shrubs and groundcover planted near perennials provide bright blooms and foliage—a neutral background that shows colors to their best advantage. When the perennials disappear during dormancy, the evergreen plants keep the landscape from appearing empty.

Rhododendron and spruce anchor a curving lawnside perennial border.

MAKE IT PERSONAL

More than any other aspect of your landscape, your garden should be personally pleasing to you. No matter what the composition, if you love it, it's just right. But if you don't know where to begin, consider these tips.

■ Play with your plants while they're in their pots. Arrange them in pleasing partnerships, creating contrasts of form and foliage.

■ Remember to consider the plant's ultimate size. Those inches-high asters in the spring may be 5-foot giants by summer. Big plants shouldn't always be banished to the back. But unless they're airy in habit, they'll swamp the shorter plants you place behind them.

■ Plant compatibles. Partners in sun, dry soil, or moist shade must take equally to their conditions and placement, or their relationship is doomed from the start.

■ If a plant ends up in the wrong place, it's usually pretty easy to move it. Don't be afraid to edit over time; the best gardens are often the result of many revisions.

A quiet nook is alive with a shade-loving mix of hosta, golden ornamental grass, and columbine.

SEASONS

Winter in the garden does not need to be a down time. Its subtle beauty lies in line and form. Cold winter gardens can hold eye-catching shapes and textures. When sturdy, structural perennials are left to stand through wind, snow, and ice, the resulting shapes can work the same magic, which transforms a meadow from stubble to sculpture.

Where mild winters are the rule (Zones 7 and higher), the garden possibilities become far more plentiful. Evergreen perennials come into their own when earlier blooming, brasher competition retreats. Grouped and given the support of compact border shrubs (evergreen herbs, rhododendrons, and dwarf conifers), even the least

showy winter flowers can make a cheerful splash.

Winter is an excellent time to study the flow and follow-through of garden color. Journal notes will help you rule out the less suitable and rearrange better performers for winter appeal. Through selection and editing, you can develop your own winter perennial palette to enliven this underappreciated season. The best way to track performance is by keeping regular records in a garden journal. Record what you've planted and where, along with rainfall and temperature. Note what's in bloom so you can have an idea of the general flow of each season through the garden year.

Flower Design: Form and Structure

To get the best performance from your garden, don't just pick plants with pretty colors. Remember texture, form, structure, and foliage.

Flower colors are important, but it's the whole plant and where it will be placed that makes up the complete picture. Formal or naturalistic, layers give the garden a relaxed, abundant look, like a meadow or woodland. Whatever the style, the first tier serves as the carpet, where low-growing plants cover the ground and sprawlers can lace layers of the bed together. Next come intermediates, which make up the middle layer and provide a ladder between the front- and back-tier layers. The middle layer is like the forest understory, knit from compact shrubs and perennials.

Third-tier plantings define the shape of the garden, so it's the place to begin. These plants create a canopy or a skyline of the tallest plants. Skyline plantings integrate the garden with surrounding trees, areas, or buildings and provide definition and balance for the garden. Whether they are trees, shrubs, oversize perennials or annuals, these big plants can enclose the space like a hedge, rise to the high point in the center of an island, or form a backdrop in the border. It's the third-tier arrangement that sets the tone, creating either a formal or casual feel. Ruffled, irregular layers help create an informal effect.

First- and second-layer plants should merge with third-tier plantings, easing the eye toward the ground. Second-tier plantings create an intermediate layer between the first tier and the back border. Larger gardens may have two or three intermediate levels. In smaller beds, one layer will suffice. In formal plantings, your intermediate layer will be uniform. Choose plants of consistent height and similar shape. For an informal setting, you can choose an assortment of plants—you won't need to rank them so strictly by their size.

The mixed borders that edge this gravel terrace die down as the growing season ends but will provide plenty of architectural interest in winter.

Front and mid-border plants often display a charming informality. Edge the front of a bed or border using low-growing plants with foliage texture and color that contrast with the lawn or the pathway. First-tier edging plants can form a continuous strip along the garden's front border for a formal effect; however, a combination of various low-growing plants is also pleasing. Alternate clusters of different types of plants to create a subtle edge that clearly states the garden begins here.

Plant by shape

An effective combination is one that emphasizes contrasts between shape and form. Many designers concentrate on the natural shape of their plants more than on any other aspect—including color. Use the innate architecture of the plants, since a wide variety of flowering plant shapes can play well against each other. Fans and fountains, mounds and sprawlers, sturdy towers and slim turrets— all can be endlessly recombined into exciting partnerships.

A colorful tulip mix provides this bed with a lively launch in springtime.

The lows mingle with the highs, the rounded with the sharps, the yellows with the reds and greens in this imaginative border of golden creeping Jenny, coral bells, lily, bugleweed, hardy geranium, and beard-tongue.

BULBS

Flower bulbs are among the most dependable and versatile plants you can incorporate into your garden scheme. You can count on such spring bloomers as crocuses, daffodils, hyacinths and tulips to lead the way into the growing season. And summer bloomers such as gladiolus, lilies, or dahlias can punctuate with distinctive shape and color, as well as help plug holes in your beds and borders. Hardy bulbs come from climates that have cold winters and hot summers, temperature extremes that tell the plant to grow or go dormant. Planted in an appropriate spot and favorable climate, hardy bulbs act like perennials, coming back to bloom yearly. Tender bulbs come from climates with wet and dry seasons, and the soil's moisture level determines the plant's start and end of growth. Tender bulbs can't handle a cold winter and generally are grown as annuals. Plant loads of hardy bulbs, such as tulips or tiger lilies, where they can enjoy their yearly moment of glory at bloom time. Plant tender summer bulbs in containers or to fill a color gap in your beds or borders when spring bloomers fade.

Above: Ornamental onion (*Allium hollandicum* 'Purple Sensation') steals the show in this contemporary garden.

At right: Poppies, torch lilies (*Kniphofia*), marguerite daisies (*Anthemis*), blue and white bellflower (*Campanula*), verbascum, and heritage roses mix it up in this bed.

Flower Design: Playing with Color

Color brings the garden to life. Flowers and colorful foliage turn the daily greenery of gardens to a pleasing harmony. Color stimulates the senses, awakens emotions, and stirs a sense of beauty. Color work is an art, not a science, and its vocabulary is simple: A hue is a pure, saturated color, such as orange or blue. The more saturated it is, the more intense it will appear against a green backdrop. Less saturated colors, such as pastels, recede. A tone is either a shade (darkened) or a tint (lightened) of a pure color. Clean pastel pink, for example, is light and bright; murky red is heavy and dark. Color charts and wheels help you understand basic color compatibilities, but there are no hard and fast rules because tastes are so personal. The bottom line is that garden color should gladden your spirit and suit your sensibilities.

Combining colors

Use your intuition and fortify it with a few techniques gleaned from artists. Painters and photographers know that light has everything to do with how color is perceived. All day long and into the night, every flower and foliage tint and shade shifts in the slanted light of morning, the floodlight of noon, and the backlight of evening. Position also matters; when light strikes plants set on a bank, it reveals subtones in the foliage—often purple or copper or burgundy—that are masked in massed bed plantings. Indirect or filtered light (what gardeners call high or dappled shade) brings out depths in soft colors that stronger light may bleach.

In successful plant combinations, foliage works as hard as flowers.

Companion plants can be partners or competitors, supportive or challenging. Partners chosen for color balance will create harmonies. Competitors will create tension and drama. For example, mix dark orange with spectrum purple and deep, singing red and you'll invoke a western sunset. Sherbet orange blended with chalky yellows and whites looks light and cool, fresh and sparkling. Clean orange and sea blue are midweight colors that balance with each other, while the same orange matched with a red of similar value will edge toward a flamboyant clash (often quite pleasurably). The same clear red looks hotter and brighter against a foliage that is bronze or burgundy, and cooler and darker when set amid pale blue forget-me-nots.

Seasonal color alters the garden constantly, from spring's pastels to summer's rainbow, autumn's sunset tints, and winter's green-gray-brown. Develop color themes for each area in the garden or the garden as a whole and repeat those same colors through the seasons. Select compatible colorways—integrated groups of related colors that you can mix and mingle interchangeably—for the separate areas. When blue is primary, all the other colors are secondary. When yellow replaces blue as primary, blue becomes secondary, and so on. Allow predominant colors to trade the lead from area to area or season to season, and support them with a united family of secondary colors.

Delicate nasturtium is edible and isn't too hard on the eyes either.

EDIBLES

Edible plants can be ornamental as well. Plant squash, thyme and smoky fennel for color and texture as well as for tasty harvests. Combine herb or vegetable plots with flowers for a charming country kitchen garden. Grow edible flowers such as nasturtiums and violas for a sprinkle of color in salads. Include herbs as a facing border for taller plants. The dense green foliage of parsley, for example, makes an excellent foreground for summer caladiums.

A rowdy annual bed of petunia, pelargonium, alyssum, lobelia, and fuschia is energetic and happy.

Flower Design: Playing With Color
(continued)

Pink poppies, blue cornflowers, and white bugbane in a cool combination.

Cool color themes

The colors clustered on the blue, green, and yellow side of the spectrum are considered cool; reds, oranges, and purples are hot. Because white is cool and black is warm, a pastel tint (which is whitened) of almost any color works well in combination with other cool colors, but French pastels (which are grayed) look best with warm colors.

Early in the 20th century, when English gardeners first began making gardens with color themes, nearly all the color combinations were cool, with white flowers and white-streaked foliage. White, as you may have discovered, is very difficult to work with because few of the endless variations of white match well.

But because white is cool, carefully chosen clear whites can function well in cool themes. Matching the whites of various flowers is a challenge, and combinations tend to make off-whites look dingy. Temper the brightness of white flowers with textured foliage plants. Be cautious with pure white; it can be glaring and harsh unless mixed with lustrous greens.

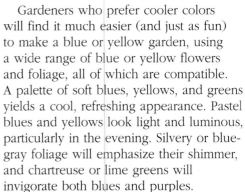

Gardeners who prefer cooler colors will find it much easier (and just as fun) to make a blue or yellow garden, using a wide range of blue or yellow flowers and foliage, all of which are compatible. A palette of soft blues, yellows, and greens yields a cool, refreshing appearance. Pastel blues and yellows look light and luminous, particularly in the evening. Silvery or blue-gray foliage will emphasize their shimmer, and chartreuse or lime greens will invigorate both blues and purples.

Pink and blue pastel gardens are even more popular, particularly when frosted with silvery gray, or blue-gray foliage. If you prefer a brighter scheme but want a cool look, try blending soft yellows with clean pastel tints—apricot, peach, and salmon—adding lots of chilly gray and muted blue foliage.

A few other general ideas apply to cool color gardens. Remember that less saturated colors recede. So, if you're using pastel shades of these colors, try to place them either close to where you want them to be viewed or in dappled or high shade. If you place them in full, noonday sun, they can't help but be washed out.

Lenten rose (*Helleborus orientalis*) is a cool-colored early bloomer.

A subtle mix of bachelor's button, ballet-pink celosia, and poppy.

Warm color themes

Cheerful, joyous, ebullient, or gaudy, hot colors create instant excitement. Reds, purples, and orange can look brash, brazen, or brilliant, depending on how they are assembled. Heat lovers delight in making salsa gardens filled with the festive, snapping colors of an open-air market. Dramatic sunsets inspire combinations with deeper tones—smoldering purples streaked with flaming reds and brassy oranges, for example.

Any combination is bound to be memorable, but unless you want unrestrained riot, it's best to be deliberate. Successful hot combinations will have partners of equal weight and value and significant assistance from surrounding foliage.

Orange is generally underused, but don't let that stop you; your garden can be stunning when you mix it with bronze, copper, brown, and other oranges. Think of these colors as the colors of fall or Halloween, then add your personal spin.

Yellow also is central to many a warm color scheme. Remember, though, that not all yellows are created equal. Some are deep, rich golds. Others are clear lemon yellows. And still others are yellow-greens.

Red adds instant energy to a planting and combines well with a variety colors. A little, however, goes a long way and the most successful warm-color themes use red judiciously.

Foliage is important in these schemes. Deep purple and silver gray foliage add interest while toning down combinations that might otherwise seem overwhelming.

In well-matched combinations, these strong colors resonate and will amplify each other—even more so if you mix in slightly lighter shades. It rarely works to blend pastels with fully saturated hues; but step the saturation down a degree or two, and you'll have successful contrasts.

Yellow *Inula magnifica* combines brilliant color, shape, and texture.

Hot, hot, hot! Canna 'Wyoming,' celosia 'Apricot Brandy,' 'Fiesta' peppers, and 'Yellow Ruffles' zinnia sizzle together.

Flower Design: Using Foliage

Background foliage is an important consideration for color too; the darkest shades of reds and purples can vanish into a dim green hedge but set them in front of gold or chartreuse foliage and the darker, somber colors really sing. If your favorites are the darker colors, remember this factor when you're choosing combinations. Also, if you want to use small, darker bedding plants, try planting gold or chartreuse bedding plants with them—they won't be tall enough to show off against a background but by placing them this way they will shine.

Alter the look of any color by changing its backdrop: Set a citrus orange marigold against deep purple or mahogany red foliage—the orange will pop out sharply. Back that same marigold with a red or purple of matching weight and the orange will merge instead. Place it in front of murky lavender or smoky blue and orange will seem cool and dark.

Leafy hosta paired with towering agapanthus are a bold element in this deck garden.

Bright narrowleaf zinnia (*Zinnia angustifolia*) accentuates the shape and color of yucca (*Yucca filamentosa*).

More than green

Many people begin gardening because they fall for flowers, but as their gardening experience deepens, the appreciation for foliage increases as well. Green is the most common color in the plant world— the basic black of gardening—though it's not often thought of when gardeners choose their plants. There are a thousand shades of green. They can give the garden body and depth and can be used in the palette just like any other color.

Coneflower, lavender, and yarrow harmonize **beautifully with yucca and ornamental grass in this perennial border.**

Bright 'Impulse' impatiens bring out the greens in miniature sedge (*carex conica* 'Variegata') and hosta 'Sagae.'

What's more, foliage presents us with hundreds of alternatives to basic green. You can make strikingly beautiful gardens simply by combining green foliage with blue- and gold-, silver- and bronze-, or red- and purple-leaved plants. Harmonious or contrasting foliage can be combined even more readily than flowers and it persists far longer. Luminous or softly gilded foliage will brighten a shady corner. Stronger sun brings out hidden undertones in deep-colored foliage and strengthens the flush of fall. Leaves present a remarkable range of shape and size as well as texture and finish.

Perennial foliage offers the opportunity to develop stunning seasonal effects, starting with earliest spring. Peonies (*Paeonia*) produce copper red new leaves on top of black or burgundy stems. Certain hardy geraniums have hot red new leaves, while many spurges (*Euphorbia*) emerge in sizzling chartreuse, glowing orange, or frosty purple. In fall, the clear gold of balloon flower (*Platycodon grandiflorus*) foliage, the shocking pink of beard-tongue (*Penstemon*), the ember red of plumbago (*Ceratostigma plumbaginoides*) all contribute to the garden's gaiety.

Variegated foliage lightens and brightens the garden tapestry, and strikingly variegated shade plants can illuminate dark spaces. Choose somewhat simple patterns—perhaps an edging of cream or pink or yellow—and large, restful leaves. Powerfully patterned plants can lend focus to a jumble and can elevate a dull planting to high art.

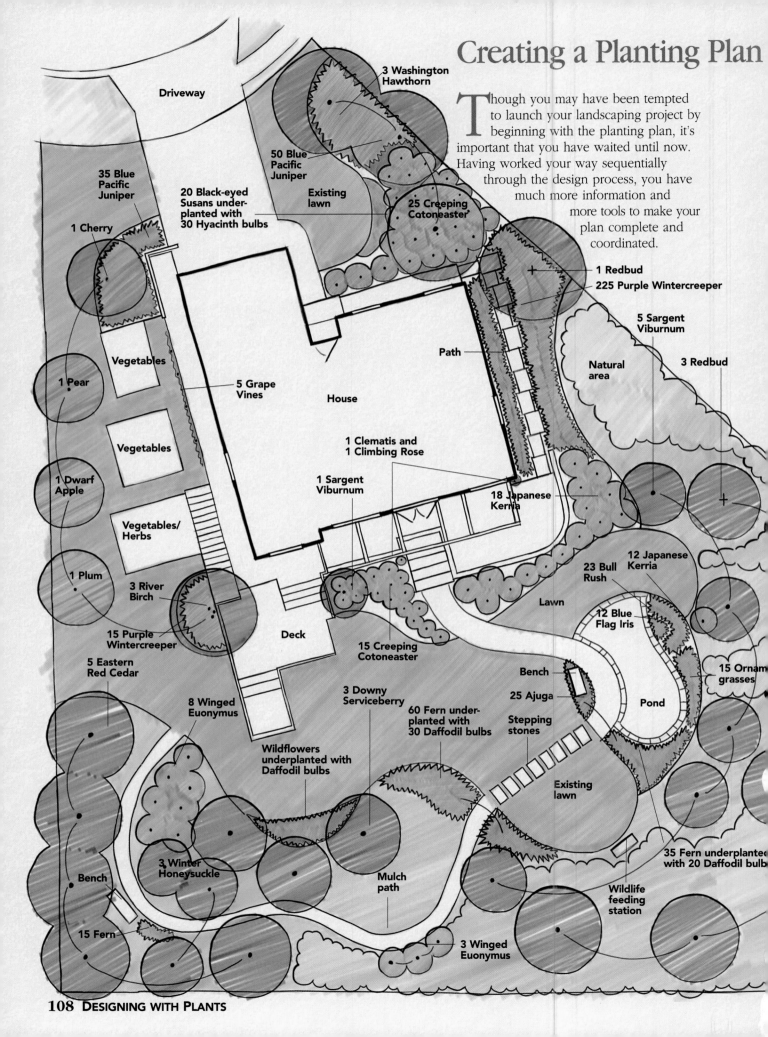

Creating a Planting Plan

Though you may have been tempted to launch your landscaping project by beginning with the planting plan, it's important that you have waited until now. Having worked your way sequentially through the design process, you have much more information and more tools to make your plan complete and coordinated.

Driveway

3 Washington Hawthorn

50 Blue Pacific Juniper

35 Blue Pacific Juniper

20 Black-eyed Susans under-planted with 30 Hyacinth bulbs

Existing lawn

25 Creeping Cotoneaster

1 Cherry

1 Redbud

225 Purple Wintercreeper

5 Sargent Viburnum

Path

Natural area

3 Redbud

Vegetables

1 Pear

5 Grape Vines

House

1 Clematis and 1 Climbing Rose

Vegetables

1 Dwarf Apple

1 Sargent Viburnum

18 Japanese Kerria

12 Japanese Kerria

Vegetables/ Herbs

23 Bull Rush

1 Plum

3 River Birch

12 Blue Flag Iris

Lawn

15 Purple Wintercreeper

Deck

15 Creeping Cotoneaster

Bench

15 Ornam grasses

5 Eastern Red Cedar

Pond

25 Ajuga

8 Winged Euonymus

3 Downy Serviceberry

60 Fern under-planted with 30 Daffodil bulbs

Stepping stones

Existing lawn

35 Fern underplanted with 20 Daffodil bulb

Wildflowers underplanted with Daffodil bulbs

Bench

3 Winter Honeysuckle

Wildlife feeding station

Mulch path

15 Fern

3 Winged Euonymus

To make the planting plan itself, lay tracing paper over your master plan and trace outlines of hardscape, house, property lines, and the existing plants you want to keep. Lightly trace bed lines too. (Make sure you're using your latest revision.) Lay this tracing over your planting schematic so you can see where you need to plant and the plant qualities you listed for each area.

As a result of all your research you should have several specific plant names written next to each quality. Narrow these selections down as you prepare your planting plan. Remember to repeat some of the same plants throughout the beds or planting areas to create unity in your planting scheme.

Refer to your notes regarding plant spacing and check your concept diagram to ensure that your final plant selections meet the design goals you intended.

Trees first

Draw trees on your planting plan first.
Put a bold dot in a spot where you need to plant a tree. Take out your large circle template and select the size that corresponds to the spread of the tree at the scale of your drawing. Draw a quick circle around the dot to represent the canopy. It's okay if your tree circles overlap patios, driveways, decks, lawn, and shrub beds. Those overlaps will show you how the tree canopies will shade these areas. Remember, your template is a tool to help you sketch at the correct scale. It is not necessary to produce a professionally drafted plan.

Bed lines and groupings

Adjust bed lines if necessary to accommodate your tree planting ideas. Next, refer to your planting schematic and divide beds into areas that represent different plant groupings. (Don't be afraid to alter an earlier plant choice.) Then determine the spacing for your plants and draw circles that touch each other, beginning and continuing along the bed lines. Each circle represents a mature or nearly mature plant. Draw a dot in the center of each circle; that will be where you're going to dig each planting hole. Shade the outline of all the plant groups.

Plants (circles) that you intend to scatter throughout a bed do not have to touch. For example, three accent plants set in a bed of groundcover would be shown as three separate circles. Instead of drawing tiny circles for groundcover, give the bed area a simple pattern to distinguish it from other areas.

Revise as you go

Don't become so engrossed in drawing circles that you are unwilling to make mistakes and start again. You may need several layers of tracing paper to get your planting design just right. Remember, the design process is ongoing. You may refine bed lines, plant choices, locations, and even hardscapes as you work. Be sure to adjust other plans that may be affected by your changes. When you're finished, compile a list of plants used on your plan. Take a tally of quantities and sizes. Use this for estimating and shopping. Trace a second copy of your planting plan to take outside when you begin the installation of your dream landscape.

3 Eastern Red Cedar

Natural area

PLANTING PLAN

Plant Selection

As with all the elements of your landscaping plan, you have your parameters—money, space, and time. Money certainly will be a driving force in deciding what plants you buy for your landscape. Whether you budget to tackle each part of the landscape now or use an over-time approach (planting certain important things initially and waiting on other plantings until you have the money), your budget will help you decide exactly what's going into your landscape.

Practical considerations

Space is another thing you need to consider when choosing plants. You need to think both in the present and the future for spacing needs. Take into account how large the plantings ultimately will be at maturity. For instance, that skinny little sapling you plant today may end up being 15 feet tall and 10 feet wide before you know it. If you haven't allowed enough space, you'll end up with an oversize, out-of-place planting that doesn't suit its surroundings. Smaller plants are easier to change if things get out of hand, but

taking the time in the planning stages to choose the right plants for your space will save lots of time in the future.

Time—how much you've got to spend to take care of your landscape and how much time you're willing to wait for it to fully take shape—is a major consideration when choosing plants. If you've got all the time in the world, go ahead and choose young plants or plants that require more attention than others. If you don't have the time to pamper a plant, choose one that doesn't require much work. If you don't want to wait long for your landscape to grow into maturity, you can plant mature plants but it will cost you. Waiting for your landscape to come together may require some patience, but you'll realize your landscape vision in the end.

Conditions

Choosing the right plant for your landscape conditions—sun, soil and moisture—is imperative. If the instructions for a plant say it needs full sun, be sure that plant will have at least eight hours of direct sunlight. If a plant needs alkaline soil, don't plant it in acidic soil and hope for the best. You'll be wasting your time and money planting things in conditions where the plant can't thrive. Pay attention to plants' requirements and choose the ones that meet both your landscape needs as well as the conditions in your yard.

Zone

Many a gardener has tried to beat the odds with plantings not suited for their hardiness zone and has ended up with dead plants and empty pockets. The zone map clearly outlines the minimum extremes in temperature,

The plants you choose to feature are key to adding yet more character to your landscape design.

creating an obvious starting place for choosing your plants. All plants are classified by the coldest temperature and zone they can endure. For example, plants hardy to Zone 6 survive where winter temperatures drop to -10°F. Those hardy to Zone 8 die long before it's that cold. Follow the zone map when you're choosing plants, and you'll have a better shot at making your plantings last the test of winter.

USDA PLANT HARDINESS ZONE MAP OF NORTH AMERICA

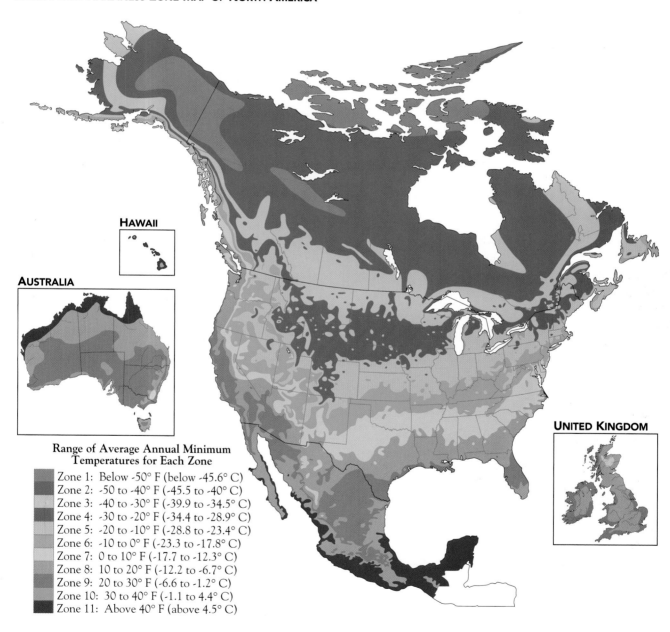

HAWAII

AUSTRALIA

UNITED KINGDOM

Range of Average Annual Minimum Temperatures for Each Zone

Zone 1: Below -50° F (below -45.6° C)
Zone 2: -50 to -40° F (-45.5 to -40° C)
Zone 3: -40 to -30° F (-39.9 to -34.5° C)
Zone 4: -30 to -20° F (-34.4 to -28.9° C)
Zone 5: -20 to -10° F (-28.8 to -23.4° C)
Zone 6: -10 to 0° F (-23.3 to -17.8° C)
Zone 7: 0 to 10° F (-17.7 to -12.3° C)
Zone 8: 10 to 20° F (-12.2 to -6.7° C)
Zone 9: 20 to 30° F (-6.6 to -1.2° C)
Zone 10: 30 to 40° F (-1.1 to 4.4° C)
Zone 11: Above 40° F (above 4.5° C)

Trees

Many trees offer short-term yet spectacular seasonal effects that provide a constantly changing drama around your home. Some trees are cloaked in beautiful flowers in spring or summer. Others provide attractive fruit in late summer and autumn, or burst into flaming foliage colors in fall. Still others come into their greatest glory after leaves drop to reveal startling sculptural form or beautiful bark.

Of course, a number of trees offer a colorful show

A tree can hold interest through the seasons, as this ornamental cherry (*Prunus*) does in winter (left) and spring (opposite right).

GOOD WILDLIFE TREES

American arborvitae
   (*Thuja occidentalis*)
American beech
   (*Fagus grandifolia*)
Paper birch
   (*Betula papyrifera*)
Colorado blue spruce
   (*Picea pungens glauca*)
Ohio buckeye
   (*Aesculus glabra*)
Easter red cedar
   (*Juniperus virginiana*)
Horsechestnut
   (*Aesculus hippocastanum*)

Amur chokeberry
   (*Prunus maackii*)
Flowering dogwood
   (*Cornus florida*)
American elm
   (*Ulmus americana*)
Balsam fir
   (*Abies balsamea*)
Black gum
   (*Nyssa sylvatica*)
Cockspur hawthorn
   (*Crataegus crusgalli*)

over a very long season. Many cultivars selected for brightly colored leaves, such as red-leaved Japanese maple or white-and-pink-variegated dogwood, provide summer-long color as effective as any flowering tree. And a wide range of evergreens offers such colorful foliage all year long.

What matters

Two main considerations for choosing a tree are the conditions in your yard and the ultimate size and configuration of the tree at maturity. Next to regional climate, the soil and available light in your yard are the most important factors in the success of your trees. Make sure the tree is adaptable to your type of soil—sand, loam, or clay—or it won't survive in your landscape. The tree should also have the right amount of sunlight in order to thrive. Take the recommendations on the tree instructions seriously when it comes to how much sunlight is required.

The ultimate shape, height, and spread of a tree should also be a consideration in choosing a tree for your yard. The space you've allotted for that tree should accommodate that tree at maturity—unless you plan to move it in the future. The size of the tree—height and spread—shouldn't be underestimated. In reality, the tree may never truly reach its fullest growth—but it could—and that's what you need to be prepared for.

Trees: All-Season All-Stars

Selecting trees that provide showy, changing effect in not just one, but two or more seasons, is an excellent way to pack the most colorful punch into your landscape and get the most effect for your money. Such hardworking, multiple-season trees are relatively rare in the horticultural world; we call them all-stars.

Billows of white, apple-like blooms on Allegheny serviceberry (*Amelanchier laevis*) announce the early spring, giving way to red-orange autumn foliage and striped gray bark in winter. Flowering dogwood (*Cornus florida*) is truly a tree for four seasons, with showy spring flowers, shiny red summer fruit, crimson autumn foliage, and fissured, black winter bark. Korean stewartia (*Stewartia pseudocamellia* 'Korean Beauty') bears flowers like single camellias in midsummer; its foliage turns gold to yellow-orange in autumn, and its multicolored bark peels off in large spectacular, rounded flakes for interest all winter long.

Use the chart below to develop a landscape with seasonal drama throughout the year.

The Japanese maple (*Acer palmatum*) is a classic multi-season performer, sustaining interest with powerful foliage from spring through fall, and with its structure in winter.

Plant name
Japanese maple (*Acer palmatum*)
Red maple (*Acer rubrum*)
Apple serviceberry (*Amelanchier grandiflora* cultivars)
Allegheny serviceberry (*Amelanchier laevis*)
Yellowwood (*Cladrastis lutea*)
Flowering dogwood (*Cornus florida*)
Kousa dogwood (*Cornus kousa*)
Washington hawthorn (*Crataegus phaenopyrum*)
Winter King hawthorn (*Crataegus viridis* 'Winter King')
Crape myrtle (*Lagerstroemia indica*)
Flowering crabapple (*Malus* cultivars)
Sourwood (*Oxydendrum arboreum*)
Sargent cherry (*Prunus sargentii*)
Japanese flowering cherry (*Prunus serrulata*)
Chinese quince (*Pseudocydonia sinensis*)
Callery pear (*Pyrus calleryana* 'Autumn Blaze', 'Redspire', or 'Chanticleer')
Sassafras (*Sassafras albidum*)
European mountain ash (*Sorbus aucuparia*)
Korean stewartia (*Stewartia pseudocamellia* 'Korean Beauty')

Korean stewartia (*Stewartia pseudocamellia* 'Korean Beauty') is a standout in the home landscape.

Pink flowering dogwood (*Cornus florida*) has it all—spectacular blooms, strong foliage and fruit, and a fine structure in winter.

MULTI-SEASON ALL STARS

Spring	Summer	Autumn	Winter
Attractive new foliage	Green summer foliage	Strong fall color	Sculptural winter form
Haze of red flowers	Good shade tree	Strong fall color	Good winter structure
White flowers	Attractive fruit	Strong fall color	Silvery bark
Bronze foliage, white flowers	Attractive fruit	Strong fall color	Good winter form
Attractive bark and foliage	Attractive white flowers	Strong fall color	Attractive structure
Spectacular flowers	Good foliage, red berries	Fall color	Horizontal winter structure
Spectacular flowers	Good foliage, red berries	Fall color	Good winter structure, bark
White flowers	Lustrous green leaves	Fall color	Showy fruit
White flowers	Lustrous green leaves	Fall color	Showy fruit and bark
	Spectacular flowers	Strong fall color	Showy bark and structure
Covered with flowers	Good foliage	Colorful fruit	Attractive structure
	White tassel-like flowers	Strong fall color, white fruit	Good winter structure
Pink flowers	Good foliage	Strong fall color	Very attractive bark
Attractive flowers	Good foliage	Occasional fall color	Attractive bark, structure
Pink flowers	Attractive fruit	Strong fall color	Attractive bark
Brilliant white flowers	Good foliage and form	Fall color	Distinctive structure
Yellow flowers before foliage	Good foliage	Neon fall color	
	White flowers	Bright, dramatic berries	Good structure
	Camellia-like flowers	Fall color	Outstanding bark

Trees: Flowering Trees

Everyone has a special place in their heart for flowering trees because of their spectacular blooms. For many trees, peak flowering is late spring and early summer, but some bloom from early spring until autumn. Yoshino cherries (*Prunus yedoensis*), for example, flower briefly; be ready or you'll miss them. Stewartia, on the other hand, remains in bloom for more than a month. A few, like bottlebrush (*Callistemon*), flower most of the year in mild climates. Choose a tree for its size and shape, in addition to its flowers. Plant medium-height trees with wide canopies in front of taller, denser trees or next to buildings. If there is room, plant several to increase the effect.

Crape myrtle (*Lagerstroemia indica*)

FLOWERING TIMES OF TREES

Tree	Spr. E	M	L	Sum. E	M	L	Fall
Red maple (*Acer rubrum*)	■						
Serviceberries (*Amelanchier* species)	■						
Bottlebrush (*Callistemon*)	████	████	████	████	████	████	████
Eastern redbud (*Cercis canadensis*)	■						
Sassafras (*Sassafras albidum*)	■						
Empress tree (*Paulownia tomentosa*)		■					
Cherry plum (*Prunus cerasifera* cultivars)	■						
Sargent cherry (*Prunus sargentii*)		■					
Japanese flowering cherries (*Prunus serrulata*)		■					
Callery pear (*Pyrus calleryana*)		■					
Flowering dogwood (*Cornus florida*)			■				
Saucer magnolia (*Magnolia ×soulangiana*)			■				
Flowering crabapples (*Malus* species and cultivars)			■				
Carolina silverbell (*Halesia tetraptera*)			■				
Bigleaf magnolia (*Magnolia macrophylla*)				■			
Red horsechestnut (*Aesculus ×carnea* 'Briotii')					■		
Horsechestnut (*Aesculus hippocastanum*)					■		
Yellowwood (*Cladrastis lutea*)					■		
Southern magnolia (*Magnolia grandiflora*)				████	████	████	

Goldenchain tree (*Laburnum ×watereri*)

Flowering crabapple (*Malus*)

Tree	Spr. E	M	L	Sum. E	M	L	Fall
White fringe tree (*Chionanthus virginicus*)			■				
Dove tree (*Davidia involucrata*)			■				
European mountain ash (*Sorbus aucuparia*)			■				
Hawthorns (*Craetagus*)			■				
Goldenchain tree (*Laburnum ×watereri*)			■				
Black locust (*Robinia pseudoacacia*)			■				
Japanese snowbell (*Styrax japonicus*)			■				
Kousa dogwood (*Cornus kousa*)				■			
Japanese tree lilac (*Syringa reticulata*)				■			
Southern catalpa (*Catalpa bignonioides*)				■			
Silk tree or mimosa (*Albizia julibrissin*)					■		
Red-flowering gum (*Eucalyptus ficifolia*)					■		
Japanese stewartia (*Stewartia pseudocamellia*)					■		
Golden rain tree (*Koelreuteria paniculata*)					■		
Crape myrtle (*Lagerstroemia indica*)					■		
Five-stamen tamarisk (*Tamarix ramosissima*)					■		
Sourwood (*Oxydendrum arboreum*)					■		
Chaste tree (*Vitex agnus-castus*)					■		
Japanese pagoda tree (*Sophora japonica*)						■	
Franklin tree (*Franklinia alatamaha*)							■

Franklin tree (*Franklinia alatamaha*)

Saucer magnolia (*Magnolia ×soulangiana*)

Japanese lilac (*Syringa reticulata*)

Trees: Fall Foliage

Variegated box elder (*Acer negundo* 'Variegata')

The most memorable feature of many trees is its foliage. Whether it's lustrous summer foliage to rival even the showiest of flowers, showstopping fall foliage, or the deep, resonant color of winter evergreens, the leaves and needles of certain trees hold center stage. Careful selection of species and cultivars with distinctive foliage can color your landscape year-round.

The summer show

Trees with strong summer foliage can command attention all summer—long after the flashy blooms of spring have come and gone. From deep, near-black purples and reds, through gentle hues of white, silver, and blue, to vibrant pinks and yellows or lively variegated leaves, trees with high-season color are worth careful consideration for your landscape. Many summer show-offs work best against a background of green. Use them sparingly—one red-leaved Japanese maple or variegated-leaf dogwood can go a long way; too many can be overbearing.

Tulip poplar (*Liriodendron tulipifera*)

A fancy fall performance

Brilliant fall foliage lets even those trees that have gone unnoticed in other seasons claim the spotlight. Some have one characteristic fall color; others display different colors all at once. Try to feature them against a dark green background of evergreens. Fall color varies depending on the climate and soil, from season to season and from tree to tree. To avoid some of this

SHOWY SUMMER FOLIAGE

Box elder cultivars
(*Acer negundo* 'Flamingo'
and 'Variegatum')
Japanese maple cultivars
(*Acer palmatum*)
Norway maple cultivars
(*Acer platanoides* 'Crimson
King' and 'Drummondii')
Eastern redbud
(*Cercis canadensis*
'Forest Pansy')
European beech
(*Fagus sylvatica* 'Purpurea',
'Riversii', 'Rohanii', 'Rosea-
marginata', and 'Zlatia')
Sweet gum
(*Liquidambar styraciflua*
'Burgundy' and 'Palo Alto'™)
Royalty flowering crabapple
(*Malus* 'Royalty')
Purple-leaved cherry plums
(*Prunus cerasifera* 'Newport'
and 'Thundercloud')
Willow-leaved pear
(*Pyrus salicifolia*)
Silver linden
(*Tilia tomentosa*)

Japanese maple (*Acer palmatum* 'Kihachijo')

Chinese dogwood (*Cornus kousa* var. *chinensis*)

Lion's head maple (*Acer palmatum* 'Shishigashira')

variability, try to buy your tree from the nursery in the fall when you can see its color. And remember that for the most part, the cooler your climate, the more intense the color of your fall foliage. A tree that looks like it's on fire in the fall in New Hampshire may give off more of a warm glow in the Carolinas. Base your expectations on the kind of color you see in the autumn where you live.

American beech (*Fagus grandifolia*)

OUTSTANDING AUTUMN FOLIAGE

Amur maple
 (*Acer ginnala*)
Japanese maple
 (*Acer palmatum*)
Red maple
 (*Acer rubrum*)
Sugar maple
 (*Acer saccharum*)
Apple serviceberry
 (*Amelanchier grandiflora*)
Allegheny serviceberry
 (*Amelanchier laevis*)
Pawpaw
 (*Asimina triloba*)
Paper birch
 (*Betula papyrifera*)
Katsura tree
 (*Cercidiphyllum japonicum*)
White fringe tree
 (*Chionanthus virginicus*)
Flowering dogwood
 (*Cornus florida*)
Kousa dogwood
 (*Cornus kousa*)
Cockspur hawthorn
 (*Crataegus crus-galli*)
Persimmon
 (*Diospyros*)
American beech
 (*Fagus grandiflora*)
Franklin tree
 (*Franklinia alatamaha*)
White ash
 (*Fraxinus americana*)
Green ash
 (*Fraxinus pennsylvanica*)
Gingko
 (*Gingko biloba*)
Crape myrtle
 (*Lagerstroemia indica*)

Sweet gum
 (*Liquidambar styraciflua*)
Tulip tree
 (*Liriodendron tulipifera*)
Black gum or tupelo
 (*Nyssa sylvatica*)
Sourwood
 (*Oxydendrum arboreum*)
Chinese pistachio
 (*Pistacia chinensis*)
Quaking aspen
 (*Populus tremuloides*)
Sargent cherry
 (*Prunus sargentii*)
Flowering cherry
 (*Prunus serrulata*)
Chinese quince
 (*Pseudocydonia sinensis*)
Golden larch
 (*Pseudolarix amabilis*)
Callery pear
 (*Pyrus calleryana*)
White oak
 (*Quercus alba*)
Scarlet oak
 (*Quercus coccinea*)
Sassafras
 (*Sassafras albidum*)
European mountain ash
 (*Sorbus aucuparia*)
Japanese stewartia
 (*Stewartia pseudocamellia*)
Bald cypress
 (*Taxodium distichum*)
Littleleaf linden
 (*Tilia cordata*)
Elm
 (*Ulmus* spp.)
Japanese zelkova
 (*Zelkova serrata*)

Himilayan white birch
(*Betula utilis* var.
jacquemontii) and black-stemmed dogwood
(*Cornus alba*
'Kesselringii') combine
for superb winter
aesthetics.

Trees:
Winter Interest

Certain trees can command interest through even the bleakest of winters, bearing fruit, featuring extraordinary bark, or displaying dramatic architecture against the seasonal backdrop.

Colorful fruit

Fruit-bearing trees often keep their fruit longer than their flowers. Some also appeal to the birds and will help animate your garden with these feathered friends. Some fruit trees, such as serviceberry (*Amelanchier*), ripen by midsummer and become food for early birds. Others, such as the flowering dogwood (*Cornus florida*). ripen in late summer. The fruit of American holly (*Ilex opaca*) and Washington hawthorn (*Crataegus phaenopyrum*) is not palatable until late winter (awaiting the birds of spring). Meanwhile, it adds touches of color to the landscape.

Distinctive bark

When was the last time you thought of a tree in terms of its bark? Its the most-often overlooked feature of a tree, but in some it is an outstanding asset that adds to the look of the tree year-round. Bark character, in fact, is the most interesting aspect of the paperbark maple (*Acer griseum*), paper birch (*Betula papyrifera*), and Amur chokecherry (*Prunus maackii*). It's an interest that is present all the time but more noticeable when the tree is without its leaves.

Evergreens, such as false cypress (*Chamaecyparis*), and redwood (*Sequoia sempervirens*) have striking bark, an up-close feature that adds to the appeal of the tree.

Winter structure

Winter is the time when the structure of trees comes into its own. No longer shrouded in a mantle of foliage or adorned with berries and flowers, the arching or upright limbs and branches are now what we see first. For certain trees, this

The brilliant berries explain
why Winter King hawthorn
(*Crataegus viridis* 'Winter King')
is winter landscape royalty.

TREES WITH SHOWY FRUIT

Amur maple
(*Acer ginnala*)
Japanese persimmon
(*Diospyros kaki*)
Flowering dogwood
(*Cornus florida*)
Kousa dogwood
(*Cornus kousa*)
Washington hawthorn
(*Crataegus phaenopyrum*)
Winter King hawthorn
(*Crataegus viridis* 'Winter King')
American holly
(*Ilex opaca*)
Golden rain tree
(*Koelreuteria paniculata*)

Flowering crabapples
(*Malus* species and cultivars)
Magnolias
(*Magnolia* spp.)
Black gum
(*Nyssa sylvatica*)
Sourwood
(*Oxydendrum arboreum*)
Chinese quince
(*Pseudocydonia sinensis*)
Pepper tree
(*Schinus molle*)
European mountain ash
(*Sorbus aucuparia*)

Kousa dogwood (*Cornus kousa*) berries are gorgeous when encapsulated in ice.

The distinctive bark of the paper birch (*Betula papyrifera*) is all the more compelling tinged with snow.

TREES WITH SHOWY BARK

Paperbark maple
   (*Acer griseum*)
River birch
   (*Betula nigra*)
Paper birch
   (*Betula papyrifera*)
Kousa dogwood
   (*Cornus kousa*)
Eucalyptus
   (*Eucalyptus* spp.)
Crape myrtle
   (*Lagerstroemia indica*)
Amur cork tree
   (*Phellodendron amurense*)
Lacebark pine
   (*Pinus bungeana*)
Plane tree, sycamore
   (*Platanus* spp.)
Quaking aspen
   (*Populus tremuloides*)
Amur chokecherry
   (*Prunus maackii*)
Sargent cherry
   (*Prunus sargentii*)
Chinese quince
   (*Pseudocydonia sinensis*)
Japanese stewartia
   (*Stewartia pseudocamellia*)
Chinese elm
   (*Ulmus parvifolia*)

framework is their most outstanding feature and it shows only after the leaves have fallen. Then sculptural trees truly dominate the winter garden. Highlight, for example, the intricate weeping habit of a cutleaf Japanese maple or the twisting branches of a contorted Hankow willow by planting one near the front walk. Visitors will never fail to comment, winter or summer, about this unusual and unique tree.

Many other weeping trees are sculptural, but those with spreading branches are also outstanding in the winter. They may take a while to reach their peak but are well worth the wait.

Colorado spruce (*Picea pungens*) gets pleasantly frosted in winter.

TREES WITH SCULPTURAL WINTER FORM

Japanese maple
   (*Acer palmatum*)
European hornbeam
   (*Carpinus betulus*)
American beech
   (*Fagus grandifolia*)
Weeping European beech
   (*Fagus sylvatica* 'Pendula')
Red Jade weeping crabapple
   (*Malus* 'Red Jade')
Dawn redwood
   (*Metasequoia glyptostroboides*)
Amur cork tree
   (*Phellodendron amurense*)
Tanyosho pine
   (*Pinus densiflora* 'Umbraculifera')
Weeping cherry
   (*Prunus subhirtella* 'Pendula')
Corkscrew willow
   (*Salix matsudana* 'Scarlet Curls' and 'Tortuosa')

The lovely shape of a crabapple (*Malus*) is highlighted in the winter scape.

Trees: Evergreens

American holly (Ilex opaca) is a classic broadleaf evergreen.

Looking for a permanent fixture in your landscape? Consider evergreens. Their year-round interest can unify your garden through the seasons. In winter they contrast with the stark outlines of deciduous trees and take on a whole different look because of this. Within this class of plants, you'll find needle and broadleaf evergreens; they vary both in the conditions they prefer and in their landscape uses.

NEEDLE EVERGREENS are called conifers because they bear cones. Most are pyramidal or conical, at least while young, and prefer full sun. Some, however, benefit from light shade; and a few, such as hemlocks (*Tsuga*) and yews (*Taxus*), will tolerate considerable shade. Most need little or no pruning if you give them growing space. Slower-growing conifers will save you time and effort (and space in small places).

BROADLEAVED EVERGREENS have leaves that overwinter. They do lose their leaves, but unlike deciduous trees, only after a new set has appeared. Most prefer mild climates, and very few will survive northern winters.

Some offer bright red berries in the winter, such as American and English hollies (*Ilex opaca* and *I. aquifolium*), while others have huge, waxy white flowers in spring and summer, such as southern magnolia (*Magnolia grandiflora*).

DECIDUOUS CONIFERS are among the few that lose their leaves in fall. Like needle evergreens, they offer an interesting combination of leaves, cones, and tree shapes with fall foliage color before they drop their leaves. And because they do lose their leaves, in the winter they bring unique silhouettes and trunk and branch shapes to the garden. They usually don't color as dramatically as deciduous trees, but instead offer a more muted color palette with which to experiment.

BROADLEAF EVERGREEN TREES

Lemon bottlebrush
  (*Callistemon citrinus*)
Camphor tree
  (*Cinnamomum camphora*)
Loquat
  (*Eriobotrya japonica*)
Eucalyptus or gum
  (*Eucalyptus* spp.)
American holly
  (*Ilex opaca*)
Southern magnolia
  (*Magnolia grandiflora*)
Olive
  (*Olea europaea*)
Cherry laurel
  (*Prunus laurocerasus*)
Coast live oak
  (*Quercus agrifolia*)
Pepper tree
  (*Schinus molle*)

DECIDUOUS CONIFERS

European larch
  (*Larix decidua*)
Japanese larch
  (*Larix kaempferi*)
Dawn redwood
  (*Metasequoia glyptostroboides*)
Golden larch
  (*Pseudolarix amabilis*)
Bald cypress
  (*Taxodium distichum*)

Canadian hemlock (Tsuga canadensis) is a graceful, low-maintenance evergreen.

ODD-SHAPED EVERGREENS have their color in common with other evergreens, but not their shape, as they can be tall pyramids or dwarf cones, or take conical, weeping, columnar, and open forms. One columnar Skyrocket juniper will punctuate a flower bed; two can bring formality to an entryway. The Tanyosho pine, wide and spreading over its trunks, almost qualifies as a sculpture in the garden.

EXTREME EVERGREENS with extra-colorful foliage can brighten your garden. Blue-toned conifers, such as blue Atlas cedar or Hoops blue spruce, mix well with other evergreens or bright flower colors. Yellow-tinged trees, such as golden chamaecyparis, work well as a focal point or as a contrast with duller colors such as gray or maroon-red.

The deodar cedar (*Cedrus deodara*) is a favorite for the open, shaggy shape it takes on as it matures.

NEEDLE EVERGREEN TREES

Firs
(*Abies* spp.)
False cypresses
(*Chamaecyparis* spp.)
Japanese cedar
(*Cryptomeria japonica*)
Leyland cypress
(*Cupressocyparis leylandii*)
Monterey cypress
(*Cupressus macrocarpa*)
Italian cypress
(*Cupressus sempervirens*)
Spruces
(*Picea* spp.)
Pines
(*Pinus* spp.)
Yew pine
(*Podocarpus macrophyllus*)
Japanese umbrella pine
(*Sciadopitys verticillata*)
Redwood
(*Sequoia sempervirens*)
Giant sequoia
(*Sequoiadendron giganteum*)
American arborvitae
(*Thuja occidentalis*)
Canada hemlock
(*Tsuga canadensis*)

Blue spruce (*Picea pungens* var. *glauca*) is a classic conical evergreen, favored for its blue-green needles.

Shrubs

Shrubs are used for practical purposes, such as privacy or wind control, as well as for aesthetics—their flowers and foliage contribute to the beauty of your landscape. The many types of shrubs from which to choose help assure you find one that will have just the right effect for just the right spot.

Consider the shrub as a whole—flowers, foliage, winter interest, and shape—when planning them into your landscape. Some shrubs lend themselves to a hedgerow quite nicely, while others can stand alone as a focal point. The shape and height of the shrub can contribute much-needed variations within the landscape or fade into the background to highlight other plantings. If a spot in your yard needs both color and privacy, plant some flowering shrubs that will grow into the perfect screen.

Mature shrubs are relatively inexpensive compared to mature trees, so you can have a more established landscape sooner than you could with trees. Even if you buy younger shrubs, many varieties grow quickly so you won't have to wait for that finished-looking landscape for long. Take into account the ultimate size and shape of the shrub when planning and buying your shrubs. As with trees, the mature size of the shrub will determine where it goes and with what other plantings; be sure it won't tower over or become dwarfed by other plants.

Flowering shrubs, when planted as a hedge, in bloom steal the show.

At left: Evergreen trees and shrubs in a variety of heights, colors, and shapes create visual drama and complete privacy all year long.

Shrubs: Flowering Types

'Yaku' rhododendron (Rhododendron yakushimanum)

When you see a shrub in bloom at a nursery or public garden and decide that you must have it, remember that the floral display that attracts you will probably last a month or less. Choose shrubs for their foliage and branching structure, not just for their flowers.

Several things should be considered when designing a planting of flowering shrubs. You can plant shrubs that flower at the same time to create attractive combinations. Be sure their colors also harmonize with bulbs and other flowers on the property, as well as with the house and other structures. You can also plant shrubs that bloom at different times for a staggered impact. Also think about which shrubs should be planted in masses or in small groups, rather than individually.

Then consider the details of flower size and prominence, fragrance, and the shrub's size and growth habit. Be sure they are compatible with the soil and other environmental needs. If your soil is not acidic, keep all ericaceous plants—such as rhododendrons (Rhododendron), azaleas (Rhododendron), and blueberries (Vaccinium)—in a planting area that can be acidified without treating the entire yard.

Common lilac (Syringa vulgaris 'Marechal Foch')

Kerria (Kerria japonica)

Japanese spirea (Spiraea japonica)

TOP SPRING FLOWERING SHRUBS

Camellia
  (*Camellia japonica*)
Common lilac
  (*Syringa vulgaris*)
Flowering quince
  (*Chaenomeles speciosa*)
Japanese andromeda
  (*Pieris japonica*)
Japanese spirea
  (*Spiraea japonica*)
Kerria
  (*Kerria japonica*)
Rhododendron and azalea
  (*Rhododendron* spp.)
Rose daphne
  (*Daphne cneorum*)
Shrubby veronica
  (*Hebe*)
Warminster broom
  (*Cystisus × praecox*)

A rhododendron border in the natural style.

TOP SUMMER FLOWERING SHRUBS

Bigleaf hydrangea
  (*Hydrangea macrophylla*)
Butterfly bush
  (*Buddleja davidii*)
Carolina allspice
  (*Calycanthus floridus*)
Crape myrtle
  (*Lagerstroemia indica*)
Harlequin glory bower
  (*Clerodendrum trichotomum*)
Mountain laurel
  (*Kalmia latifolia*)
Rose
  (*Rosa* spp.)
Tree peony
  (*Paeonia suffruticosa*)

Bigleaf hydrangea (*Hydrangea macrophylia* 'Tokyo Delight')

Floribunda rose (*Rosa* 'Europeana')

Common hydrangea (*Hydrangea hortensia*)

Guelder rose (*Viburnum opulus*)

Star magnolia (*Magnolia stellata*)

Shrubs: Interesting Foliage

While seasonal gardens benefit from the careful use of flowering shrubs, it's not the color of the flowers but of the leaves that has the greater impact on the landscape. Leaves are present throughout the growing season (or year-round on evergreen shrubs). By using foliage color to paint the landscape, you can create a long-lasting, harmonious setting for your home.

Silverthorn (*Elaeagnus pungens* 'Maculata')

Japanese aucuba (*Aucuba japonica* 'Variegata')

A leaf color of emerald green has a restful, neutral effect. Likewise, shades of cool blue, gray, and variegated green and white tend to recede visually in the border. Variegated shrubs such as Japanese aucuba (*Aucuba japonicus*) can enliven a shady corner of the garden, the green of the leaves blending the plant into its surroundings while the white reflects the dim light and stands out. The typical yellow-leaved deciduous or evergreen shrub has a golden greenish tint that can be jarring if overused in the garden but which makes an outstanding highlight in a sunny border. Red, another accent color, is the complement of green on standard color charts. Therefore, a shrub with bright red leaves creates a vibrant contrast against a green background. A shrub with dark purple leaves has a blackish effect on the landscape and creates a dramatic visual hole in a bed or border.

Fall foliage color is as arresting as the color of flowers. It may not last long but while it does, red, orange, purple, and yellow leaves weave a spectacular tapestry of brilliant color.

Vanhoutte Spiraea (*Spirea* × *vanhouttei*)

Variegated gold boxwood (*Buxus sempervirens* 'Aurea Variegata')

Yellow Japanese barberry (*Berberis thunbergii* 'Aurea')

Variegated wintercreeper (*Euonymus fortunei*)

SHRUBS FOR FALL COLORS

Barberry
   (*Berberis*)
Beautyberry
   (*Callicarpa*)
Blueberry
   (*Vaccinium*)
Burning bush
   (*Euonymus alatus*)
Cotoneaster
   (*Cotoneaster* spp.)
Fothergilla
   (*Fothergilla major*)
Glossy abelia
   (*Abelia grandiflora*)
Heavenly bamboo
   (*Nandina domestica*)
Japanese maple
   (*Acer palmatum*)
Oakleaf hydrangea
   (*Hydrangea quercifolia*)
Red chokeberry
   (*Aronia arbutifolia*)
Redvein enkianthus
   (*Enkianthus campanulatus*)
Smoke bush
   (*Cotinus*)
Sumac
   (*Rhus*)
Viburnum
   (*Vibernum* spp.)
Virginia sweetspire
   (*Itea virginica*)
Witch hazel
   (*Hamamelis virginiana*)

Shrubs: Winter Interest

Many deciduous shrubs still look terrific after the last fall leaf has dropped. Some bear flashy fruit in red, yellow, orange, purple, or blue that will last until spring. Others carry vibrant berries for hungry birds and visiting wildlife to devour.

Colorful or textured bark also makes an effective winter display in the home landscape. Blueberry *(Vaccinium)* bushes, for example, bear fruit in late summer, while in winter their young stems turn a deep purplish shade of red. Similarly, Japanese kerria *(Kerria japonica)* boasts vivid arching green stems that stand out against winter's palette of whites, browns, and grays in the woodland garden.

Late-season interest is not confined to berries and bark. Harry Lauder's walking stick *(Corylus avellana* 'Contorta'), for example, rises like an expressionist sculpture from the landscape. Here is a shrub with greater impact in winter than in summer, when coarse leaves obscure its curious, twisted branches. These intriguing branches are useful for indoor arrangements.

This viburnum's winter berries dangle like jewels.

Hemlock topiaries dominate a winter landscape.

WINTER FLOWERS

Jump-start the growing season by planting shrubs that blossom in winter or by forcing branches of early spring-flowering shrubs indoors. Winter-blooming deciduous shrubs include familiar plants such as witch hazel *(Hamamelis ×intermedia)* and pussy willow *(Salix discolor)*. Among favorite winter-blooming evergreens are common camellia *(Camellia japonica)* and winter daphne *(Daphne odora)*.

Shrubs that bloom in early spring are the best for forcing. Forsythia *(Forsythia intermedia)*, buttercup winter hazel *(Corylopsis pauciflora)*, and lilac *(Syringa vulgaris)* all work well. Forcing time varies, but the nearer it is to a plant's natural flowering time, the faster the stems will bloom. Simply cut the stems up to 3 feet long, then set them in a tall container of clean water until they flower. For quicker forcing, use warm water and set the container in bright, warm, indirect sunlight. Continue to add warm water as necessary. To delay blooming, place the vase in a cooler part of the room and, if necessary, add ice to the water.

Witch hazel (*Hamamelis ×intermedia*) teases with winter blooms.

SHRUBS WITH EDIBLE FRUIT

Shrubs often produce enticing fruits, some of which are edible and some of which are toxic. Don't sample the berries in your landscape without knowing with certainty which species produce fruit edible to humans. Fruit may be red, orange, yellow to green, blue, or purple, thus integrating colorfully into your landscape design. Fruit also may attract birds and other wildlife, adding another dimension to the garden. But if you want the fruit for your own table, you may need to cover the shrubs with netting while they ripen.

Attractive shrubs with edible fruit include flowering quince *(Chaenomeles speciosa)*, pomegranate *(Punica granatum* 'Wonderful'), beach rose *(Rosa rugosa* 'Frau Dagmar Hartopp'), highbush and lowbush blueberry *(Vaccinium corymbosum* and *V. angustifolium)*, and American cranberrybush *(viburnum trilobum)*.

Blueberry (*Vaccinium*) bushes (above) and pomegranate (right) (*Punica granatum*) are good-looking shrubs with edible fruit.

Shrubs: Year-Round Stars

Choosing shrubs for year-round interest guarantees the ever-changing beauty of a garden for the longest possible time. Moreover, because top-quality plants can also be expensive, selecting shrubs that are attractive for more than a few weeks a year gives value for your money.

While evergreens offer year-round color and greater consistency, deciduous shrubs change from season to season. Some are noticeable only for a few weeks when in bloom. Others provide months of seasonal interest. For instance, dwarf fothergilla (*Fothergilla gardenii*) produces three seasons of beauty, with charming white bottlebrush flowers in the spring, attractive medium-textured bright green leaves during the growing season, and luminous orange foliage

Redtwig dogwood (*Cornus alba*) offers remarkable red bark in the bare of winter.

in the fall. Cream-edged tatarian dogwood (*Cornus alba* 'Argenteomarginata') stands out all four seasons with its spring flowers, variegated foliage, and colorful bark (in this case, glowing red stems) after the leaves drop. Sometimes bark peels off shrubby stems, giving them a lively three-dimensionality.

DECIDUOUS SHRUBS FOR MULTISEASON EFFECT

American cranberrybush
(*Viburnum trilobum*)
Cream-edged tatarian dogwood
(*Cornus alba*
'Argenteomarginata')
Double-file viburnum
(*Viburnum plicatum*
f. *tomentosum* 'Mariesii')
Dwarf fothergilla
(*Fothergilla gardenii*)
Enkianthus
(*Enkianthus* spp.)
Flame azalea
(*Rhododendron
calendulaceum*)
Harry Lauder's walking stick
(*Corylus avellana* 'Contorta')
Highbush blueberry
(*Vaccinium corymbosum*)
Large fothergilla
(*Fothergilla major*)
Lowbush blueberry
(*Vaccinium angustifolium*)
Oakleaf hydrangea
(*Hydrangea quercifolia*
'SnowQueen')
Red chokeberry
(*Aronia arbutifolia*
'Brilliantissima')
Royal azalea
(*Rhododendron
schlippenbachii*)
Seven-son flower
(*Heptacodium miconioides*)
Variegated yellow-twig dogwood
(*Cornus stolonifera*
'Silver and Gold')
Warminster broom
(*Cytisus* × *praecox*)

Oakleaf hydrangea (*Hydrangea quercifolia*) delivers gorgeous spring blooms and exemplary fall foliage.

Evergreens

Evergreens give year-round stability to a landscape, bringing together many different parts of the yard throughout all four seasons.

Broadleaved evergreens can have striking flowers and unusual leaves. For example, yaku rhododendron *(Rhododendron yakushimanum)* bears white, pink, or rose flowers in May on a shrub covered with leaves that are glossy green on top and felted with heavy brown hair below. The effect of the color and textural contrasts within each leaf gives this shrub a subtle richness. Oregon grapeholly *(Mahonia aquifolium)* and leatherleaf mahonia *(Mahonia bealei)* add showy berries to the winning combination of yellow flowers and evergreen leaves.

Because conifers add year-round color to the garden, you may be tempted to overuse them. Their density, however, can mire the composition in textural sameness. Especially in foundation plantings, use conifers with rounded forms to bring the gaze back to the earth. Conifers with pyramidal shapes sometimes grow tall and lead the eye up the walls of the house, emphasizing the disparity between the elements in constructed and natural environments. When designing with conifers, check their mature size before buying. With their wide palette of colors and the proliferation of dwarf and slow-growing varieties, conifers are fundamental to the well-landscaped home.

Evergreens combined with accents of seasonal color provide interest throughout the year.

Azaleas are at their most colorful in spring but have attractive foliage in summer and fall too.

EVERGREEN SHRUBS FOR MULTISEASON EFFECT

Common juniper
   (Juniperus communis 'Berkshire')
Drooping leucothoe
   (Leucotho fontanesiana 'Girard's Rainbow')
Firethorn
   (Pyracantha)
Heaths and heathers
   (Erica spp.)
Rocky Mountain juniper
   (Juniperus scopulorum 'Table Top Blue')
Sawara cypress
   (Chamaecyparis pisifera 'Golden Mop')
Wintergreen cotoneaster
   (Cotoneaster conspicuus)

Shrubs: Using in Hedges

Hedges define areas of the landscape, as well as provide privacy and control wind and noise. Grow hedges that are right for the space you've allotted them in your yard. Small hedges are perfect for areas within the landscape (as opposed to lining the outer edges of the yard) that need some definition and shape. For instance, a row of small hedges can partition interior areas of a garden, creating natural walking paths. Larger shrubs can be grouped to create hedge walls around the perimeter of the yard or to screen an unwanted sight. Sheared hedges can give your landscape an air of formality, while loose, unclipped hedges (and even some unconventional hedges) give your landscape a more informal look.

Carefully shaped shrubs and boxwood hedges define the paths of a formal garden.

SHRUBS FOR SHEARED HEDGES

American arborvitae
  (*Thuja occidentalis*)
Cotoneaster
  (*Cotoneaster* spp.)
Chinese Holly
  (*Ilex cornuta*)
Japanese Holly
  (*Ilex crenata*)
Junipers
  (*Juniperus* spp.)
Privet
  (*Ligustrum* spp.)
Yew
  (*Taxus* spp.)

PLANTS FOR UNCONVENTIONAL HEDGES

Castor beans
  (*Ricinus communis*)
Spider flowers
  (*Cleome hassleriana*)
Sunflowers
  (*Helianthus*)
False indigo
  (*Baptisia*)
Peonies
  (*Paeonia*)
Cacti
Ornamental grasses

SHRUBS FOR SMALL HEDGES

Dwarf conifers
Common boxwood
  (*Buxus sempervirens*)
Winter daphne
  (*Daphne odora*)
Rosemary
  (*Rosmarinus officinalis*)

Low boxwood hedges contain an abundant bed of 'Jenny Duval' roses.

A loose hedge of 'Mohave' red and 'Teton' yellow pyracantha spill over a stone wall.

SHRUBS FOR LOOSE HEDGES

Azaleas
  (*Rhododendron* spp.)
Bigleaf hydrangea
  (*Hydrangea macrophylla*)
Burning Bush
  (*Euonymus alatus*)
Oakleaf hydrangea
  (*Hydrangea quercifolia*)
Kerria
  (*Kerria japonica*)
Mexican orange
  (*Choisya ternata*)
Oleander
  (*Nerium oleander*)
Rose
  (*Rosa* spp.)
Rose of Sharon
  (*Hibiscus syriacus*)
Viburnum
  (*Viburnum* spp.)

Vines

All eyes are on this lovely grape arbor, not the garage, as the vine gracefully softens hard edges.

Whether you need to plant vines for privacy or you want to train a vine up an arbor to use as a focal point, choosing the right plant can make all the difference in the overall effect of your landscape. Refer to your planting plan and look at the areas you designated for vines of climbers. Now decide what characteristics you'd like in your plant. Are flowers important? Will you need to have year-round color or will one-season color suffice? The aspects of a vine or climber—color, texture, and seasonal interest—will help narrow your choices.

VINES FOR HOT SUN

Trumpet vine (*Campsis radicans*)
Virginia creeper (*Parthenocissus quinquefolia*)
English ivy (*Hedera helix*)
Rose (*Rosa* spp.)
Coral vine (*Antigonon leptopus*)
Kiwi (*Actinidia deliciosa*)
Siberian gooseberry (*Actinidia arguta*)
Grape (*Vitis* spp.)
Bougainvillea (*Bougainvillea glabra*)
Mandevilla (*Mandevilla × amabilis*)
Golden trumpet (*Allamanda cathartica*)
Sweet potato vine (*Ipomoea batatas*)

VINES FOR SHADE

Kolomikta vine (*Actinidia kolomikta*)
Akebia (*Akebia quinata*)
Dutchman's pipe (*Aristolochia macrophylla*)
Climbing hydrangea (*Hydrangea petiolaris*)
False climbing hydrangea (*Schizophragma hydrangeoides*)
Wood vamp (*Decumaria barbara*)
Honeysuckle (*Lonicera* spp.)
Creeping fig (*Ficus pumila*)

The color and texture of English ivy make this terra-cotta-colored wall a work of art.

VINES FOR COLD CLIMATES

Climbing hydrangea (*Hydrangea petiolaris*)
Virginia creeper (*Parthenocissus quinquefolia*)
Boston ivy (*Parthenocissus tricuspidata*)
Siberian gooseberry (*Actinidia arguta*)
Hops, European (*Humulus lupulus*)
Trumpet honeysuckle (*Lonicera sempervirens*)
Dutchman's pipe (*Aristolochia macrophylla*)
Trumpet vine (*Campsis radicans*)
Silver lace vine (*Polygonum aubertii*)
American bittersweet (*Celastrus scandens*)
Wintercreeper (*Euonymus fortunei*)
Kentucky wisteria (*Wisteria macrostachya*)
Large-flowered hybrid clematis (*Clematis* spp.)

Clematis makes merry with a red rambler rose.

Choosing the right vine or climber will also depend on your climate and where the vines will be in the yard. Don't ignore the recommended growing conditions when purchasing a vine. If a vine needs full sun, it should be placed in an area that receives at least eight hours of direct sunlight. If a vine isn't recommended for your climate zone, don't plant it anyway and hope for the best. So many varieties of vines exist, you won't be at a loss to find just the right one for your needs.

VINES FOR AREAS WITH MILD WINTERS

Coral vine (*Antigonon leptopus*)
Evergreen clematis (*Clematis cirrhosa, C. armandii*)
Ivies (*Hedera* spp.)
Jessamine (*Gelsemium sempervirens*)
Cross vine (*Bignonia capreolata*)
Maypop (*Passiflora incarnata*)
Wood vamp (*Decumaria barbara*)
False climbing hydrangea (*Schizophragma hydrangeoides*)
Wisteria (*Wisteria* spp.)
Grape (*Vitis* spp.)
Rose (*Rosa* spp.)
Climbing bleeding heart (*Dicentra scandens*)
Trumpet vine (*Campsis radicans*)
Confederate jasmine (*Trachelospermum jasminoides*)

White wisteria showers down the side of a brick wall.

Vines: Hiding and Screening

Just as you might use a slipcover to give an old chair a new look, you can use vines as a "fabric" in your landscape to cover up its blemishes. By choosing an attractive vine, you can even turn an eyesore into a beautiful focal point. First take a look at what you want to hide or screen. The vine you choose should not only cover up something, it should have its own effect in the landscape. If you're covering up a chain link fence, for instance, decide what you want the vine-covered fence to become in the yard. A vine with great green foliage can serve as a backdrop to other elements in the landscape, while a blooming vine-covered fence can become a focal point. When choosing vines, consider the original need for the vine (a coverup or screen) as well as the secondary purpose it will serve in the landscape (as a highlight or background).

VINES FOR POSTS

Dutchman's pipe
  (*Aristolochia macrophylla*)
American bittersweet
  (*Celastrus scandens*)
Carolina jessamine
  (*Gelsemium sempervirens*)
Large-flowered hybrid clematis
  (*Clematis* spp.)
Hops, European (*Humulus lupulus*)
Trumpet honeysuckle
  (*Lonicera sempervirens*)
Rose (if tied) (*Rosa* spp.)
American wisteria (*Wisteria frutescens*)
Kolomikta vine (*Actinidia kolomikta*)

Dense European hops (*Humulus lupulus*) makes a perfectly private retreat of this arbor.

A June riot of 'Red Cardinal' clematis makes a chain link fence disappear.

VINES FOR TREE STUMPS OR ROCK PILES

Virginia creeper (*Parthenocissus quinquefolia*)
Trumpet vine (*Campsis radicans*)
Wintercreeper (*Euonymus fortunei*)
Creeping fig (*Ficus pumila*)
Ivies (*Hedera* spp.)
Climbing hydrangea (*Hydrangea petiolaris*)
False climbing hydrangea
  (*Schizophragma hydrangeoides*)

VINES FOR LATTICE

Hybrid clematis
  (*Clematis* spp.)
Rose (*Rosa* spp.)
Kolomikta vine
  (*Actinidia kolomikta*)
Mandevilla
  (*Mandevilla × amabilis*)
Golden trumpet
  (*Allamanda cathartica*)
Coral vine
  (*Antigonon leptopus*)

Violet wisteria showers down the side of a brick wall.

Elegant white clematis cloaks a nondescript lamppost.

VINES FOR CHAIN LINK AND WROUGHT IRON

Morning glory (annual *Ipomoea*)
Kentucky wisteria (*Wisteria macrostachya*)
Ivy (*Hedera helix*)
Moonseed (*Menispermum canadense*)
Silver lace vine (*Polygonum aubertii*)
Confederate jasmine
  (*Trachelospermum jasminoides*)

139

Vines: Color

Blackie sweet potato vine (*Ipomoea batatas* 'Blackie') is showy with its deep purple foliage.

Vines can be bold or they can be subtle. They can be showy for a moment or a season. Or they can quietly impress with shimmering shades of rich greens. Spring and summer bloomers can bring a wall of color to your garden. Their effect may be fleeting—as it is with the gorgeous rambling rose—or long-lasting, as with mandevilla or golden trumpet. They can perform solo or extend harmoniously the colors of other plants.

A Silver Moon rambler rose in a Japanese tree lilac doubles the effect of cream-colored flowers in June. Such complementary plantings enhance the beauty of both.

Don't be mistaken—showy doesn't always mean a riot of color. It can also mean quiet, understated, elegant. And it's not just flowers that put on such a show. The foliage of vines, their fruit, and winter structure all make equal statements in your landscape.

PURPLES

Purple sweet potato
   (*Ipomoea batatas* 'Blackie')
Purple-leaved wintercreeper
   (*Euonymus fortunei*)
Hyacinth bean
   (*Lablab purpureus*)
Purple-leaved grape
   (*Vitis vinifera* 'Purpurea')

Sweet potato vine cultivars have purple or yellow foliage throughout the summer. The yellow autumn color of climbing hydrangea is followed by dry, pinkish buff flowers and flaky cinnamon winter bark. Boston ivy and Virginia creeper have exceptionally attractive autumn red leaves. Textures abound in vines; the large leaves of Dutchman's pipe, moonflower, and kiwi contrast with the small leaves of cypress vine, clematis, and climbing snapdragons.

The foliage of vines can be as splashy and dramatic as their flowers, and since leaf color can be both a constant and a changing element in the garden, plan for it with care. Consider all the flowers that will appear through the season so you avoid unwanted combinations. Be sure you won't tire of the leaf color halfway through the summer, and remember that some leaves will change color in both the spring and fall.

An assortment of colors

Foliage color offers a wide variety of choices. There are vines with leaves that are entirely purple, yellow, or chartreuse. Others have variegated leaves that are usually marked by a mix of green with white, yellow, or even pink.

Play with foliage colors. Try purple leaves with pink flowers. Mix them with petunias, roses, and other pink-flowered plants. Orange can be smashing with purple. Consider annual zinnias, Mexican sunflowers, and other orange flowers near purple-leaved

Delicate-looking sweet pea (*Lathyrus odoratus* 'Angela Ann') is as fragrant as it is pretty.

vines. Blue foliage, especially blue conifers, goes well with purple.

Plant a hyacinth bean to grow up a fir, or a Blackie sweet potato vine in a container at the base of a dwarf Japanese white pine.

Yellow leaves brighten dark areas and can match the yellows of flowers grown among them. A yellow vine in front of dark brown timbers is a knockout. The chartreuse of the Margarita sweet potato vine will brighten a dark container of evergreens. And if you have a bed of black-eyed susans, try a bamboo tripod with black-eyed susan vine nearby to give some height and to repeat the gold and brown.

The lime green leaves of this sweet potato vine (Ipomoea batatas 'Terrace Lime') make a great contrast to dark-leaved plants and flowers.

The distinctive yellow flowers of Clematis tibetana give way to the fabulous seedheads that stick around for winter interest.

Vines: Texture

Green, of course, is the fundamental color of the garden. It's the "ground" on which the other colors show. It ties the space together through the seasons and allows the eye to rest. But look again. This single color is not so simple after all. It's a range of shades from the light and yellow green of spring to the dark blue-green of summer growth. It's glossy and it's dull, and with the foliage of your vines, their hues and textures, you can make a quiet place—a space with an elegance all its own.

The layered look

Experiment with two- and three-dimensional effects. Some vines, such as Boston ivy, are flat and tightly clinging. They create a fantastic wall of green. Contrast this with a vine that grows horizontally. Climbing hydrangea and false climbing hydrangea escape the plane by sending out horizontal shoots on which their flowers bloom. English ivy, bougainvillea, and trumpet vine also stand out from walls.

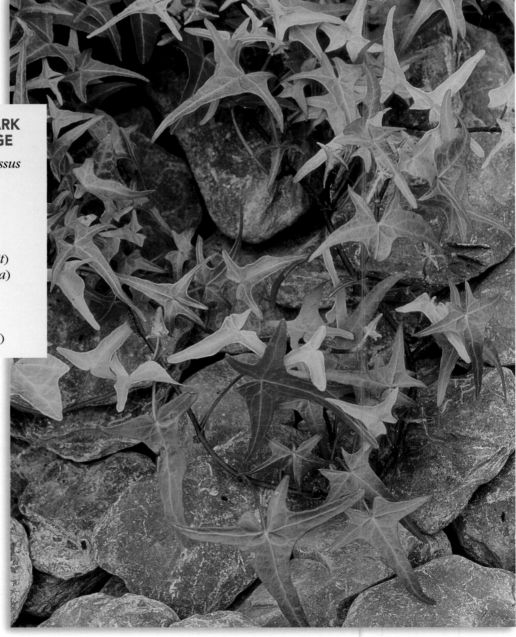

The lacy leaves of this English ivy (*Hedera helix* 'Light Fingers') contrast with the hefty stones.

VINES WITH DARK GREEN FOLIAGE

Boston ivy (*Parthenocissus tricuspidata*)
Dutchman's pipe (*Aristolochia macrophylla*)
Cardinal climber (*Ipomoea quamoclit*)
Akebia (*Akebia quinata*)
Morning glory (*Ipomoea tricolor*)
Evergreen clematis (*Clematis armandii*)

VINES WITH BOLD TEXTURE

Dutchman's pipe (*Aristolochia macrophylla*)
Moonflower (*Ipomoea alba*)
Kiwi (*Actinidia deliciosa*)
Algerian ivy (*Hedera canariensis*)
Wood vamp (*Decumaria barbara*)
Trumpet vine (*Campsis radicans*)
Cup-and-saucer vine (*Cobaea scandens*)
Ornamental gourd (*Cucurbita pepo*)
Hops, European (*Humulus lupulus*)
Bottle gourd (*Lagenaria siceraria*)
Crimson glory vine (*Vitis coignetiae*)

This ivy (*Hedera helix* 'Eileen') masses to create a deeply textured groundcover.

The leaves of Dutchman's pipe are bold and dark. They grow in layers and lend a tropical three-dimensional effect to the garden. The foliage of kiwi is even larger, and new growth is covered with orange hairs. Look closely for the shimmer of color.

Fine-textured grace

Fine-textured and translucent leaves bring lightness and grace to the garden, and counter any heaviness in the landscape. Plant kiwi in a sunny spot and notice the fine-textured veins in the leaves as the sun shines through them. Use an Italian clematis as a screen; its sense of lacy intrigue offers glimpses of what is beyond. The 'Lowii' cultivar of Boston ivy has small leaves like many clematis. For the smallest and finest leaves of all, plant cypress vine.

Glossy or muted leaves

Glossy green leaves shimmer in the sun. Some of the cultivars of English ivy glisten all year long. Wintercreeper and evergreen clematis are two other shiny evergreens; Boston ivy is deciduous. In contrast are the muted shades of Virginia creeper, akebia, and Siberian gooseberry, as well as the matte finish of *schizophragma* 'Moonlight'. These are much quieter in the landscape and make great backdrops.

VINES WITH FINE TEXTURE

Climbing bleeding heart
   (*Dicentra scandens*)
Anemone clematis (*Clematis montana*)
Cardinal climber (*Ipomoea ×multifida*)
Pink Chinese jasmine
   (*Jasminum polyanthum*)
Silver lace vine (*Polygonum aubertii*)
Confederate jasmine
   (*Trachelospermum jasminoides*)
Climbing snapdragon
   (*Asarina scandens*)
Italian clematis (*Clematis virginiana*)
Sweet autumn clematis (*C. terniflora*)
Cypress vine (*Ipomoea quamoclit*)

Variegated leaves give a distinctive twist to this trumpet vine (*Campsis radicans* 'Summer Snowfall').

Vines: Seasonal Interest

Vines with showy flowers are a joy to use. They add luxuriant color and do not take up space. Some bloom with one brief burst of color; others blossom throughout the growing season. Trumpet honeysuckle blooms from May until October. Tropical vines such as mandevilla and golden trumpet (planted as annuals) bloom the entire summer. Three selections of clematis will give you spring-to-fall flowers: anemone clematis in spring, Jackman clematis in summer, and sweet autumn clematis in fall. With planning, flowers will span the seasons.

The leaves of Boston ivy (*Parthenocissus tricuspidata*) turn from green to scarlet in fall.

Autumn color

Autumn color is one of the joys of living in a climate with four distinct seasons. Trees usually come to mind with thoughts of fall color, but there are vines that are equally vibrant. They let you mix and match. Grow a vine with yellow fall foliage (climbing hydrangea) on the trunk of a tree with red fall color (pin oak, sour gum, sweet gum) for a trunk of yellow and a blaze of red or purple in the crown. Reverse the effect with the red of Boston ivy or Virginia creeper on a tulip tree.

AUTUMN COLOR

Boston ivy (*Parthenocissus tricuspidata*)

Virginia creeper (*Parthenocissus quinquefolia*)

Climbing hydrangea (*Hydrangea petiolaris*)

Crimson glory vine (*Vitis coignetiae*)

Winter silhouettes

A fascinating garden is more than just flowers and foliage. And at the end of the growing season, when other colors pale, vines can be dramatic. They bring an upward moving brightness to the fall and winter.

Winter is a wonderful time to appreciate the "bones" of vines. The bark of climbing hydrangea sheds to reveal papery reddish brown layers that become more beautiful as the plant ages. The bark of grapes peels off in distinctive long strips; an aged grape vine is a sight to behold. Old wisteria trunks twine around themselves in amazingly beautiful patterns, especially when outlined in snow.

Boston ivy forms a flat, fine-textured tracery upon surfaces, especially in contrast to a yellow or ochre-colored masonry wall.

Evergreens

The presence of evergreens can help you get through the winter. Wintercreeper is one of the hardiest of the evergreen vines. Its cultivar 'Vegetus' climbs well and can eventually reach the top of a three-story building.

Some English ivy cultivars, such as 'Bulgaria' and 'Baltica', are nearly as hardy as euonymus. In far northern areas where they are borderline hardy, plant them along a sheltered wall and protect them from the winter sun. Some cultivars have yellow leaves; others have shapes that are distinctly different. Algerian ivy offers bolder leaves than English ivy, although it is not hardy north of Zone 8.

Sweet autumn clematis (*Clematis paniculata*) twines a porch railing.

VINES FOR SPRING BLOOM

Anemone clematis
  (*Clematis montana*)
Golden clematis
  (*Clematis tangutica*)
Roses (*Rosa* spp.)
Evergreen clematis
  (*Clematis cirrhosa*
  and *C. armandii*)
Wisteria (*Wisteria* spp.)
Sweet pea
  (*Lathyrus odoratus*)
Carolina jessamine
  (*Gelsemium sempervirens*)

EVERGREEN VINES

Wintercreeper (*Euonymus
  fortunei*)
English ivy (*Hedera helix*)
Algerian ivy
  (*Hedera canariensis*)
Creeping fig
  (*Ficus pumila*)
Evergreen clematis
  (*Clematis cirrhosa,
  C. armandii*)
Cross vine (*Bignonia
  capreolata*)
Carolina jessamine
  (*Gelsemium
  sempervirens*)

**English ivy
evergreen**

VINES FOR SUMMER BLOOM

Moonflower (*Ipomoea alba*)
Jackman clematis
  (*Clematis jackmanii*)
Hyacinth bean
  (*Lablab purpureus*)
Climbing rose (some)
  (*Rosa* spp.)
Coral vine
  (*Antigonon leptopus*)
Cross vine
  (*Bignonia capreolata*)
Trumpet vine
  (*Campsis radicans*)
Mandevilla
  (*Mandevilla ×amabilis*)
Golden trumpet
  (*Allamanda cathartica*)
Bougainvillea
  (*Bougainvillea glabra*)

**The brilliant red flowers
of the scarlet runner bean
(*Phaseolus coccineus*
'Pulsar') bloom from
midsummer until frost.**

VINES FOR WINTER EFFECT

Climbing hydrangea
  (*Hydrangea petiolaris*)
Grape (*Vitis* spp.)
Wisteria (*Wisteria* spp.)
Siberian gooseberry
  (*Actinidia arguta*)
False climbing hydrangea
  (*Schizophragma
  hydrangeoides*)
Trumpet vine
  (*Campsis radicans*)

**Trumpet creeper is a
vigorous growing vine
that gives nearly year-
round interest with
flower, foliage, and form.**

With the right grass in the right conditions, every lawn can be a perfect lawn.

Lawns

Growing just the right grass in just the right place is the most important step in making a fine lawn. Turfgrass species vary considerably in climactic, environmental, and cultural preferences. Chances are there's one that's just right for your lawn, or even that corner with which you've had so much trouble.

Maybe it's the grass variety you already have growing in your yard. Maybe another species would do better. In either case,

whether you're improving your care program to match your lawn or starting a new lawn, the following information will help you choose the best grass for your landscape.

Warm season grasses

ZOYSIAGRASS (*Zoysia* species) is a tough, aggressive, creeping warm-season perennial with leaf texture that ranges from coarse to fine, depending on variety.

This is the grass that you often see advertised as miracle grass, and it does have some outstanding characteristics. Tolerant of heat and drought, yet able to endure some shade and cool temperatures, zoysiagrass forms a dense, wiry, low-maintenance lawn that crowds out weeds. However, the needlelike blades of many zoysiagrass can be sharp underfoot.

It is often grown in the transition zone between warm- and cool-season areas, as far north as New Jersey in the East and Oregon in the West. It will survive winters, but at the first hint of cold weather, zoysiagrass goes dormant and turns brown while cool-season grasses are still bright green.

BERMUDAGRASS (*Cynodon* species) is to the South what Kentucky Bluegrass is to

Zoysiagrass

the North—the stuff of which most lawns are made. This creeping turfgrass is easily grown in most soils and takes both low- and high-maintenance regimes. Depending on the variety, bermudagrass resists many diseases and can take considerable wear and abuse. Deep roots allow it to tolerate heat and drought. It doesn't grow well in shade and often goes dormant, turning yellow or brown when temperatures drop below 50–60° F.

Bermudagrass grows throughout the warm-season turfgrass area and well into some areas of the cool-season region. However, it is best adapted to lower elevations in the Southwest and in a region bounded by Maryland, Florida, Texas, and Kansas. When bermudagrass invades cool-season turf, it is considered a weed.

St. Augustinegrass

ST. AUGUSTINEGRASS (*Stenotaphrum secundatum*) is a robust, fast-growing, coarse-textured, warm-season perennial with broad, dark green blades. Suitable for lawns and other turfgrass areas where a fine texture is not required, St. Augustinegrass is among the most shade tolerant of the warm-season grasses. On the minus side, it requires frequent watering and tends to lose its color as soon as the weather turns cold. It requires a fertile, well-drained soil, but even in good soil, it requires regular fertilization. It is also susceptible to insect damage and disease.

It has adapted to southern California, Hawaii, mild areas of the Southwest, Florida, and other Gulf Coast states, as it withstands heat well and is tolerant of salt spray and salty soil. St. Augustinegrass doesn't produce viable seed so it must be planted by sprigs or sod.

CENTIPEDEGRASS (*Eremochloa ophiuroides*), a coarse-textured, light green grass is sometimes called "lazy man's grass" because of its low-maintenance requirements. It needs less mowing than other grasses and it adapts to poor soil, resists chinch bugs and brown patch disease, and is aggressive enough to crowd out weeds. These qualities make it an excellent choice for general-purpose lawns in the Southeast and Gulf Coast states.

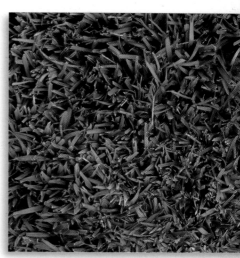

Centipedegrass

Its shallow roots give it only moderate drought tolerance, and it's among the first of the warm-season grasses to turn brown during extended hot, dry periods. It's also sensitive to low temperatures and tends to go dormant when cold. It won't withstand much traffic and is slow to recover when damaged.

CARPETGRASS (*Axonopus fissifolius*) is a specialized creeping grass that forms a dense, fast-growing, wear-tolerant turf that grows well in the lower coastal plains of the United States. It is cold-sensitive and cannot survive winter temperatures north of Central Georgia. Even in the Deep South, it will go dormant and turn brown during the relatively cooler winter months.

The blades are quite coarse and the plant forms unattractive seed heads if allowed to grow more than an inch tall; frequent mowing is required to keep it below that height. However, if well maintained, carpetgrass is a disease- and insect-tolerant turfgrass that stands up to heavy wear.

Carpetgrass

Plant Selection: Lawns
(continued)

Buffalograss

Blue gramagrass

Kentucky bluegrass

BUFFALOGRASS (*Buchloe dactyloides*) is only one of two native grasses grown as turfgrass in North America. It has fine-texture, curling blades, and outstanding heat tolerance. Often planted for its low maintenance, buffalograss thrives in areas that receive only 12 to 15 inches of rain per year. It takes hard wear and looks fairly good with little summer watering.

BLUE GRAMAGRASS (*Bouteloua gracilis*) is another native of the prairies of the Great Plains. It has been frequently put to use on lawns because it can serve as low-maintenance turf. It is often mixed with buffalograss for a better-looking lawn. Grayish green with fine-textured, curling leaves, it has excellent pest and disease resistance and tolerance to heat, cold, drought, and alkaline soils. Although technically a warm-season grass, it remains hardy to −40° F. It can be left unmowed or, for a more turflike appearance, mowed three to four times per year.

Cool season grasses

KENTUCKY BLUEGRASS (*Poa pratensis*) is a cool-season, fine-textured perennial with good color and vigorous spreading ability. Its appearance is the standard against which all other turfgrasses are measured. It is perhaps the most cold-hardy of all turfgrass, making it a dependable lawn in the northern reaches of the United States. It's noted for its fine texture and dense, thick turf. It needs more fertilizing and more frequent mowing than many other cool-season grasses, and it doesn't tolerate shade.

Rough bluegrass (*Poa trivialis*) is a bright-green, fine-textured, shallow-rooted relative of Kentucky bluegrass. It is soft-bladed, and in mild climates, retains its color over winter. It can survive without full sun so it makes a good component in shady lawn mixtures. Canada bluegrass (*Poa compressa*) is a cold-tolerant, fine-textured bluegrass that is well adapted to Canada and the northern United States. It is a good substitute for high-maintenance turf in conservation areas, on banks, and in hard-to-access areas.

Annual bluegrass (*Poa annua*), a low-growing, creeping grass, is a weed. Stay away from any seed mixtures containing it.

Fine fescue

FINE FESCUES are very fine-textured grasses with needlish blades. Chewings fescue (*Festuca rubra commutata*) is an aggressive fine fescue that can overtake other grasses. It is sometimes used to overseed shady lawns, often in mixtures with perennial ryegrass and Kentucky bluegrass. It is adapted to cooler areas in the northern United States and Canada, and to the coastal regions of the Northeast and Pacific Northwest. It is a good choice for low-maintenance turf in shaded, low-traffic areas in lawns.

Hard fescue (*Festuca longifolia*) is a fine-textured grass grown mostly at high elevations in the northern United States and Canada. It requires low fertilization and its short growth and slow growth rate mean less frequent mowings. It is very well suited to covering slopes and banks.

Red fescue (*Festuca rubra*), also known as creeping red fescue, is often combined with Kentucky bluegrass in good-quality

Tall fescue

lawn seed mixes. A fine-textured, low-maintenance grass with narrow, dark green blades, it blends well and grows well in shade and drought. It grows well on banks and slopes, and creates an especially lush effect when left unmowed. It is best adapted to the coastal Northwest and high elevations, and it is widely planted in the Great Lakes region.

Sheep fescue (*Festuca ovina*) is a cool-season perennial that requires little water. Once established, it is persistent and winter hardy. Though it doesn't make an elegant lawn, it is a good low-maintenance grass for off-the-beaten-path areas in lawns. It does well in cool, dry areas and requires infrequent mowing and minimal fertilizing.

TALL FESCUE (*Festuca arundinacea*), a dense grass that is able to grow in sun or shade, is a good low-maintenance choice for home lawns. It performs best in areas with mild winters and warm summers and in mild-temperature regions of the Southwest. It is one of the best turf choices for the transition zone and will stay green all year where the winters are mild. It tolerates high and infrequent mowing.

PERENNIAL RYEGRASS (*Lolium perenne*) exhibits the best wear tolerance of any cool-season grass. It can be successfully grown throughout the cool-season turfgrass regions and in cooler parts and higher elevations of the warm-season region. It likes full sun but will tolerate some shade.

Annual ryegrass (*Lolium multiflorum*), also known as Italian ryegrass, forms a medium- to coarse-textured lawn with moderate wear tolerance. It is often found in inexpensive grass mixes, but it does not belong in a permanent lawn because it lives for only one year. It is sometimes used as a temporary lawn and can be used to overseed warm-season lawns to provide winter color.

CREEPING BENTGRASS (*Agrostis palustris*) is the finest-textured and lowest-growing of all. This is the grass that's used on putting and bowling greens. It forms a soft, dense carpetlike lawn, but requires good drainage, frequent low mowing, watering, and fertilizing.

Colonial bentgrass (*A. tenuis*) is a bit more user friendly. It tolerates higher mowing and less fertilizer. When left unmowed, it can serve as a conservation grass, stabilizing banks. It is well adapted to the Pacific Northwest.

Redtop (*A. alba*) often is included in inexpensive cool-season and construction-grade mixes because it germinates and spreads rapidly. It will often out-compete other, more desirable grasses.

Perennial ryegrass

Creeping bentgrass

Lawns: Grasses for Trouble Spots

The right variety and species of grass can yield a trouble-free lawn even in moderately shaded areas.

GLOSSARY

As you do your turfgrass homework, you'll find a few descriptive terms repeated. Here's what they mean:

Low maintenance: A maintenance regime in which fertilizer, water, and mowing are at much lower than optimum rates.

High maintenance: A maintenance regime that provides optimum, or better than optimum, amounts of water and fertilizer combined with frequent mowing.

Tolerates low mowing: The ability of a variety to tolerate a much shorter mowing height than other varieties in the species while retaining color and vigor.

Tolerates infrequent mowing: The ability of a variety to grow slow enough to need little mowing or to look fine even when allowed to reach 3 or 4 inches tall.

Disease resistance: The ability of a variety to thrive despite the presence of disease-causing fungi.

Wear tolerance: The ability of a variety to tolerate frequent foot or other type of traffic.

Spring green-up: The time when a variety breaks dormancy.

Density: The number of shoots in an area; the greater the number, the denser, or thicker, the turf.

If your lawn seems to be struggling, you might be trying to grow the wrong grass. Maintaining a lawn is easy in good soil in the sun, but most of us are not so blessed. Fortunately, however, there are many turf grass species that thrive even in troublesome areas. The key is to find the species that matches your conditions.

Shady

Along with shade tolerance, look for good drought-tolerant grass because shade is often caused by trees that compete for soil moisture. Try cool-season grasses, such as rough bluegrass, fine fescue and tall fescue, and warm-season grasses such as St. Augustinegrass, centipede grass, and bahiagrass.

Dry

The best drought-tolerant grasses are usually the ones that grow long roots to tap into all the available soil moisture. The best are tall fescue and fine fescue for cool-season grasses, and bermudagrass, zoysiagrass, bahiagrass, and buffalograss in warm-season areas.

Hot

Heat tolerance is relative. Warm-season grass, of course, can take the heat better than cool-season varieties. Some cool-season grasses, on the other hand, show moderate and even good heat tolerance and can be planted in cooler areas of the South. Use perennial ryegrass, tall fescue, fine fescue, and Kentucky bluegrass in cool-season regions. For warm-season regions, plant bermudagrass, centipedegrass, zoysiagrass, St. Augusinegrass, and buffalograss.

Cold

Most cool-season grasses survive even the severest winters, except those in the far North. Some, however, bounce back more quickly from the cold. The best cold-tolerant cool-season grasses are fine fescue, creeping bentgrass, and Canada and Kentucky bluegrass. Bermudagrass, zoysiagrass, and hybrid St. Augustinegrass are the most cold-tolerant of the warm-season grasses.

Slopes

Grass for lawns on slopes need to tolerate infrequent mowing, little to no fertilization and dry soil (slopes dry out faster than flat ground). Plant hard fescue and sheep fescue in cool-season areas and buffalograss and blue gramagrass in warm-season areas.

Traffic

For heavily used areas, grasses should have good vigor and strong crowns that can produce blades even under constant traffic. In cool-season regions, plant tall fescue, perennial ryegrass, and Kentucky bluegrass. In warm-season regions, plant bermudagrass, bahiagrass and zoysiagass.

HOW GRASSES MEASURE UP

Grasses	Establishment Speed	Heat Tolerance	Cold Tolerance	Drought Tolerance	Shade Tolerance	Wearability	Low Mowing	Fertilizer Needs
COOL-SEASON GRASSES								
Creeping bentgrass	moderate	poor	good	poor	moderate	poor	good	high
Kentucky bluegrass	poor	moderate	good	moderate	moderate	moderate	moderate	moderate
Rough bluegrass	moderate	poor	good	poor	good	moderate	moderate	moderate
Canada bluegrass	poor	poor	good	moderate	moderate	poor	poor	low
Fine fescues	moderate	moderate	good	moderate	good	good	poor	moderate
Perennial ryegrass	good	moderate	moderate	moderate	moderate	good	moderate	moderate
Tall fescues	good	good	poor	good	moderate	good	poor	moderate
WARM-SEASON GRASSES								
Bahiagrass	moderate	good	poor	moderate	moderate	good	poor	low
Hybrid bermudagrass	good	good	moderate	good	poor	good	good	moderate
Blue gramagrass	moderate	good	moderate	good	poor	poor	moderate	low
Buffalograss	moderate	good	good	good	poor	moderate	good	good
Carpetgrass	moderate	high	poor	moderate	poor	poor	good	low
Centipedegrass	moderate	good	poor	moderate	moderate	poor	moderate	moderate
St. Augustinegrass	moderate	good	poor	poor	good	moderate	poor	moderate
Zoysiagrass	poor	good	moderate	good	moderate	good	good	low

Groundcovers

Selecting the best groundcovers for your landscape depends on where you live, the conditions in your yard, and the design effect you're looking for. It's easy to narrow down your choices based on where you live. It's not worth the time and money to tinker with plants that ultimately won't survive in your landscape, so from the start, choose plants that will grow in your hardiness zone.

Now take a look at your landscape plan and identify the areas you want to place groundcovers. Next, determine the conditions in these areas. Is it sunny or shady? Is the area wet or dry? Figuring out the details of the areas you want groundcovers will help you narrow down the field even more. Choose plants that will survive in these microclimates in your yard so you won't have to struggle to keep the plants alive.

Mesh function and design into your selection of groundcover plants, because function and design are dictated by a plant's type. Woody plants give permanence to a landscape, while herbaceous plants offer a lush, carpeted impression only during the growing season. Evergreen plants bring year-round color and structure to a landscape; deciduous plants lose their leaves in winter, which may reveal different stem colors or add new textures to the landscape. Or they may simply seem to disappear.

You can mix and match these different qualities— woody, herbaceous,

evergreen, and deciduous—the options are almost endless.

Herbaceous or woody

Plants are described as either herbaceous or woody. Both types make fine groundcovers; however, each brings a different element to the landscape and fills different roles.

Herbaceous groundcovers have little or no woody tissue. Their stems are fleshy and supple rather than rigid, and aboveground portions tend to be leaflike in structure and texture. Herbaceous groundcovers grow in a wide range of shapes, sizes, and colors. For example, lilyturf provides height and grassy shape and texture; ajuga and vinca create a low carpet; lavender cotton forms a silvery ball of foliage.

Perennial herbaceous plants die back to the ground each winter, then produce new shoots and leaves each spring, which is how they cope with cold. For that reason, they don't provide the same year-round visual structure as woody plants. But they are lush during the growing season and often have showier flowers, foliage, and

Lily-of-the-valley

Juniper dwarf

A SAMPLING OF HERBACEOUS GROUNDCOVERS

Cinquefoil (*Ptentilla* spp.)
Goutweed
  (*Aegopodium podagraria*)
Hostas (*Hosta* spp.)
Lily-of-the-valley
  (*Convallaria majalis*)
Moneywort
  (*Lysimachia nummularia*)
Vinca (*Vinca* spp.)
Wild strawberry
  (*Fragaria chiloensis*)
Yellow archangel
  (*Lamium galeobdolon*)

A FEW WOODY GROUNDCOVERS

Barberry (*Berberis thunbergii*)
Broom (*Cytisus* spp.)
Bush honeysuckle (*Lonicera pileata*)
Cotoneaster (*Cotoneaster* spp.)
Coyote brush (*Baccharis pilularis*)
Indigo (*Indigofera* spp.)
Ivy (*Hedera* spp.)
Juniper (*Juniperus* spp.)
Rose (*Rosa* spp.)
Russian cypress (*Microbiota decussata*)
Virginia creeper (*Parthenocissus quinquefolia*)
Wintergreen (*Gaultheria* spp.)

GROUNDCOVERS FOR FULL SUN

Artemisia (*Artemisia* spp.)
Broom (*Cytisus* spp.)
Cotoneaster (*Cotoneaster* spp.)
Coyote brush (*Baccharis pilularis*)
Creeping manzanita
    (*Arctostaphylos uva-ursi*)
Fleabane (*Erigeron karvinskianus*)
Juniper (*Juniperus* spp.)
Lavender (*Lavendula* spp.)
Lippia (*Phyla nodiflora*)
Moss phlox (*Phlox subulata*)
Rock rose (*Cistus* spp.)
Rose (*Rosa* spp.)
Sedum (*Sedum* spp.)
Snow-in-summer
    (*Cerastium tomentosum*)
Sun rose
    (*Helianthemum nummularium*)
Trailing lantana
    (*Lantana montevidensis*)
Woolly yarrow (*Achillea tomentosas*)

Chicks and hens
(*Sedum rosularia*)

seeds than woody groundcovers. They also supply seasonal diversity to your setting as they grow, bloom, and later die back.

Most herbaceous groundcovers have fibrous roots and dense growth, which help stabilize soil and prevents erosion.

Woody groundcovers include trees, shrubs, and many shrubby groundcovers such as junipers, cotoneasters, barberries, and vines.

Unlike herbaceous plants, woody plant cells contain lignin, a cellulose fiber that produces rigid rather than pliable stems and limbs. For that reason, woody plants maintain their form year-round. Even without their leaves, deciduous woody groundcovers form lovely silhouettes in the landscape.

There are no set rules about when and where to use woody groundcovers instead of herbaceous groundcovers, but they're ideal for spots requiring a year-round presence, such as where boundary plants are called for. Woody groundcovers can be superb boundary plants because when placed close together, they provide a solid, year-round barrier. For example, the thorns and height of groundcover barberries prevent people walking in certain areas, even when snow covers them.

Because the stems of most woody groundcovers don't form roots wherever their branches touch the ground, they don't prevent erosion until their canopies

Sedum kamtsenaticum
"Aurea"

Cotoneaster

GROUNDCOVERS FOR DRY SITES

Cotoneaster (*Cotoneaster* spp.)
Gazania (*Gazania rigens*)
Grapeholly (*Mahonia* spp.)
Juniper (*Juniper* spp.)
Rosemary (*Rosemarinus oficinalis*)
St. Johnswort (*Hypercium* spp.)
Trailing lantana (*Lantana
    montevidensis*)
Yarrow (*Achillea* spp.)

Groundcovers
(continued)

completely cover the ground. Once that happens and their root systems fill the soil, they do a good job of holding the soil.

Deciduous or evergreen

Like all plants, groundcovers can be deciduous or evergreen. Both types fill design and functional roles in landscapes.

Deciduous plants lose their leaves in fall and are bare in winter. Evergreens retain their foliage, staying green and functional year-round. However, they tend to be less colorful and seasonally diverse than deciduous plants.

Some plant groups have deciduous and evergreen members. For example, creeping cotoneaster is deciduous, while bearberry cotoneaster is evergreen. Other plants are deciduous or evergreen depending on climatic conditions. For example, in warm areas, New Zealand brass buttons tends to be evergreen, but in cold climates, it is deciduous. Check with the nursery or garden center to ensure you select a true evergreen (if that is what your landscape requires).

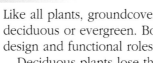

Hosta 'Sum and Substance'

Japanese painted fern

Barberry

Plants for special effects

Some groundcovers, such as mosses and ornamental grasses, readily fill special landscaping needs.

MOSSES: Mosses are a lush and enchanting groundcover option. Although they are sometimes difficult to establish and slow to spread, once they take hold they are practically maintenance-free and resilient to foot traffic. Use mosses where the soil is poor and between stepping-stones and rocks. Star, fern, broom, cedar, and hairy-cap mosses grow in almost any climate.

GRASSES: Ornamental grasses bring subtle color and texture to a groundcover bed. They are lovely as edging plants and spread well to fill large areas. Grasses often have a longer growing season than other herbaceous perennials. Although their foliage dies back in winter, you can leave it in place to provide a winter presence. In addition, most have lovely seed heads that dress up a winter landscape. Some ornamental grasses, such as blue fescue, grow in clumps rather than spreading to form a solid mat of plants.

GROUNDCOVERS FOR WET SITES

Chinese astilbe (*Astilbe chinensis*)
Ferns (*Adiantum* spp., *Dryopteris* spp.)
Forget-me-not (*Myosotis scorpioides*)
Hostas (*Hosta* spp.)
Lilyturf (*Liriope* spp.)
Moneywort (*Lysimachia nummularia*)
Ribbon grass (*Phalaris arundinacea*)
Yellow-root (*Xanthoriza simplicissima*)

Mother-of-thyme

GROUNDCOVERS FOR TRAFFIC

Blue star creeper (*Laurentia fluviatilis*)
Chamomile (*Chamaemelum nobile*)
Creeping speedwell (*Veronica repens*)
Irish moss (*Arenaria verna*)
Lippia (*Phyla nudiflora*)
Mock strawberry (*Duchesnea indica*)
New Zealand brass buttons (*Leptinella squalida*)
Thyme (*Thymus* spp.)

Moss path

GROUNDCOVERS FOR DESERT REGIONS

Bush morning glory (*Convolvulis cneorum*)
Dwarf coyote brush (*Baccharis pilularis*)
Gazania (*Gazania rigens*)
Manzanita (*Arctostaphylos edmundsii*)
Mother-of-thyme (*Thymus serpyllum*)
Rosemary (*Rosmarinus officinalis*)
Snow-in-summer (*Cerastium tomentosum*)
Trailing indigo bush (*Dalea greggii*)

and present a low, massed appearance. More importantly, they contribute unique design qualities to a landscape.

Typically, most people think of nonliving materials as surfaces only for paths, patios, or other hardscaping or for mulching. However, nonliving materials offer as much design potential in a landscape as groundcover plants. The design effects they create are quite different from those of groundcover plants but are just as beautiful. Like plants, they add texture (from fine to coarse) and color (generally neutral shades of tan or brown, but also black and other colors). Use nonliving groundcovers to create a swath of color through a landscape, to draw a pattern, to add textural or color contrast between plants and hardscapes, or as substitutes for lawn.

Alternative groundcovers

The broad definition of groundcovers encompasses nonliving materials as well as plants. It includes organic materials, such as wood and bark chips, and inorganic materials, such as rock, pebbles, gravel, and pavers. These materials help stabilize soil, discourage weeds,

Creeping manzanita

GROUNDCOVERS FOR DEEP SHADE

Barrenwort (*Epimedium* spp.)
Bunchberry (*Cornus Canadensis*)
Cast-iron plant (*Aspidistra elatior*)
English ivy (*Hedera helix*)
Ferns (*Dryopteris* spp.)
Hostas (*Hosta* spp.)
Lily-of-the-valley (*Convallaria majalis*)
Pachysandra (*Pachysandra* spp.)
Sweet woodruff (*Galium odoratum*)
Wandflower (*Galax ureceolata*)
Wild ginger (*Asarum* spp.)

GROUNDCOVERS FOR THE SEASIDE

Broom (*Cytisus* spp.)
Ice plants (*Delosperma* spp.)
Lantana (*Lantana* spp.)
Manzanita (*Arctostaphylos edmundsii*)
Speedwell (*Veronica* spp.)
Wedelia (*Wedelia trilobata*)

Pachysandra in bloom

A June garden crowded with daylilies, black-eyed Susans, and complementary annuals isn't shy about color.

Flowers

The most fun—and perhaps most daunting—thing to choose for the landscape is the flowers. The sheer numbers of flowering plants from which to choose can boggle the mind and make choosing the right plant for the right place downright intimidating. First, always take into consideration your practical requirements; that is, what you need to accomplish in your landscape. Once you have that firmly fixed in your mind, you can begin to narrow down your choices.

Truly, there isn't much to learning how to choose the right flower to plant— you just have to understand the basic categories. Perennials to annuals, early bloomers to late bloomers, warm colors to cool colors, and from small to large, once you know the basics, you can easily whittle your choices down to plants that you love and will work well in your landscape design.

SPRING BLOOMERS

FOR SUN
Cushion spurge (*Euphorbia polychroma*)
Heartleaf bergenia (*Bergenia cordifolia*)
Leopard's bane (*Doronicum caucasicum*)
Marsh marigold (*Caltha palustris*)
Rock cress (*Aurinia saxatilis*)

FOR SHADE
Bishop's hat (*Epimedium grandiflorum*)
Bleeding heart (*Dicentra spectabilis*)
Blue corydalis (*Corydalis flexuosa*)
Columbine (*Aquilegia*)
Lenten rose (*Helleborus orientalis*)
Lungwort (*Pulmonaria officinalis*)
Primrose (*Primula*)
Sweet violet (*Viola odorata*)
Wood anemone (*Anemone nemerosa*)

Bleeding heart (*Dicentra spectabilis*) and Siberian bugloss (*Brunnera macrophylla*) brightly announce that spring is here.

Flowers: Great Perennials

If trees, shrubs, and vines are the workhorses of a garden, then perennials are the stars. A well-chosen succession of perennials will supply gardens with months of colorful, ever-changing drama.

First flowers

In early spring, garden beds and borders green up fast. Sleepy perennials stretch skyward as temperatures rise. Some of the hardiest begin to bloom as the snow melts. Others leaf out first, then their fresh foliage is quickly followed by plump buds and cheerful flowers.

Combine blooms to develop vivid early color. Arrange these first-flowering plants in clusters in sufficient quantities to make an impact.

Plant for a sequence of blooms, so first flowers are followed by second and third waves in the same location. Spring flowers don't have to simply appear on trees and shrubs or bulbs. Look to nature and you'll find plenty of perennial early risers, such as sweet violet *(Viola)* and fringed bleeding heart *(Dicentra)*. Dozens of other native species flower in spring, as do their hybrid cousins. Consider tucking clumps of early perennials between larger and later-rising plants; they will bloom early then remain as a groundcover.

Early summer

By early summer, many gardens are fragrant with roses, lilies, and honeysuckle, but apart from peonies *(Paeonia)*, foxglove *(Digitalis)*, and coral bells *(Heuchera)*, perennials appear in short supply. Some gardeners select flowers that all bloom at approximately the same time for a garden filled with color. This creates a brief but spectacular display. Unfortunately, it also means there is little or no perennial bloom for the rest of the season.

Gardeners who prefer a longer duration of early summer color plant for a continuous succession of bloom, with new flowers coming as spring flowers fade past bloom. This may seem to dilute the impact of the overall color scheme, but it actually reveals more of the complete character of the plants. In general, even when the garden is planned and planted with succession in mind, three or four peak periods during the season are interspersed with periods of quiet green relief.

With the variations in blossoming times and the duration of bloom, the possibilities for the early summer perennial garden are immense. Sequencers—plants that remain effective throughout the seasons—help bridge the gap between peak periods. Meadow rue *(Thalictrum),* for example, makes a super sequencer; its airy scrim adds a sense of mystery to the small garden and screens over sweeps of browning bulb foliage. Ornamental grasses, mounded spirea shrubs, and woolly lamb's-ear *(Stachys byzantina)* are all excellent sequencers.

Make it last

Many early summer perennials can also provide you with decorative effects over additional seasons. In early summer, false indigo *(Baptisia),* with its sweet pealike flowers in blue or white, doubles as a splendid foliage plant. Its lustrous blue-gray foliage partners pleasantly with long-fingered peonies and the slender wands of peach-leaf bellflower *(Campanula persicifolia)*. Indigo foliage remains sturdy into winter and provides a handsome backdrop for late bloomers. In shady sites, try clumps of foxglove and aster, which are long-blooming. Bellflower, too, lasts longer than a single season. And if spent blooms are cut back, they'll likely send up a fresh flush of flowers.

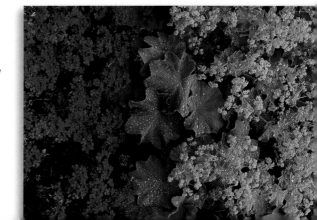

Strong colors combine forces in the royal purple of verbena and vibrant green of lady's mantle.

Flowers: High-Summer Perennials

Use flowers to concoct potent combinations by interweaving flowers and foliage. When one plant takes a breather, another can step in and take its place. Track their performance in a garden journal or notebook.

How to grow a great variety

The best way to enjoy an unbroken sequence of bloom is to develop a full palette of perennial color. (It helps to shop all year round, choosing seasonal bests.) Variety ensures that despite quirky weather, disease, or nuisance animals, something will succeed. Begin with garden workhorses, plants with staying power in almost any situation. Yarrow *(Achillea)*, sedum, daylily *(Hemerocallis)*, and similar tireless plants come in a range of sizes and colors.

Don't stop with color. Group your choices by shape and texture as well. Many perennials are basically mound-shaped and need contrasts to keep their own identity. Choose among yucca, Chinese rhubarb *(Rheum palmatum)*, mullein *(Verbascum)*, sea holly *(Eryngium)*, and fountain grass *(Pennisetum)*, for starters.

Sun and shade

Sunny gardens can host a tremendous number of summer bloomers. Among them are many native flowers that adapt effortlessly to the home landscape, growing larger and blooming longer than they do in the wild. Purple coneflower *(Echinacea purpurea)*, blanket flower *(Gaillardia)*, black-eyed Susan *(Rudbeckia)*, and beard-tongue *(Penstemon)* all provide multiple possibilities throughout the summer season.

Shady woodland gardens are often quite dry by midsummer. Where water is an issue, select drought-tolerant plants. If it's damp shade you have, dozens of perennials suit it to a "T," from spiky ligularia to bold rodgersia. Damp or dry, shade gardens can hold marvelous tapestries of foliage perennials such as hosta and lungwort *(Pulmonaria)*. For contrast, mix in rounded and ruffled coral bells *(Heuchera)*, lacy ferns, and fine-textured astilbes.

HIGH-SUMMER PERENNIALS

FOR SUN

Blazing star *(Liatris spicata)*
Daylily *(Hemerocallis)*
Hollyhock mallow *(Malva alcea)*
Joe-Pye weed *(Eupatorium purpureum)*
Queen-of-the-prairie *(Filipendula rubra)*
Red valerian *(Centranthus ruber)*
Sea holly *(Eryngium amethystinum)*
Tree mallow *(Lavatera thuringiaca)*
Yarrow *(Achillea)*

FOR SHADE

Astilbe *(Astilbe arendsii)*
Goatsbeard *(Aruncus dioicus)*
Hosta *(Hosta)*
Japanese painted fern *(Athyrium nipponicum)*
Lady fern *(Athyrium filix-femina)*
Maidenhair fern *(Adiantum pedatum)*

Above: Bee balm (*Monarda didyma*) is a dependable plant in the midsummer garden, attracting butterflies and hummingbirds. Below: Hollyhock, black-eyed Susan, and bee balm cheerfully mix and mingle in this porch-side bed.

Chrysanthemums, blazing star (*Liatris spicata*), and coneflower (*Echinacea purpurea*) fill this autumn bed.

Flowers: Late Bloomers

As late summer melts into autumn, warm days and cool nights can waken the hidden flames of foliage. Blue star *(Amsonia taberaemontana)* and balloon flower *(Platycodon)* turn to fiery gold. Variegated obedient plant *(Physostegia)* reblooms above foliage streaked with raspberry and cream.

Extending autumn

In order to have a good autumnal show, you must dedicate significant garden space to some of these late bloomers. It need not mean a summer sacrifice: If 10 to 20 percent of your plants offer strong fall flower or foliage color, they will carry the season. Keep in mind, many late performers are large plants with plenty of character. What's more, you can place them behind rebloomers, (yarrow, blanket flower, and daylily), whose contribution will then be amplified by their dramatic neighbors.

To maximize your autumn display, group late bloomers in clusters and sweeps, and give them supportive companions (such as long-season foliage plants and additional reliable rebloomers), so the fall performers do not appear forlorn or as an afterthought in the home landscape. And select fall flowers that can pull their weight over several seasons, such as sedum, black-eyed Susan *(Rudbeckia fulgida),* and the structurally fascinating *Aster lateriflorus* var. *horizontalis.*

Seedheads of rudbeckia and upright ornamental grasses keep the garden interesting even in the white of winter.

LATER PERFORMERS

FOR SUN
Blue star (*Amsonia tabernaemontana*)
Boltonia (*Boltonia asteroides*)
Goldenrod (*Solidago*)
Hardy aster (*Aster*)
Helen's flower (*Helenium autumnale*)
Plumbago (*Ceratostigma plumbaginoides*)
Stonecrop (*Sedum spectabile*)

FOR SHADE
Bugbane (*Cimicifuga racemosa*)
Cardinal flower (*Lobelia cardinalis*)
Japanese anemone (*Anemone ×hybrida*)
Monkshood (*Aconitum*)
Toad lily (*Tricyrtis hirta*)

COLD-WINTER INTEREST

FOR SUN
Black-eyed Susan (*Rudbeckia fulgida*)
False indigo (*Baptisia australis*)
Giant feather grass (*Stipa gigantean*)
Globe thistle (*Echinops bannaticus*)
Sea Holly (*Eryngium amethystinum*)
Yucca (*Yucca filamentosa*)

FOR SHADE
Barrenwort (*Epimedium ×rubrum*)
Golden Grass (*Hakonechloa macra*)

MILD-WINTER INTEREST

FOR SUN
Anise hyssop (*Agastache foeniculum*)
Maiden grass (*Miscanthus sinensis*)
New Zealand flax (*Phormium tenax*)
Switch grass (*Panicum virgatum*)

FOR SHADE
Bergenia (*Bergenia cordifolia*)
Stokes' aster (*Stokesia laevis*)
Varigated Japanese sedge (*Carex morrowii* 'Varigata')

Use this chart to help you plan for overlapping seasons of bloom for color all year. Because perennials are listed in order of bloom and broken into early, mid-, and late season, you can easily see at a glance which bloom together, which bloom in succession, and which bloom for extra long times. Remember that any bloom chart will only be a rough guide, as bloom seasons can differ according to the region, the weather, microclimates, and cultivars. Blue bars represent bloom seasons; orange bars represent fall foliage and fruit effects.

(Bloom key: **B** = blue bar / bloom season; **O** = orange bar / fall foliage and fruit effects)

Plant Name	Spr. E	Spr. M	Spr. L	Sum. E	Sum. M	Sum. L	Fall E	Fall M	Fall L	Win. E	Win. M	Win. L
Basket-of-gold (Aurinia saxatilis)	B	B										
Bergenia (Bergenia cordifolia)	B	B					O	O	O			
Marsh marigold (Caltha palustris)	B	B										
Red barrenwort (Epimedium ×rubrum)	B	B					O	O				
Cushion spurge (Euphorbia polychroma)	B	B	B									
Mediterranean spurge (Euphorbia characias)	B	B						O	O			
Lenten rose (Helleborus orientalis)	B	B						O	O			
Creeping phlox (Phlox subulata)	B	B										
Bethlehem sage (Pulmonaria saccharata)	B	B	B									
Sweet violet (Viola odorata)	B											
Bleeding heart (Dicentra spectabilis)		B	B									
Luxuriant bleeding heart (Dicentra 'Luxuriant')			B	B	B							
Myrtle spurge (Euphorbia myrsinites)	B	B	B					O				
English primrose (Primula vulgaris)		B	B									
Columbine (Aquilegia)			B	B								
False indigo (Baptisia australis)			B				O	O				
Dwarf crested iris (Iris cristata)			B									
Cheddar pink (Dianthus gratianopolitanus)			B	B								
Woodland phlox (Phlox divaricata)			B									
Allegheny foam flower (Tiarella cordifolia)			B	B								
Lady's mantle (Alchemilla mollis)				B								
Blue star (Amsonia tabernaemontana)			B	B				O				
Astilbe (Astilbe ×arendsii)			B	B			O	O	O			
Masterwort (Astrantia major)			B	B								
Yellow corydalis (Corydalis lutea)				B	B	B						
Japanese primrose (Primula japonica)				B	B							
Peach-leaf bellflower (Campanula persicifolia)				B	B							
Red valerian (Centranthus ruber)				B	B	B						
Twinspur (Diascia barberae)				B	B		O					
Foxglove (Digitalis purpurea)				B	B							
Bloody cranesbill (Geranium sanguineum)				B	B		O					
Johnson's Blue hardy geranium (Geranium 'Johnson's Blue')				B	B							
Geum (Geum)				B	B							
Creeping baby's breath (Gypsophila repens)				B	B	B						

Plant Name	Spr. E	Spr. M	Spr. L	Sum. E	Sum. M	Sum. L	Fall E	Fall M	Fall L	Win. E	Win. M	Win. L
Stella de Oro daylily (Hemerocallis 'Stella de Oro')				B	B	B						
Coral bells (Heuchera hybrids)				B								
Bearded iris, early season (Iris hybrids)			B	B								
Siberian iris (Iris sibirica)			B	B		O	O					
Lupine (Lupinus 'Russell Hybrid')			B	B								
Catmint (Nepeta ×faassenii)			B	B	B	B						
Peony (Paeonia hybrids)			B	B								
Oriental poppy (Papaver orientale)			B	B								
Beard-tongue (Penstemon)			B	B								
Lamb's-ear (Stachys byzantina)			B	B								
Columbine meadow rue (Thalictrum aquilegifolium)			B	B								
Variegated Solomon's seal (Polygonatum odoratum 'Variegatum')			B			O	O					
Coronation Gold yarrow (Achillea 'Coronation Gold')				B	B	B			O	O		
Hollyhock (Alcea rosea)				B	B	B						
Goatsbeard (Aruncus dioicus)				B								
Hybrid sage (Salvia ×sylvestris)				B								
Delphinium (Delphinium elatum)				B	B							
Butterfly weed (Asclepias tuberosa)				B	B		O					
Speedwell (Veronica hybrids)				B	B							
Kamtschatka stonecrop (Sedum kamtschaticum)				B								
Mullein (Verbascum chaixii)				B	B	B			O	O		
Carpathian bellflower (Campanula carpatica)				B								
Common yarrow (Achillea millefolium)				B	B							
Maiden pink (Dianthus deltoides)				B	B							
Modern pink (Dianthus 'Allwoodii' hybrids)				B	B							
Baby's breath (Gypsophila paniculata)				B	B		O					
Daylily (Hemerocallis)				B	B			O				
Bearded iris, late season (Iris hybrids)				B								
Shasta daisy (Leucanthemum ×superbum)				B	B							
Leopard's bane (Doronicum orientale)				B								
Threadleaf coreopsis (Coreopsis verticillata)				B	B							
Hardy geranium (Geranium psilostemon 'Bressingham Flair')				B	B		O					
Daylily, early season (Hemerocallis)				B								

Plant Name	Spr. E	Spr. M	Spr. L	Sum. E	Sum. M	Sum. L	Fall E	Fall M	Fall L	Win. E	Win. M	Win. L
Japanese iris (*Iris ensata*)				■								
Crimson pincushion (*Knautia macedonica*)				■	■							
Torch lily (*Kniphofia uvaria*)				■	■							
Tree mallow (*Lavatera thuringiaca*)				■	■							
Hollyhock mallow (*Malva alcea*)				■	■	■	■					
Golden lace (*Patrinia*)				■								
Chinese rhubarb (*Rheum palmatum*)				■								
Butterfly Blue pincushion flower (*Scabiosa columbaria* 'Butterfly Blue')				■	■							
Creeping verbena (*Verbena* hybrids)				■	■							
Sunny Border Blue speedwell (*Veronica* 'Sunny Border Blue')				■	■							
Feather reed grass (*Calamagrostis × acutiflora* 'Stricta')				■	■	▒	▒	▒				
Tickseed (*Coreopsis grandiflora*)				■	■							
Blanket flower (*Gaillardia ×grandiflora*)				■	■							
Frances Williams hosta (*Hosta sieboldiana* 'Frances Williams')				■								
Crocosmia (*Crocosmia* hybrids)				■	■							
Tufted hair grass (*Deschampsia caespitosa*)				■	■	▒	▒					
Globe thistle (*Echinops bannaticus*)				■	■	▒	▒					
Fleabane (*Erigeron* hybrids)				■								
Autumn Joy stonecrop (*Sedum/Hylotelephium* 'Autumn Joy'/ 'Herbstfreude')					■	■	■					
Yucca (*Yucca filamentosa*)				■	▒	▒	▒					
Plumbago (*Ceratostigma plumbaginoides*)					■	▒	▒					
Queen-of-the-prairie (*Filipendula rubra*)				■	■							
Blue oat grass (*Helictotrichon sempervirens*)				■	■		▒	▒				
Purple moor grass (*Molinia caerulea* 'Variegata')				■	■		▒	▒				
Bee balm (*Monarda didyma*)				■	■							
Russian sage (*Perovskia atriplicifolia*)				■	■	▒						
Rodgersia (*Rodgersia pinnata*)				■	■							
Stokes' aster (*Stokesia laevis*)				■	■							
Plume poppy (*Macleaya cordata*)				■	■							
Giant feather grass (*Stipa gigantea*)				■	■	▒	▒					
Monch Frikart's aster (*Aster frikartii* 'Monch')				■	■							
Chinese astilbe (*Astilbe chinensis*)				■	■							
Bugbane (*Cimicifuga racemosa*)					■							
Purple coneflower (*Echinacea purpurea*)				■	■	▒	▒					

Plant Name	Spr. E	Spr. M	Spr. L	Sum. E	Sum. M	Sum. L	Fall E	Fall M	Fall L	Win. E	Win. M	Win. L
Sea holly (*Eryngium amethystinum*)					■	■				▒		
Perennial sunflower (*Helianthus × multiflorus*)					■	■						
False sunflower (*Heliopsis helianthoides scabra*)					■	■						
Daylily, midseason (*Hemerocallis*)					■							
Rose mallow (*Hibiscus moscheutos*)					■	■						
Blazing star (*Liatris spicata*)					■	■						
Ligularia (*Ligularia*)					■	■						
Cardinal flower (*Lobelia cardinalis*)					■	■						
Gooseneck loosestrife (*Lysimachia clethroides*)					■	▒						
Purple loosestrife (*Lythrum salicaria*)					■	■						
Switch grass (*Panicum virgatum*)					■	▒	▒	▒				
Perennial fountain grass (*Pennisetum alopecuroides*)					■	▒	▒	▒				
Garden phlox (*Phlox paniculata*)					■	■						
Pokeweed (*Phytolacca americana*)					■	▒	▒					
Balloon flower (*Platycodon grandiflorus*)					■	▒						
Black-eyed Susan (*Rudbeckia fulgida*)					■	■						
Silver spike grass (*Spodiopogon sibiricus*)					■	■						
Anise hyssop (*Agastache foeniculum*)					■	■	▒					
Joe-Pye weed (*Eupatorium purpureum*)					■	■						
Helen's flower (*Helenium autumnale*)					■	■						
Maiden grass (*Miscanthus sinensis*)					■	▒	▒	▒				
Goldenrod (*Solidago* hybrids)					■	▒	▒					
Daylily, late season (*Hemerocallis*)					■							
August lily (*Hosta plantaginea*)					■							
Obedient plant (*Physostegia virginiana*)					■	■						
Monkshood (*Aconitum*)					■	■						
Hardy aster (*Aster*)					■	■						
Boltonia (*Boltonia asteroides*)					■	■						
Northern sea oats (*Chasmanthium latifolium*)						■	▒	▒				
Japanese anemone (*Anemone hupehensis*)						■	▒	▒				
Pampas grass (*Cortaderia selloana*)						■	■	▒				
Meadow rue (*Thalictrum rochebrunianum*)					■							
Toad lily (*Tricyrtis hirta*)					■	■						
White Pearl bugbane (*Cimicifuga simplex* 'White Pearl')							■					
Hardy chrysanthemum (*Chrysanthemum* hybrids)							■					

A combination of hostas ('Zounds,' 'Lemon Lime,' 'Patriot,' and 'Pearl Drops') makes for a varied combination of foliage.

Flowers: Bold-Shaped Plants

Modern life is full of straight lines and rigid routines, but a garden in which plants dominate and nature rules with its own wild ways is a constant refreshment to the spirit. More and more designers are stressing plant-driven rather than florally driven gardenscapes. Garden gigantism can give you the opportunity to be utterly embraced by plants. In these new gardens, boldly shaped and oversize plants often play the space-defining role traditionally assigned to hardscaping (walls, trellises, and arbors). But even in the smaller garden, large plants have their place, lending it a surprising sense of the dramatic.

In warm climates where a wide range of true tropical plants flourish, it's easy to give any garden a lush, junglelike appearance. No substitutes are needed; warm climates support the real thing. Gunnera *(Gunnera manicata)* and New Zealand flax *(Phormium tenax)* grow to amazing proportions where heat and

moisture are in ample supply. Drier, hot climates nourish a wide range of astonishing desert plants, including dozens of spurges *(Euphorbia)* as well as broad-bladed grasses and swirling, sword-leaved yuccas.

Mild-winter areas allow hardy tropicals and large-leaved foliage plants to create the impression of jungle abundance yet take moderate frosts in stride. In recent years, plant explorers have increased the palette with dozens of (somewhat) cold-hardy perennial forms of former tropical house plants. Many of these new introductions are finding their way into "Tropicalismo gardens," a school of thought that celebrates joyful gigantism. Characterized by a sense of exuberance, this style features sculptural character with spunky style. Ambitious designers mingle large-scale native plants from their own regions with allies and exotics from all over the world, creating a world-mix of plants that cohabitate with ease.

THE BIG AND THE BOLD

Cardinal flower (*Lobelia cardinalis*)
Chinese rhubarb (*Rheum palmatum*)
Goatsbeard (*Aruncus dioicus*)
Gunnera (*Gunnera manicata*)
Hosta (*Hosta sieboldiana elegans*)
Joe-Pye weed (*Eupatorium purpureum*)
Ostrich fern (*Matteuccia struthiopteris*)
Pampas grass (*Cortaderia selloana*)
Plume poppy (*Macleaya cordata*)
Pokeweed (*Phytolacca americana*)
Rodgersia (*Rodgersia pinnata*)
Rose mallow (*Hibiscus moscheutos*)
Tatarian aster (*Aster tataricus*)
Zebra grass (*Miscanthus sinensis* 'Zebrinus')

A giant clump of zebra grass brings distinctive stripes and dramatic scale to the show.

Cinnamon fern (*Osmunda cinnamomea*) dazzles with its spiky spores and lush fronds.

Big, bold junglelike plants, oversize ferns, and yucca can give the backyard garden a tropical flavor.

163

Perennials from Small to Large

Use this chart to help you combine perennials according to size and form. They are organized in order of their height from short to tall so that you can quickly find a perennial of the correct size at a glance. Each perennial listed is accompanied by a sketch of its typical form, approximately to scale. Remember that this chart is a rough guide; the size given and the form shown can vary according to the cultivar selected, as well as region, weather, and horticultural practice.

Creeping phlox (*Phlox subulata*) 3–6"

Kamtschatka stonecrop (*Sedum kamtschaticum*) 4–9"

Dwarf crested iris (*Iris cristata*) 6"

English primrose (*Primula vulgaris*) 6–9"

Allegheny foam flower (*Tiarella cordifolia*) 6–12"

Sweet violet (*Viola odorata*) 8"

Plumbago (*Ceratostigma plumbaginoides*) 8–12"

Barrenwort (*Epimedium ×rubrum*) 8–12"

Fringed bleeding heart (*Dicentra eximia*) 9–18"

Basket-of-gold (*Aurinia saxatilis*) 12"

Yellow corydalis (*Corydalis lutea*) 12"

Japanese painted fern (*Athyrium nipponicum* 'Pictum') 12"

Bergenia (*Bergenia cordifolia*) 12"

Pink (*Dianthus*) 12"

Twinspur (*Diascia*) 12"

Lungwort (*Pulmonaria saccharata*) 12"

'Georgia Blue' speedwell (*Veronica peduncularis* 'Georgia Blue') 12"

Dwarf blue fescue (*Festuca glauca*) 12"

Lamb's-ear (*Stachys byzantina*) 12"

Vial's primrose (*Primula vialii*) 12–15"

Columbine (*Aquilegia*) 1–2'

Marsh marigold (*Caltha palustris*) 12–18"

Fleabane (*Erigeron* hybrids) 1–2'

Lenten rose (*Helleborus orientalis*) 12–18"

Patrinia (*Patrinia scabiosifolia*) 12–18"

Japanese blood grass (*Imperata cylindrica* 'Red Baron') 12–18"

Variegated Japanese sedge (*Carex morrowii* 'Variegata') 12–18"

Hardy geranium (*Geranium*) 1–2'

Maidenhair fern (*Adiantum pedatum*) 12–20"

Golden grass (*Hakonechloa macra* 'Aureola') 1–2'

Creeping verbena (*Verbena* hybrids) 12–18"

Spiked speedwell (*Veronica spicata*) 10–36"

Coral bells (*Heuchera* hybrids) 12–24"

Stoke's aster (*Stokesia laevis*) 12–24"

Lady's mantle (*Alchemilla mollis*) 18"

Threadleaf coreopsis (*Coreopsis verticillata*) 18"

Leopard's bane (*Doronicum orientale*) 18–24"

Geum (*Geum*) 18"

Catmint (*Nepeta ×faassenii*) 18–24"

Pincushion flower (*Scabiosa caucasica*) 18–24"

Hardy chrysanthemum (*Chrysanthemum/ Dendranthema* hybrids) 1–3'

Wormwood (*Artemisia ludoviciana*) 2'

Sea holly (*Eryngium amethystinum*) 2'

Crimson pincushion (*Knautia macedonica*) 2'

Shasta daisy (*Leucanthemum ×superbum*) 2'

Christmas fern (*Polystichum acrostichoides*) 2'

Japanese primrose (*Primula japonica*) 2'

Stonecrop (*Sedum spectabile*) (*Hylotelephium spectabile*) 2'

Blanket flower (*Gaillardia ×grandiflora*) 2–3'

Beard-tongue (*Penstemon*) 2–3'

Fern-leaf yarrow (*Achillea filipendulina*) 2–3"

Masterwort (*Astrantia major*) 2–3'

Gooseneck lysimachia (*Lysimachia clethroides*) 2–3'

Hybrid sage (*Salvia ×sylvestris*) 2–3'

Toad lily (*Tricyrtis hirta*) 2–3'

Peach-leaf bellflower (*Campanula persicifolia*) 2–3'

Red valerian (*Centranthus ruber*) 2–3'

Crocosmia (*Crocosmia* hybrids) 2–3'

Hay-scented fern (*Dennstaedtia punctilobula*) 2–3'

Tufted hair grass (*Deschampsia caespitosa*) 2–3'

Bleeding heart (*Dicentra spectabilis*) 2–3'

Baby's breath (*Gypsophila paniculata*) 2–3'

Daylily (*Hemerocallis*) 1–3'

Bee balm (*Monarda didyma*) 2–3'

Japanese iris (*Iris ensata*) 2–3'

Balloon flower (*Platycodon grandiflorus*) 2–3'

Variegated Solomon's seal (*Polygonatum odoratum* 'Variegatum') 2–3'

Black-eyed Susan (*Rudbeckia fulgida*) 2–3'

Arendsii hybrid astilbe (*Astilbe ×arendsii*) 2–4'

Hardy aster (*Aster*) 2–4'

Northern sea oats (*Chasmanthium latifolium*) 30"

Male woodfern (*Dryopteris filix-mas*) 2–4'

Purple coneflower (*Echinacea purpurea*) 2–4'

Bearded iris (*Iris* hybrids) 2–4'

Siberian iris (*Iris sibirica*) 2–4'

Purple moor grass (*Molinia caerulea* 'Variegata') 2–4'

Oriental poppy (*Papaver orientale*) 2–4'

Garden phlox (*Phlox paniculata*) 2–4'

Obedient plant (*Physostegia virginiana*) 2–4'

 Goldenrod (*Solidago* hybrids) 2–4'

 Foxglove (*Digitalis purpurea*) 2–5'

 Meadow rue (*Thalictrum*) 2–6'

 Anise hyssop (*Agastache foeniculum*) 3'

 Blue star (*Amsonia tabernaemontana*) 3'

 Butterfly weed (*Asclepias tuberosa*) 3'

 Blue oat grass (*Helictotrichon sempervirens*) 3'

 Frances Williams hosta (*Hosta sieboldiana* 'Frances Williams') 3'

 Blazing star (*Liatris spicata*) 3'

 Lupine (*Lupinus* 'Russell Hybrid') 3'

 Cinnamon fern (*Osmunda cinnamonea*) 3'

 Peony (*Paeonia* hybrids) 3'

Mullein (*Verbascum chaixii*) 3'

 Japanese anemone (*Anemone × hybrida*) 2–4'

 False indigo (*Baptisia australis*) 3–4'

 Globe thistle (*Echinops bannaticus*) 3–4'

 False sunflower (*Heliopsis helianthoides scabra*) 3–4'

 Ligularia (*Ligularia*) 3–4'

 Cardinal flower (*Lobelia cardinalis*) 3–4'

Hollyhock mallow (*Malva alcea*) 3–4'

 Perennial fountain Grass (*Pennisetum alopecuroides*) 3–4'

 Russian sage (*Perovskia atriplicifolia*) 3–4'

 Rodgersia (*Rodgersia pinnata*) 3–4'

 Helen's flower (*Helenium autumnale*) 3–5'

 Purple loosestrife (*Lythrum salicaria*) 3–5'

 Cushion spurge (*Euphorbia polychroma*) 3–5'

 Monkshood (*Aconitum*) 3–6'

 Torch lily (*Kniphofia uvaria*) 4'

 Ostrich fern (*Matteuccia struthiopteris*) 4'

 Feather reed grass

(*Calamagrostis ×acutiflora* 'Stricta') 4–5'

 Tree mallow (*Lavatera thuringiaca*) 4–5'

 Silver spike grass (*Spodiopogon sibiricus*) 4–5'

 Perennial sunflower (*Helianthus ×multiflorus*) 4–6'

 Goatsbeard (*Aruncus dioicus*) 4–6'

 Bugbane (*Cimicifuga*) 4–6'

 Delphinium (*Delphinium elatum*) 4–6'

 **Pokeweed** (*Phytolacca americana*) 4–6'

 Joe-Pye weed (*Eupatorium maculatum*) 4–7'

 Hollyhock (*Alcea rosea*) 4–8'

 **Boltonia** (*Boltonia asteroides*) 5'

 **Rose mallow** (*Hibiscus moscheutos*) 5'

 Switch grass (*Panicum virgatum*) 5'

 Giant feather grass (*Stipa gigantea*) 5'

 **Pampas grass** (*Cortaderia selloana*) 5–12'

SUB. CHS. ART 149
YUCCA FILAMENTOSA

Yucca (*Yucca filamentosa*) 2–12'

 Queen-of-the-prairie (*Filipendula rubra*) 6–8'

 Gunnera (*Gunnera*) 6–10'

 Ornamental rhubarb (*Rheum palmatum*) 6–10'

Plume poppy (*Macleaya cordata*) 8'

Maiden grass (*Miscanthus sinensis*) 8'

New Zealand flax (*Phormium tenax*) 8–10'

Flowers: Cool-Color Perennials

Bugbane (*Cimicifuga racemosa*) and fairy candles (*Cimicifuga dahurica*) are cultivated in a shady woodland border.

Foxglove and geranium, along with ornamental grass, cool it under a Kousa dogwood.

English garden designer Gertrude Jekyll popularized color theme gardens in the early 19th century. She was the first to suggest grouping plants that bloom at the same time and insisted that no color can be fully appreciated on its own. Color values are relative, she explained, so any color comes into its own only in relationship to others. A white garden, for instance, could contain plants with white or near-white flowers but also contain silvery leaves or white-variegated foliage.

Working with white

White can seem difficult to work with but is especially valuable for those who enjoy their gardens in the evenings. Jekyll preferred off-white shades she called skim milk, eggshell, or bone, and yellowed tints like butter and cream. Blended with plenty of gray, sage, and olive foliage, these gentle colors weave a sumptuous tapestry. Jekyll thought sticking too closely to a theme was silly.

If off-whites look best, or if pale blue, pastel peach, or shell pink will emphasize the cool quality of white, use it! Don't sacrifice effect for strict consistency.

Astilbe (*Astilbe ×arendsii* 'Deutschland') has feathery white blooms.

Left: Balloon flower (*Platycodon grandiflorus* 'Hakone Blue') is a favorite of the cool summer garden.

Below: Sea holly (*Eryngium alpinum*) offers a tinge of amethyst and a hint of thistle.

Cooling it off

Colors on the blue side of the spectrum are considered cool, while those on the red side are hot. Chilly tints of peach with icy apricot, salmon, and chalky yellows with gray and blue foliage make a frosty color scheme. Matte, muted purple foliage like that of common sage *(Salvia officinalis),* whose fuzzy texture turns it pewtery, is likewise cooling.

The unusual blooms of *Corydalis flexuosa* 'Blue Panda' are true blue.

Salvia and artemisia are a dynamic duo in this bright border.

Vibrant dahlias stand out against black-eyed Susans.

Flowers: Warm-Color Perennials

Hot colors create drama in the landscape. A successful hot combination will have partners of equal weight and value, and significant assistance from surrounding foliage. Screaming orange demands a dazzling red. Soft pink would look insignificant next to orange. When the main colors—perhaps plum purple and apple red—are both saturated, dark green foliage will anchor them firmly. Rich, deep reds and purples can disappear into the background. Lighter reds mixed with shocking pinks and purples will make those murky colors sing, especially with a lift of chartreuse foliage. Silver, gray, and blue-green foliage make darker oranges and smudgy reds volcanic. Purple and blue leaves lend weight and depth to bright oranges and fresh greens; high colors that seem to float on their own.

A ruffled yellow and orange daylily is the perfect selection for a hot bed.

Oriental poppy (*Papaver orientale*)

How to develop a theme

In choosing the palette for your garden, consider the overall effect you want to achieve; solid sheets of unbroken color work well in larger landscapes but seem relentless in smaller gardens, especially when many of your plants are long bloomers. It's most effective to repeat colorful vignettes—small groups of related color plants—throughout the entire garden. For multiseason color, give each vignette some spring, summer, autumn, and even winter performers. In formal settings, space these repetitions precisely. Remember, cottage or naturalistic gardens call for informality. Avoid a boring sameness; vary form, height, mass, and texture within your color groupings themselves.

False sunflower (*Heliopsis*), yarrow (*Achillea*), and Helen's flower (*Helenium*) make a rowdy bunch.

Torch lily (*Kniphofia uvaria* 'Red Hot Poker') lives up to its name.

Red roses, Helen's flower, crocosmia, and New Guinea impatiens make a festive mix.

This mix of lilies, roses, and celosia is so hot you can practically warm your hands by it.

Flowers: Great Annuals

Fast growing, free flowering, and festive, annuals live for the moment. They have to—their lifespan is less than a year, and often only a few months. Early annuals leap from the ground and bloom before perennials know it's spring. Some summer annuals party from June until frost. Later bloomers carry on past Labor Day, their flowers fading into winter. Tougher relatives even survive mild winters.

Annuals come in almost every color, size, and shape and can be quite trouble-free. And you can pick annuals to bloom in most seasons. You can mingle pink and blue forget-me-nots among your tulips in the spring and tuck apricot and burgundy winter pansies beneath your chrysanthemums in the fall. Annuals are ready to jazz up the garden with instant color almost any time of the year.

First flowers

Some annuals are almost synonymous with spring. Pansies and forget-me-nots have shouted, "Spring is here!" for centuries, and modern versions of these old favorites now come in a wide range of tints and tones. These two certainly aren't your only choices—annuals abound that thrive in this cool season.

Enjoy the cheery chorus of a bed of annuals in a summer garden.

FAVORITE EARLY BLOOMERS

English daisy (*Bellis perennis*)
Pot marigold (*Calendula*)
Wallflower (*Chieranthus cheiri and Erysimum species*)
Godetia (*Clarkia*)
Siberian wallflower (*Erysimum asperum*)
California poppy (*Eschscholzia californica*)
Forget-me-not (*Myosotis sylvatica*)
Baby blue-eyes (*Nemophila menziesii*)
Pansy (*Viola ×wittrockiana*)
Viola (*Viola species*)

Godetia, here in bright pink, is a favorite for massing in the annual bed.

One of the best ways to show off early birds is to mass them as underplanting for spring bulbs. Blue forget-me-nots foaming through ranks of white tulips make a fetching picture, as do sheets of pink pansies amid yellow daffodils. Livelier pairings can be memorable—pink and purple pansies under rose-toned tulips or spicy orange tulips rising above blue forget-me-nots.

Other early bloomers can keep spring bulbs company. Wallflowers, cheerful or sizzling hot, have a delicate fragrance: Set a few beneath a window with some narcissus and the perfume of spring will waft indoors.

Rock walls make lovely homes for the delicate blossoms of baby blue eyes and species tulips. Golden calendulas can soften the edge of a driveway or sidewalk. Plant shady areas (often sunny before the leaves emerge) with a mix of bulbs and wildflowers (grape hyacinth and fried-egg flower, for example). Cheerful, starry English daisies and small violas can nestle naturally beside a mossy rock.

First-wave flowers show up early and bow out fast; but before their blooms are fully faded, have replacements ready.

Early summer

Beds and borders are filling up fast now. Leaves unfold and buds open. Annuals ease the transition from the tulips to the full magnificence of summer.

Use stop-gap annuals to keep your garden full of life while you wait for the glory of high summer. Instead of weeding, carpet the ground with blooms while you wait for your groundcovers to mature. By high summer, groundcovers fill in and you can cut the annuals away. Also, early summer bloomers, like the spring annuals that preceded them, can hide the browning leaves of bulbs and serve as heralds of plants yet to come. Scented sweet alyssum will foam in pastel clouds where Siberian iris will later show. In dappled shade, welsh poppies grow happily under hostas and rodgersias, whose leaves are slow to wake.

If you want to test new varieties, try sprinkling seed into paving cracks or along the sidewalk or retaining walls. Sow a pinch of seed in walls and the clinging plants will hang like a living sculpture.

Annual wildflowers are excellent early summer bloomers. California poppies, blue flax, and lupines are splendid self-sowers. In new gardens where grass is not yet planted, wildflower mixes fill summer with delight before you sow or sod. You don't need a meadow for these mixtures; scatter them in sweeps under shrubs and around trees. Plant wildflower mixes that don't contain grasses, which are likely to elbow out your flowers.

A casual bed of marigolds keeps company with a rustic zigzag fence.

California poppy (*Eschscholzia californica*) will reseed freely in most gardens.

FAVORITE EARLY SUMMER ANNUALS

Swan River daisy (*Brachycome*)
Honeywort (*Cerinthe major*)
Godetia (*Clarkia hybrids*)
Chinese forget-me-not (*Cynoglossum*)
China pink (*Dianthus chinensis*)
Sweet William (*Dianthus barbatus*)
Toadflax (*Linaria maroccana*)
Edging lobelia (*Lobelia erinus*)
Sweet alyssum (*Lobularia maritima*)
Stock (*Matthiola incana*)
Iceland poppy (*Papaver nudicaule*)
Shirley poppy (*Papaver rhoeas*)

Flowers: High-Summer Annuals

Summer annuals are showboaters; they'll carry your garden through the season with their flurry of flowers and foliage. This is often the most eye-catching season of the year. Ranks of tall purple cleomes and red amaranths behind swaths of zinnias, 'Orange Zest' salvias, and African marigolds—a classic combination—will remind you of an open-air market. White salvias, blue and purple larkspur, and yellow French marigolds or ferny bidens, 'Golden Eye,' look nautically crisp. For a more subtle touch, try mingling flowering tobaccos with baby's breath and blue lace flower for a tea-garden display. Cool and pale, Marguerites bloom on lacy foliage all summer. White and pastel cosmos are gentle at the back border, with white cleome and trumpet-flowered woodland tobacco.

A tiny yard packed full of sunflowers is unforgettable. Top them off with a bang—thread a firecracker vine through the tall stalks. Morning glories are astonishing as they reach for the sky from the sunflowers' golden embrace.

For the tantalizingly tropical, combine big-belled *Datura* 'Evening Fragrance' with bold banana trees and variegated cannas like 'Pretoria.' Tree-like brugmansias reach flowering size in a single season and may produce flaring flowers by the dozen.

Lantana and portulaca thrive in high summer.

Black Tuscan kale (*Brassica* 'Nero di Toscano') and verbena ('Snow Flurry') make a bold pairing.

TOP NONSTOP SUMMER ANNUALS

Begonia (*Begonia*)
Vinca (*Catharanthus roseus*)
Coleus (*Coleus ×hybridus*)
Cosmos (*Cosmos bipinnatus*)
Globe amaranth (*Gomphrena globosa*)
Impatiens (*Impatiens hybrids*)
Flowering tobacco (*Nicotiana*)
Geranium (*Pelargonium*)
Petunia (*Petunia ×hybrida*)
Salvia (*Salvia* spp.)
Marigold (*Tagetes hybrids*)
Narrowleaf zinnia (*Zinnia angustifolia*)

French marigolds (*Tagetes* 'Forever Red') are among the hardiest and most dependable of summer annuals.

Pansies provide color in cool temperatures.

Ornamental kale, depending on the variety, looks good even in winter.

Flowers: Cool-Season Annuals

Where winters are short and mild, cold-tolerant annuals will keep things lively from late fall until spring. Bright calendulas, beloved for their constant bloom, will often carry on all winter. Violet cress, a fragrant, dainty crack filler, will entice you outdoors.

Pansies are cool-season classics. New strains include some baby blues and purples, yellows and rosy pinks, mahoganies, spicy oranges, and copper browns. Winter-flowering primroses are equally pleasant, adding height to pansies. Their bright-eyed abundance earns them a place as temporaries anywhere. Mixed with winter bulbs and evergreen perennials and grasses, these stalwarts bring cheer to window boxes and containers.

Compact ponytail grass adds high drama to winter combinations. Its flossy bloom persists through winter. Or add clumps of bronze and coppery carex, tender grasses grown as annuals in colder climates. Like ponytail grass, the thready carex brings light-textured movement to stiff winter compositions.

Gardeners also have great fun with the cabbage family and its dozens of winter-hardy members. To bring out the best of their great, rounded heads, give the cabbages companions with contrasting shapes and complementary colors. Rosettes of 'Red Giant' mustard will set off to perfection frilly 'Peacock' kale. Ruffled 'Northern Lights' kale forms a cabbage-like mound in an array of colors. These plumpers will look dignified with rose- and purple-stemmed kales and darker winter pansies.

WINTER ANNUALS

Snapdragon (*Antirrhinum majus*)
Ornamental cabbage and kale (*Brassica oleracea*)
Pot marigold (*Calendula officinalis*)
Annual chrysanthemum (*Chrysanthemum multicaule*)
African daisy (*Dimorphotheca sinuate*)
Strawflower (*Helichrysum*)
Diamond flower (*Ionopsidium acaule*)
Ponytail grass (*Stipa tenuissima*)
Pansy (*Viola ×wittrockiana*)
Viola (*Viola* spp.)

ANNUALS BLOOM SEASON CHART

Use this chart to help you plan overlapping seasons of bloom. Annuals are listed in order of bloom and broken into early, mid-, and late season, so you can see at a glance which bloom together, which bloom in succession, and which bloom for extra-long times. Remember, bloom charts are only rough guides, as bloom seasons differ according to region, weather, microclimates, and cultivars. Blue bars represent bloom seasons. Pink bars represent bloom seasons in mild climates. Broken bars show periods of intermittent bloom.

(In the tables below, bloom seasons are shown by bars. ● = blue bar (bloom season); ○ = pink bar (mild-climate bloom).)

Plant Name	Spr. E	Spr. M	Spr. L	Sum. E	Sum. M	Sum. L	Fall E	Fall M	Fall L	Win. E	Win. M	Win. L
ANNUALS BLOOM CHART												
English daisy (Bellis perennis)	●	●									○	
Ornamental cabbage or kale (foliage) (Brassica oleracea, Acephala group)	●						○	○	○	○	○	
Wallflower (Cheiranthus cheirii)	●	●										○
Forget-me-not (Myosotis sylvatica)	●	●										
Pansy or viola (Viola)	●	●							○	○	○	
California poppy (Eschscholzia californica)	●	●										
Clarkia/Godetia (Clarkia hybrids)		●	●									
Flowering flax (Linum grandiflorum)		●										
Annual chrysanthemum (Chrysanthemum multicaule)	○			●	●		○	○	○			
Canterbury bells (Campanula medium)				●								
Annual sweet pea (Lathyrus odoratus)				●								
Annual poppy (Papaver species)				●								
Pot marigold (Calendula officinalis)			○	●	●	●	○					
Begonia (Begonia)				●	●	●						
Blanket flower (Gaillardia pulchella)				●	●	●						
African daisy (Dimorphotheca sinuata)				●	●		○	○				
Heliotrope (Heliotropium arborescens)				●	●	●						
Sweet alyssum (Lobularia maritima)				●	●	●						
Laurentia (Laurentia axillaris)				●	●	●						
Stock (Matthiola incana)	○			●	●		○					
Ice plant (Mesembryanthemum)	○			●	●		○	○				
Monkey flower (Mimulus ×hybridus)				●	●	●						
Nemesia (Nemesia strumosa)				●	●	●						
Baby blue-eyes (Nemophila menziesii)	○			●	●							
Nolana (Nolana paradoxa)				●	●							
California bluebell (Phacelia campanularia)	○			●	●		○					
Annual phlox (Phlox drummondii)				●	●							

Plant Name	Spr. E	Spr. M	Spr. L	Sum. E	Sum. M	Sum. L	Fall E	Fall M	Fall L	Win. E	Win. M	Win. L
Snapdragon (Antirrhinum majus)	○			●	●	●	●		○	○	○	
Bidens (Bidens)				●	●	●						
Larkspur (Consolida ambigua)				●	●							
Dwarf morning glory (Convolvulus tricolor)				●	●	●						
Chinese forget-me-not (Cynoglossum amabile)				●	●							
Hare's tail grass (Lagurus ovatus)				●	●							
Flossflower (Ageratum houstonianum)				●	●	●						
African daisy (Arctotis stoechadifolia grandis)				●	●							
Swan River daisy (Brachycome iberidifolia)				●								
Browallia (Browallia speciosa)				●	●	●						
Calibrachoa (Calibrachoa hybrid)				●	●	●	●					
Coleus (foliage) (Coleus ×hybridus)				●	●	●						
China pink (Dianthus chinensis)				●	●							
Sweet William (Dianthus barbatus)	○			●								○
Globe candytuft (Iberis umbellata)				●	●	●		○	○			
Toadflax (Linaria maroccana)				●	●							
Petunia (Petunia ×hybrida)				●	●	●						
Butterfly flower (Schizanthus ×wisetonensis)				●	●							
Vinca (Catharanthus roseus)				●	●	●	○	○				
Statice (Limonium sinuatum)				●	●	●						
Lisianthus (Lisianthus)				●	●	●						
Lobelia, all types (Lobelia species)				●	●	●						
Geranium (Pelargonium ×hortorum)				●	●	●						
Fan flower (Scaevola)				●	●	●						
Dahlberg daisy (Thymophylla tenuiloba)				●	●							
Joseph's coat (foliage) (Amaranthus tricolor)				●	●	●						
Summer forget-me-not (Anchusa capensis)				●	●							
Chickabiddy (Asarina)				●	●	●						

Plant Selection

Bloom time chart. Columns: Spr. (E, M, L), Sum. (E, M, L), Fall (E, M, L), Win. (E, M, L). █ = black bar, ▒ = gray bar.

Plant Name	Spr. E	Spr. M	Spr. L	Sum. E	Sum. M	Sum. L	Fall E	Fall M	Fall L	Win. E	Win. M	Win. L
Caladium (foliage) (*Caladium ×hortulanum*)				█	█	█						
Canna (*Canna ×generalis*)				█	█	█						
Bachelor's button (*Centaurea cyanus*)				█	█	█						
Honeywort (*Cerinthe major purpurascens*)	▒	▒		█	█			▒	▒	▒		
Dahlia (*Dahlia*)				█	█	█						
Snow-on-the-mountain (*Euphorbia marginata*)				█	█	█						
Gazania (*Gazania rigens*)				█	█	█	█					
Globe amaranth (*Gomphrena globosa*)				█	█	█	█					
Annual baby's breath (*Gypsophila elegans*)				█	█	█						
Ginger lily (*Hedychium*)				█	█	█						
Strawflower (*Helichrysum bracteatum*)				█	█	█						
Impatiens (*Impatiens* species)				█	█	█						
Diamond flower (*Ionopsidium acaule*)				█	█							
Hartweg lupine (*Lupinus hartwegii*)				█	█							
Melampodium (*Melampodium paludosum*)				█	█	█						
Flowering tobacco (*Nicotiana* species)				█	█	█						
Love-in-a-mist (*Nigella damascena*)				█	█	█						
Basil (*Ocimum*)					█	█						
Penstemon (*Penstemon* hybrids)				█	█							
Moss rose (*Portulaca grandiflora*)					█	█						
Scarlet runner bean (*Phaseolus coccineus*)				█	█							
Painted tongue (*Salpiglossis sinuata*)				█	█	█						
Salvia (*Salvia* species)				█	█	█	█					
Creeping zinnia (*Sanvitalia procumbens*)				█	█	█						
Dusty miller (*Senecio cineraria*)				█	█							
Catchfly (*Silene*)				█	█							
Ponytail grass (*Stipa tenuissima*)				█	█	█	▒	▒	▒			
Marigold (*Tagetes*)				█	█	█						

Plant Name	Spr. E	Spr. M	Spr. L	Sum. E	Sum. M	Sum. L	Fall E	Fall M	Fall L	Win. E	Win. M	Win. L
Black-eyed Susan vine (*Thunbergia alata*)				█	█	█						
Canary creeper (*Tropaeolum peregrinum*)				█	█	█						
Garden verbena (*Verbena ×hybrida*)				█	█	█						
Rockbell (*Wahlenbergia*)				█	█							
Calla lily (*Zantedeschia*)				█	█	█						
Spider flower (*Cleome hassleriana*)				█	█	█						
Cosmos (*Cosmos* species)					█	█						
Wishbone flower (*Torenia fournieri*)				█	█	█						
Zinnia (*Zinnia*)				█	█	█						
Ornamental pepper (*Capsicum annuum*)					█	█						
Celosia (*Celosia* species)					█	█						
Morning glory, moonflower, cypress vine (*Ipomoea* species)					█	█						
Four-o'clock (*Mirabilis jalapa*)					█	█						
Nasturtium (*Tropaeolum majus*)					█	█						
Ornamental gourds (*Cucurbita pepo*)					█							
Hyacinth bean (*Lablab purpureus*)					█	█						
Sunflower (*Helianthus*)					█	█						
Tree mallow (*Lavatera* hybrids)					█	█						
Annual fountain grass (*Pennisetum setaceum*)					█	█						
Castor bean (*Ricinus communis*)					█	█						
Gloriosa daisy (*Rudbeckia hirta pulcherrima*)				█	█							
China aster (*Callistephus chinensis*)					█							
Datura (*Datura meteloides*)					█	█						
Firecracker vine (*Mina lobata*)					█	█						
Perilla (*Perilla frutescens*)						█	█					
Mexican sunflower (*Tithonia rotundifolia*)					█	█						

Flowers: Annual All-Stars

Impatiens 'Mosaic Lilac'

Coleus, mixed varieties

Petunia 'Born Free Purple'

Verbena 'Peaches & Cream' and 'Imagine'

Impatiens

Impatiens have become the most popular annual of our time because of its mounds of glossy foliage, constant bloom, luminous flower colors and shapes, and ability to flourish in shade. Impatiens are useful throughout the garden, in beds, borders, and containers, for edging and massing, and as groundcover under trees. Shorter varieties include the 'Accent' and 'Super Elfin' series, while 'Blitz' is taller. 'Frost,' 'Swirl,' and 'Mosaic' offer interesting patterns, while 'Confection' and 'Victorian Rose' offer double blooms.

Coleus

At one time a darling of the Victorian garden, coleus are available again in a huge variety of leaf colors, patterns, shapes, and sizes. They are worthwhile landscape additions for bedding, borders, or containers.

Petunia

Dependability, versatility, and variety are the hallmarks of the petunia. The flowers can be single or double, smooth or ruffled, clear, edged, striped, or veined in every color except orange, mounded or cascading, but always abundant, fragrant, and tolerant. Grandifloras have the largest flowers, single or double, and do best in containers. Multifloras, floribunda, and milliflora hybrids have an abundance of smaller flowers and do well in gardens or containers. Look for the 'Wave' series, as well as 'Supertunia' and 'Surfinia' for intense color and trailing habit.

Verbena

Verbena is one of the easiest ways to brighten sunny spots. It has deep green or grayish aromatic foliage. The flowers may be neon blue, red, white, pink, or purple. Use as groundcover in beds, in borders, containers, rock gardens, or over walls. Larger varieties include 'Amour Light Pink' and vivid red 'Blaze'. Hybrids 'Tapien' and 'Temari' are smaller and come in a wide variety of colors.

Zinnia

Many heights (from 6 to 40 inches) and forms means that there is a zinnia for nearly every garden. It comes in an enormous range of bright, festive colors. Use zinnia in borders, beds, for edging, cut flowers, and in containers. The huge range of varieties includes dwarf bedding types ('Dasher', 'Dreamland', and 'Small World' hybrids), tall cutting types ('Blue Point', 'Big Red', 'Ruffles Hybrid') and unusual colors ('Envy', which is chartreuse; 'Peppermint Stick', which is streaked).

Zinnias 'Whirlygig' and 'Chippendale'

Salvia

The genus Salvia, also known as the sages, is full of many exquisite species. Blue and scarlet salvia provide season-long color and combine wonderfully with other flowering plants. Use Salvia for bedding and borders, in containers, and for cut flowers. Scarlet sage has many varieties of different heights and colors; for example, the 'Salsa' series. Blue salvia varieties include 'Victoria' and 'Strata', while Texas sage offers 'Cherry Blossom' and 'Lady in Red.'

Salvia "Lady in Red"

Flowers: Tender Tropicals

Joe-Pye weed (*Eupatorium*), South African lilies (*Agapanthus*), banana plant (*Ensete ventricosa*), and dahlia are living large.

A century ago, tender tropicals were all the rage. All across the country, front yards boasted mounded beds, usually set in grass or gravel and packed with striped cannas and eye-catching banana trees. Huge, flaunting dahlias had pride of place in such bedding schemes, as did stiff sprays of cheerful gladiolas and mounds of brilliantly colored amaranths. That innocent Victorian delight in the gaudy soon gave way to more quietly tasteful border plantings. The brash, oversized plants were banished to parks and public places where they continue to please the eye—if not the arbiters of horticultural taste.

In your own garden, you can re-create the old tropical paradise look by arranging groups of tender tropicals in beds or containers. These days, many gardeners prefer to make more naturalistic arrangements, in which the strong lines and potent forms of the plants are played off to full advantage. However, those with Victorian homes may enjoy re-creating the exotic formalism of those heritage bedding schemes.

These were very often based on luxuriant foliage plants such as elephant's ear. For a strong combination, pair it with colorful caladiums—the smaller plants mirror the ear shapes of the larger plants and create a repetition of form. A black or green elephant's ear is the perfect background for variegated white, green, or red caladiums underneath it. Ginger lily is another plant, usually thought of mostly for its showy blooms, that has impressive foliage. The long, straplike leaves spill over in profusion and create a mound of shiny foliage.

In hot climates, many jungle understory plants, such as angel's trumpets and silverleaf, prefer some shade. A site that offers both reflected heat (as from a nearby street or sidewalk) and plenty of indirect light suits many jungle plants to a nicety. This is especially true in areas with long, humid summers. The shelter of a covered but open-sided porch often makes a happy home for showy foliage plants that tend to scorch in hot, open gardens.

Canna 'Red King Humbert' with yucca and amaranthus

Fancy-leafed caladium (*Caladium* × *hortulanum*)

THE BEST OF THE TENDER TROPICALS

Angel's trumpet (*Datura and Brugmansia*)
Caladium (*Caladium*)
Canna (*Canna*)
Elephant's ear (*Colocasia esculenta*)
Ginger lily (*Hedychium*)
Four-o'clock (*Mirabilis jalapa*)
Banana (*Musa*)
Castor bean (*Ricinis*)
Calla lily (*Zantedeschia*)

Castor bean (*Ricinus communis*)

ANNUALS FROM SMALL TO LARGE

Use this chart to help you combine annuals according to size and form. They are organized in order of their height from short to tall so you can find an annual of the correct size at a glance. Each annual listed is accompanied by a sketch of its typical form, approximately to scale. Remember, this chart is a rough guide; the size given and the form shown can vary according to the cultivar selected, as well as region, weather, and horticultural practice.

ANNUALS HEIGHT AND FORM CHART

Diamond flower (*Ionopsidium acaule*) 2"

Edging lobelia (*Lobelia erinus*) 4"

Sweet alyssum (*Lobularia maritima*) 4"

Ice plant (*Mesembryanthemum*) 4"

Baby blue-eyes (*Nemophila menziesii*) 4"

Swedish ivy (*Plectranthus*) 4"

Dahlberg daisy (*Thymophylla tenuiloba*) 4"

English daisy (*Bellis perennis*) 6"

Sweet potato vine (*Ipomoea batatas*) 6"

Monkey flower (*Mimulus* ×*hybridus*) 6"

Forget-me-not (*Myosotis sylvatica*) 6"

Moss rose (*Portulaca grandiflora*) 6"

Creeping zinnia (*Sanvitalia procumbens*) 6"

Pansy (*Viola* ×*wittrockiana*) 6"

Viola (*Viola*) 6"

Flossflower, dwarf (*Ageratum houstonianum*) 8"

Wax begonia (*Begonia* ×*semperflorens-cultorum*) 8"

Calibrachoa (*Calibrachoa* hybrid) 8"

Annual chrysanthemum (*Chrysanthemum multicaule*) 8"

China pink (*Dianthus chinensis*) 8"

Laurentia (*Laurentia axillaris*) 8"

Annual phlox (*Phlox drummondii*) 8"

Garden verbena (*Verbena* ×*hybrida*) 8"

Impatiens (*Impatiens*) 8–12"

Snapdragon, dwarf (*Antirrhinum majus*) 9"

Swan River daisy (*Brachycome iberidifoli*) 9"

Nemesia (*Nemesia strumosa*) 9"

California bluebell (*Phacelia campanularia*) 9"

Wishbone flower (*Torenia fournieri*) 9"

Summer forget-me-not (*Anchusa capensis*) 10"

Browallia (*Browallia*) 10"

Gazania (*Gazania rigens*) 10"

Melampodium (*Melampodium paludosum*) 10"

Chilean bellflower (*Nolana paradoxa*) 10"

Basil, miniature (*Ocimum*) 10"

Fan flower (*Scaevola*) 10"

Dusty miller (*Senecio cineraria*) 10"

Catchfly (*Silene*) 10"

Tuberous begonia (*Begonia* Tuberhybrida) 12"

Ornamental cabbage (*Brassica oleracea*, Acephala group) 12"

Ornamental kale (*Brassica oleracea*, Acephala group) 12"

Vinca (*Catharanthus roseus*) 12"

Plume celosia (*Celosia plumosa*) 12"

Wallflower (*Erysimum linifolium*) 12"

African daisy (*Dimorphotheca sinuata*) 12"

California poppy (*Eschscholzia californica*) 12"

Globe candytuft (*Iberis crenata*) 12"

Toadflax (*Linaria maroccana*) 12"

Petunia (*Petunia* ×*hybrida*) 12"

Flowering tobacco (*Nicotiana* hybrid) 12"

Shirley poppy (*Papaver rhoeas*) 12"

Butterfly flower (*Schizanthus* ×*wisetonensis*) 12"

French single marigold (*Tagetes patula*) 12"

Nasturtium (*Tropaeolum majus*) 12"

Rockbell (*Wahlenbergia*) 12"

Zinnia angustifolia (*Zinnia angustifolia*) 12"

Blanket flower (*Gaillardia pulchella*) 14"

Ornamental pepper (*Capsicum annuum*) 15"

Cockscomb (*Celosia cristata*) 15"

Wallflower (*Cheiranthus cheirii*) 15"

Dwarf morning glory (*Convolvulus tricolor*) 15"

Dahlia hybrids, low-growing seed-grown type (*Dahlia*) 15"

Love-in-a-mist (*Nigella damascena*) 15"

Scarlet sage (*Salvia splendens*) 15"

Snapdragon, medium (*Antirrhinum majus*) 18"

Rex begonia (*Begonia*, Rex cultorum hybrids) 18"

Bidens (*Bidens*) 18"

China aster (*Callistephus chinensis*) 18"

Bachelor's button (*Centaurea cyanus*) 18"

Honeywort (*Cerinthe major purpurascens*) 18"

Clarkia/Godetia (*Clarkia* hybrids) 18"

Chinese forget-me-not (*Cynoglossum amabile*) 18"

Sweet William (*Dianthus barbatus*) 18"

Globe amaranth (*Gomphrena globosa*) 18"

Annual baby's breath (*Gypsophila elegans*) 18"

Hare's tail grass (*Lagurus ovatus*) 18"

Flowering flax (*Linum grandiflorum*) 18"

Lisianthus (*Lisianthus*) 18"

Stock (*Matthiola incana*) 18"

Geranium (*Pelargonium* ×*hortorum*) 18"

Hybrid penstemon (*Penstemon* hybrids) 18"

Blue salvia (*Salvia farinacea*) 18"

Clary sage (*Salvia horminium*) 18"

African daisy (*Arctotis stoechadifolia* var. *grandis*) 20"

Pot marigold (*Calendula officinalis*) 20"

Yellow cosmos (*Cosmos sulphureus*) 20"

Snow-on-the-mountain (*Euphorbia marginata*) 20"

Statice (*Limonium sinuatum*) 20"

Iceland poppy (*Papaver nudicaule*) 20"

Painted tongue (*Salpiglossis sinuata*) 20"

Heliotrope (*Heliotropium arborescens*) 22"

 Swiss Chard (*Beta vulgaris cicla*) 24"

 Caladium (*Caladium bicolor*) 24"

 Canterbury bells (*Campanula medium*) 24"

 Coleus (*Coleus ×hybridus*) 24"

 Strawflower (*Helichrysum bracteatum*) 24"

 Fan hybrid lobelia (*Lobelia ×speciosa* 'Fan') 24"

 Four-o'clock (*Mirabilis jalapa*) 24"

 Basil (*Ocimum*) 24"

 Gloriosa daisy (*Rudbeckia hirta pulcherrima*) 24"

 Texas sage (*Salvia coccinea*) 24"

 African marigold (*Tagetes erecta*) 24"

 Zinnia (*Zinnia elegans*) 24"

 Sunflower, dwarf (*Helianthus*) 2–3'

 Larkspur (*Consolida ambigua*) 30"

 Tree mallow (*Lavatera* hybrids) 30"

 Pony tail grass (*Stipa tenuissima*) 30"

 Snapdragon, tall varieties (*Antirrhinum majus*) 30"

 Joseph's coat (*Amaranthus tricolor*) 3'

 Canna (*Canna ×generalis*) 3'

 Wheat celosia (*Celosia argentea spicata*) 3'

 Cosmos (*Cosmos bipinnatus*) 3'

 Hartweg lupine (*Lupinus hartwegii*) 3'

 Flowering tobacco (*Nicotiana alata*) 3'

 Breadbox poppy (*Papaver somniferum*) 3'

 Annual fountain grass (*Pennisetum setaceum*) 3'

 Penstemon (*Penstemon barbatus*) 3–4'

 Perilla (*Perilla frutescens*) 3'

 Calla lily (*Zantedeschia aethiopica*) 3'

 Spider flower (*Cleome hassleriana*) 4'

 Dahlia, giant-flowered exhibition type (*Dahlia*) 4'

 Datura (*Datura meteloides*) 4'

 Flowering tobacco (*Nicotiana sylvestris*) 4'

 **Sunflower, midheight** (*Helianthus*) 4-6'

 Annual sweet pea (*Lathyrus odoratus*) 4-6'

 Firecracker vine (*Mina lobata*) 4-6'

 Elephant's ear (*Colocasia esculenta*) 5'

 Ginger lily (*Hedychium*) 5'

 Mexican sunflower (*Tithonia rotundifolia*) 5'

Castor bean (*Ricinus communis*) 5–15'

 Canary creeper (*Tropaeolum peregrinum*) 6-10'

 **Sunflower, tall** (*Helianthus*) 7-11'

 Banana (*Musa*) 8'

Morning glory (*Ipomoea tricolor*) 9'

Hyacinth bean (*Lablab purpureus*) 10–20'

Flowers: Cool-Color Annuals

Colors on the blue, green, and yellow side of the spectrum are regarded as cool colors. White is cool also, so pastel hues (which are whitened colors) work well when mixed with other cool colors. Blue is among the coolest of garden colors. For added chill, complement it with pale yellow. Pairing 'Victoria' blue salvia and 'Gold Wizard' coleus creates a stunning combination. Or use different shades of

Torenia 'Summer Wave'

Roses (Rosa 'Bonica') mix with flowering tobacco (Nicotania sylvestris), wishbone flower (Torenia fournieri), and impatiens.

blue together; for instance, the combination of larkspur and phlox creates a cool-themed garden. To create a pink and blue garden, add silvery gray or blue-gray foliage to complement the more vibrant cool colors.

White is a difficult color to use in gardens because few of the many variations of white match each other well. That's not to say white has no place in the garden; carefully chosen clear whites can be an attractive addition in a cool theme. When good whites are matched with the cool, clear morning sun, the whites in the garden really shine. Or white impatiens can cheer a shady corner. And even though white can be difficult to match perfectly, many gardeners enjoy creating all-white gardens, which are not quite as demanding.

Play with different cool color combinations. Try planting some cool-colored mixes together in a container to see how you like them. Or take a container of blues, one of whites, and one of yellows and move them around each other so you can see how the different hues come alive when placed with other cool colors.

Above: Salvia 'Victoria Blue'
Below: Pincushion flower (*Scabiosa columnaria* 'Butterfly Blue') with butterfly bush

The foliage of kale and eucalyptus is punched up a notch next to white salvia and purple petunias.

Blue browallia (*Browallia speciosa*) cozies up to pink impatiens.

181

Flowers: Warm-Color Annuals

The warm side of the spectrum—red, orange, and purple—offers irresistible opportunities to indulge in theatrics with pure, fully saturated color. A garden of salsa colors pops with bright hot reds, oranges, and yellows for a warm color theme.

Mix orange with bronze, copper, brown, and other orange variations for a dazzling warm color garden. These strong, autumn colors in well-matched combinations intensify each other, especially if mixed with slightly lighter shades of the same colors. Pastels don't work well among these fully saturated colors, but tone down the saturation a degree or two and you'll end up with radiant, winning combinations.

Don't forget foliage when planting a warm theme garden. Warm shades of magenta and red darken against dim green leaves, but they will sparkle with electricity against chartreuse. Try combining the deep purple foliage of 'Red Russian' kale with the warm oranges and golds of marigold flowers to make the colors of the blooms pop.

Heliotrope, salvia, and celosia show how gorgeous an orange and purple color mix can be.

Fiery spikes of wheat celosia (*Celosia argentea spicata*) stand at attention.

Canna 'Wyoming', celosia 'Apricot Brandy', and zinnia 'Yellow Ruffles', 'Pepper', and 'Fiesta' make for an intensely vibrant garden.

Regal geranium (*Pelargonium × hortorum* 'Rimfire') would be ideal for a warm-color scheme in a pot or planter.

Narrowleaf zinnia (*Zinnia angustifolia* 'Star Series') is an excellent addition to a warm-color scheme.

The soft yellow of this South African daisy (*Osteospermum* 'Lemon Symphony') adds gentle color and contrast to a warm-color garden.

Flowers: Annuals for Special Spots

Petunias, fuchsia, and fan flowers burst out of this windowbox.

Sweetpeas and beans trained on tripods make a summer screen.

Containers

If your space is limited, or if you want to make a welcome entryway, enliven a poolside, or emphasize a staircase, pack annuals into containers. Choose from literally hundreds of container alternatives from window boxes and hanging baskets stuffed with trailing vines and cascading petunias to olive cans crammed with red geraniums. Bigger is better. It's easier to keep large pots well watered; small ones dry out quickly.

To dress up permanent evergreen plantings with seasonal annuals, plan ahead. Sink placeholder pots (bulb pans or 4-inch square pots) around the container edge. Then slip in your array of annuals, and you won't damage the evergreen roots.

Climbers

Annual climbers will decorate any surface you like. They can play the role of groundcover, paint a wall in living color, or fill the air with fragrance. Drape them on a slope or grow them on supports as curtains or as screening for private parts of the yard.

While waiting for foundation shrubs to grow, disguise new-house siding with annuals. Simply stretch netting across the area to be covered, then plant a few Mexican bell vines at its base. A single cathedral bell vine or goldfish vine will cover half the house by high summer. Canary creeper vine sounds slow, but this determined traveler can cover a garage or a mature fruit tree in one season.

Give spring-flowering shrubs a second season; set lightweight scramblers, such as firecracker vine or sweet peas, about their skirts. Heavier vines such as fernleaf cypress vine need sturdy hosts. Grow the fernleaf in a large tree, not a shrub. Send moonflower vines or morning glories up an old ladder leaning on a tree or give

Classic morning glory needs a tall trellis.

them runner guides of rubber-coated wire or twine that won't sag under their weight.

Shade

Shade offers the opportunity to combine colorful flowers with beautifully textured and shaped foliage. But the type of shade will determine what you plant.

Dappled, airy, light shade is ideal; it offers plenty of light and air but blocks the fierceness of the summer sun. Woodland understory annuals such as forget-me-nots will thrive in filtered shade.

Damp, moist shade makes streamside annuals—from native monkey flower to tropical begonia and fuchsia—feel at home.

Dry shade is difficult, but a handful of tough annuals will attempt it. Cheerful fried-egg flower, baby blue eyes, and foxglove will tolerate dry shade if given periodic boosts with supplemental watering.

Extremely dense, dank, or bone-dry shades are challenging; but in such situations, raised beds, pots, and containers offer ample alternatives. They can help control the soil and therefore make everything a little easier on plants in these tough spots.

And if your shade gives way to fuller light, there are all kinds of climbing and trailing annuals to expand your palette. A tremendous range of annuals grows beautifully in partial shade, especially where summers are hot, so don't hesitate to experiment to find out what does best in your garden.

Heat

If summer heat leaves gardens limp and languid, try an infusion of sun-loving annuals to keep them fresh all season. Finding the right plants for the job, however, isn't quite as simple as it sounds because heat lovers don't divide themselves neatly into categories. This is one situation that rewards some experimentation. Some annuals, such as vinca and moss rose, are extremely adaptable, thriving equally in high desert and humid lowland settings. Others, such as African daisy and gazania, thrive in dry heat but fade quickly where summer nights are muggy.

Transvaal daisies adore hot days and humid nights, but turn sulky where nights are cool, no matter how warm the days may be.

A lot of annuals can be persuaded to take the heat as long as other needs are met. Generally, humus-rich, well-drained soil and plenty of water will do the trick; and sometimes just one supplement is enough. Calendula, baby's breath, geranium, and dusty miller perform brilliantly in hot spots—even if the soil is lean and poor—with ample and regular watering. Prairie plants, such as blanket flower and tickseed, can tolerate an amazing amount of heat and drought when grown in deep, rich soils.

Nasturtium, zinnia, and sunflowers love the hot sun.

The many varieties of sunflowers, from dwarfs to giants, in colors ranging from white, yellow, and gold to red, are stars in full sun.

Installing Your Landscape

Now that you've created a master plan showing planting and hardscape areas as well as major garden amenities, it's time to think about turning those plans into physical realities. To make sure everything goes as smoothly as possible, there's still a bit more preparation to do before breaking out the shovels.

Dollars and cents

All of the things you've dreamed up and put into your landscape plan are, in reality, going to be driven by money and time. The way you're going to be able to estimate both the money and time required to implement your landscape plan is to use your working drawings.

WHEN TO HIRE A PRO

There often comes a point in a project when you must decide whether you can accomplish a task yourself or need to hire an expert to help. It's tempting to base this decision solely on the cost of hiring the contractor, but there are other expenditures to consider as well. Your time is valuable. If a grading project will require four weekends of hard labor, you may decide that spending up to $500 to hire someone to do the job on a single Saturday would be money well spent. You'll get things going faster and be able to move on to tasks you are better equipped to perform yourself.

Craftsmen can also contribute a level of skill that may be beyond your abilities. If you have limited experience, professional carpenters and masons may build portions of your hardscape more skillfully than you can. They can also be sure everything is up to code and may even be able to get all the permits for you. Study your master plan and question what you can realistically do yourself.

Getting things done right will be the most cost-effective part of your plan. Calling in a professional to help with more intricate parts of the job can be a wise decision that improves the look of your project and can save you time now and money in the long run.

The working drawings

Your layout plan shows the location, dimensions, and the materials you'll use in the construction of additions to your landscape—driveways, decks, patios, pools, walkways, parking courts, and gazebos, for example. A layout plan is like a blueprint for your hardscapes—it will help guide the construction.

A grading and drainage plan lays out the specifics of any earthwork necessary before hardscape and planting begins. This plan is prepared after the layout plan so the earth can be shaped to accommodate your design ideas. The level of detail on this plan is dependent on the complexity of your design, your existing terrain (steep sites may require more grading), and any existing drainage problems that need to be resolved.

Your planting plan translates the general ideas of your master plan into real instructions for getting the work done. Specific plant species, sizes, spacing, and locations are shown on the planting plan. You can make a list and shop from this plan; you can also take it outside with you to figure out what goes where.

The maintenance plan can help you formulate ideas that will save you time for years to come. Study your master plan so you can find shortcuts on chores that won't sacrifice the quality of your design.

Cost and time

Now is when you study your master plan and start thinking about how much it's actually going to cost to get the work done. The costs of hardscape materials, plantings, amenities, and contractors are all expenses that will have to be figured in to the overall cost of the project. You may or may not already have spent a lot of money to work with a designer to get you this far, but there's still going to be a lot to spend on the actual landscaping.

Choose a safe, convenient location for storage of materials and equipment during landscape construction.

If you've discovered that your budget won't cover the cost of your entire landscape plan, there's no reason to despair. Lots of people implement their plans in stages as they can afford it. For example, you may decide to get the deck installed and do the plantings in the front yard now, and leave the new paved sidewalk and most of the backyard plantings for next year. Or if a backyard hideaway is really important to you, you can put in your quiet, private place first and leave the some of the other things for later. Decide what's most important to you, and make those parts of the plan a priority in your budget. Then later, as money becomes available, you can work on other areas of the landscape.

Also, be sure that you plan to have work done first that will affect other parts of the landscape. For instance, you may need to have the entire yard graded, even if you're not doing all the planting and the hardscapes at once. Be aware of the domino effect of implementing your plan in stages.

Finally, consider the amount of time it will take to actually implement your design. If you're a do-it-yourselfer, be realistic in figuring how much time you have to devote to the project. You may find that hiring a contractor for some things will allow you to do the things you find more enjoyable—such as planting flower beds instead of struggling to build the deck yourself.

PERMITS AND CODES

Always check with zoning and regulation boards to determine which codes you must comply with and what permits they require. It may be necessary to revise your design to achieve compliance. Don't forget to check restrictions set by homeowners' associations. Stopping in the middle of a project to request a variance is no fun, and boards of review may not meet on a regular basis, stalling your progress. Permits usually incur some expense, so plan ahead to include these costs in your budget.

Existing lawn is killed (below, left) to make way for regrading, retaining wall construction, and finally, (below, right) a snappy new lawn.

TIMELINE

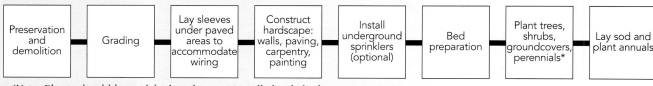

| Preservation and demolition | Grading | Lay sleeves under paved areas to accommodate wiring | Construct hardscape: walls, paving, carpentry, painting | Install underground sprinklers (optional) | Bed preparation | Plant trees, shrubs, groundcovers, perennials* | Lay sod and plant annuals |

Note: Plants should be mulched as they are installed to help them retain moisture.

Landscape Preparation

Make any tree-removal instructions crystal clear to avoid an unfortunate mistake.

There is a myriad of tasks and conditions to consider when preparing to implement your landscape plan. You may need to identify plants and elements from your current landscape that you want to preserve in order to protect them during the process. There may be demolition or extensive grading that needs to be arranged. And all of these tasks need to be accomplished in the right order. Don't skimp on time or energy devoted to preparing to launch your landscape plans—the more carefully you prepare, the less the chances costly mistakes will be made along the way.

Preservation and demolition

What you keep and what you get rid of are very important decisions. Protecting everything you want to preserve is the very first thing you should do on site. This crucial step is frequently omitted. There's nothing more distressing than buying a wooded lot because you love the trees only to discover that the contractor has cleared it.

Protecting site assets on new lots before houses are built is as important as saving features on existing properties that are being renovated.

WORK FLOW

Work flow is part of the critical path that must be followed to build your project. Examine the order of construction as it applies to your design. Can materials be delivered close to the related work area? Will working on one part of the project block access to another? Is there adequate space for a temporary holding area for materials? Look for ways to reduce construction man-hours on the job to cut costs. Doing things in the proper order will prevent subcontractors from damaging each other's work and spending time on repairs. Though it may be preferable to complete the front yard before starting on the back, you may get a better price by having your front walk and back patio poured at the same time. Talk to your contractors to understand their needs and pricing strategies. Make a timeline to direct the work schedule, even if you are doing it yourself.

Communication is the name of the game. No one working on your property will know what you want to save unless you make it very clear. Don't merely wrap flagging tape around the trees you want to save; your contractor may think that is the signal that you want them removed!

Discuss plans with workers to be sure everyone understands your wishes. It's not enough to talk only to the general contractor; subcontractors must understand your goals too. Be certain that signs, flags, or barriers communicate your wishes at a glance. It only takes one worker to make an irreversible or costly mistake.

If there is a complicated strategy for making your new design work with existing site elements, consider producing a site preparation plan. Trace a copy of your master plan and use color codes and labels to convey your intentions. Identify trees and features that remain and those that should be removed. Mark construction access routes and storage areas on your plan and give it to your contractor as soon as he or she arrives on site.

Tree strategies

Here's how to protect trees you wish to preserve: Stake the perimeter of the area beneath each tree canopy and enclose the entire area with flagging tape to keep it cleared. Flag each tree, writing KEEP in bold, black permanent marker on each flag.

Demolition should be carefully controlled. Meet with tree cutters to discuss felling strategies. Always move your car and your neighbors', just to be safe. Ask anyone doing work on your property to provide proof of bonding. Otherwise, your homeowners insurance may have to pay for any damage.

When doing earthwork, take care to avoid disturbing soil around trees you want to preserve. Exposing roots can dehydrate a tree and invite insect problems. Adding soil on top of the existing surface can kill a tree by suffocating feeder roots. A common construction mistake is to allow heavy equipment or cars to drive or park beneath trees. Stockpiling material near a tree trunk is a bad idea too.

Anything that compacts the soil can potentially kill a tree. Chemicals should never be dumped on site. Be diligent in protecting your trees because contractors may not consider the long-term health of your trees.

Safety first

Be aware that you may be liable for anyone injured on your property, including workers and even trespassers. Insist on good safety practices and proper protective gear. Secure the job site to prevent injuries to both invited and uninvited guests. Construction areas are appealing to children; require workers to remove all tools and hazardous materials when they leave each day. Holes should be barricaded, and swimming pools should not be filled with water until fences, gates, latches, and lifesaving equipment are in place.

Cost concerns

Demolition and disposal are sometimes hidden costs that drive a project over budget. Get estimates for demolition before work begins. In addition to labor and equipment expenses, permits, hauling, and dump fees can be unpleasant surprises. Know what you're getting into from the beginning. Ask contractors to itemize their costs to see if there's any work you can do yourself. If you have a truck, removing debris yourself can be a good way to save money. Make sure your local dump will accept construction rubble and that it is open during your free hours. Recycle what you can.

Grinding out a tree stump is one of those seemingly small expenses that can really add up.

PROTECTING TREES DURING CONSTRUCTION

Mature trees are assets and you should protect them from construction damage as much as possible. Temporary barriers will alert contractors to keep heavy equipment and construction debris off tree-root areas. Siltation fences can protect trees by preventing displaced soil from building up over their root zone.

LIMIT ACCESS

Designate and clearly mark a construction entrance for contractors. Place barriers across existing paving to prevent heavy equipment from cracking hard surfaces. If there's no way to avoid driving across an underground sprinkler system, cap one zone and remove the heads to minimize damage. Limit equipment in the protected zone. Though pipe breaks may be unavoidable, leaks will not occur if the zone has been disconnected from the system.

Grading

Grading is nothing more than moving earth. You will need to grade your property if you are changing the shape of your land in any way. Creating level areas for play spaces, patios, or walkways requires grading. So will cutting into slopes with retaining walls or adding soil to contribute interest to a flat site. Mounded soil—known as berms—can give shrubs and trees planted for privacy a head start by making them seem taller right away. Terracing can tame a steep site. Different levels can create distinctions between outdoor rooms within your landscape.

You will make your grading design after you design your hardscape so the earthwork can conform to construction. However, it's a good idea to keep grading in mind while designing both hardscape and planting schemes. A patio proposed on slope will cost more to build than one designed for a naturally level area. If you really want a seating area in that particular spot, consider building a deck instead. Think about the natural characteristics of your site as you plan.

CUT AND FILL

Minimizing the amount of earth that must be cut from slopes or moved to fill low areas will save money and disturb fewer existing plants. If you need to do this type of work, try to remove the same amount of soil needed elsewhere on site. Known as balancing cut and fill, this strategy saves money: You'll avoid hauling expenses to remove soil as well as the cost of buying fill dirt.

Grading order

The actual work is done in the reverse order from planning: Rough grading is completed before hardscape projects begin. Finish grades—usually accomplished by hand-raking the surface of the soil—may be set as late as the bed preparation phase of work, just before planting begins. Rough grading may or may not involve large equipment. If there are several contractors on the job, make sure one has included finish grading in his price or you could get stuck with an unplanned expense. Often the landscape contractor will plan to do some grading by hand but expects the general contractor will create rough grades that are fairly accurate.

Retaining walls

Retaining walls allow you to terrace a site, creating a level area from a hill with a cut into the slope. Retaining walls can also add height to a flat area by building up soil behind the wall. Stone, brick, concrete, concrete block, or wood treated for ground contact can be used for building retaining walls. Groundwater pressure can build and cause a wall to lean and finally overturn. Small holes, called weep holes, penetrate wall faces to allow water from the soil side to seep through. French drains—perforated pipe centered in a gravel bed—at the back foot of the wall can help alleviate water pressure, but weep holes are still needed. Supports that extend behind the wall into the soil, known as dead men, are needed for tall or wooden walls. Proper footings are also important to keep retaining walls upright.

Sleeves

After grading is done, don't forget to lay conduit beneath areas that will be paved. These empty pipes make it easy to accommodate wires or small pipe that crosses though a hardscape area. Two-inch schedule 40 PVC usually does the

After rough grading is complete, the hand-raked finish grade is established.

A retaining wall cuts in a slope and allows leveling of the area at its base.

job. Lay a few beneath each area that will be paved. Conduit should be laid perpendicular to paving so pipe reaches from one side to another. The location of sleeves isn't critical; just make sure you have a way to thread wire beneath paved areas without the expense of boring a passageway. These sleeves will come in handy if you want to add lighting or security systems in the future.

EARTHMOVERS

Large grading projects require earthmoving equipment such as front-end loaders. Their expense is usually calculated by the hour, combining an equipment fee with operator's expense, so try to have as much grading done at one time as possible. It is necessary to consider access to your property for such equipment. A temporary construction entrance is often a good idea to prevent cracking caused by driving machinery across existing paving or planting areas.

Retaining walls gently terrace this sloping lawn.

Drainage

Where is the water going to go? This important question should be asked before the first hole is dug or the first brick is laid. Standing water can cause patios, driveways, and walks to become slick with mud or moss. Even shallow puddles can become breeding sites for mosquitoes. Wood that stays damp will eventually rot. Rapidly flowing water can wash away plants and mulch, and cause erosion. Poor dispersal of rainwater can drown some plants while leaving others too dry.

Runoff water

Rain often falls faster than the ground can absorb, causing "runoff" water to flow across surfaces. When water finds a level spot, it stays there until it penetrates into the soil, evaporates, is absorbed by plants, or is moved by artificial means to a drainage system.

Runoff is increased by water shed from impermeable surfaces such as roofs and paved areas. The less porous a surface, the faster water will flow and the less likely the ground will absorb it. Whenever possible, return runoff to groundwater aquifers by disposing it within the bounds of your property. Runoff that seeps into the soil follows a natural course, which also allows plants to serve as a natural filter. Runoff that empties into a storm sewer collects impurities as it flows.

Always direct runoff away from your house and other structures. Water collected near foundations can seep into basements and crawlspaces and cause structural damage. Clay repeatedly wet and dried will expand and contract, causing foundations to shift and floors, walls, and ceilings to crack. Direct runoff away from swimming pools to prevent overflow and possible contamination. Raise copings slightly and slope pool decks away from the water's edge. Before you surround your pool deck with paving, think about how you will use the space and consider alternatives such as smaller, more intimate seating areas and more planting space near your pool.

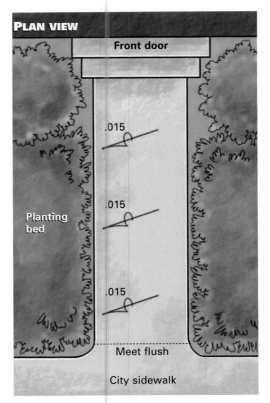

PLAN VIEW

Front door

.015

Planting bed

.015

.015

Meet flush

City sidewalk

Even walkways require a slight angle to move water away. Sheet drainage slopes the paving to one side to send runoff into existing beds.

Solutions for drainage problems

SWALES are small ditches that intercept the flow of water and redirect it around structures. Swales may be planted with grass or lined with concrete or drainage tiles. You can add flexible piping to continue the work of swales beneath features in your yard. Plan where the pipe will daylight—open an end onto the surface of the soil—so you can unobtrusively empty water elsewhere on your lawn. (It is illegal to alter drainage patterns to increase the flow of runoff onto adjacent properties.) The mat-like characteristic of lawns slows the water so it can be absorbed into the ground. Dumping runoff into planting beds can wash mulch away and drown plants.

Most swales are inconspicuous. If yours is unsightly, consider installing decking over it to hide it. Always include a trap door above pipe connections so you can remove debris that may obstruct the flow of water.

POSITIVE DRAINAGE

A finish grade should enable water to flow away from buildings and structures— positive drainage. Emphasize to anyone working on the property that you need positive drainage. This means that you expect paving and earth work to slope enough to move water away from structures and prevent standing water. Check the building codes in your area— many are very specific about foundation drainage, and you can specify the exact slope of the earth away from your house.

CATCH BASINS are underground collection devices. They hold water entering from surface drains and direct it through underground pipes to other destinations, most often storm sewer systems. It is important to set surface drains at the right elevation to capture water. Pipes must slope correctly to move water and connect to existing systems. Underground systems such as those using catch basins should be planned and installed before hardscape is constructed. A landscape architect or civil engineer can assist you with catch-basin design, if needed.

FRENCH DRAINS move water in a different manner. Perforated pipe set in a gravel bed can collect excess water and move it away from structures or boggy planting areas. French drains are easy to install yourself. It's a good idea to wrap pipes in filter fabric to keep soil particles from clogging the perforations. Use large, rinsed gravel to fill the trenches.

DETENTION AREAS are artificial depressions made to collect water and hold it temporarily until it can be absorbed into the soil. As concerns about water supplies increase, detention areas are becoming a

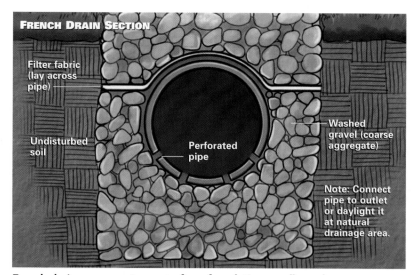

FRENCH DRAIN SECTION

Filter fabric (lay across pipe)

Undisturbed soil

Perforated pipe

Washed gravel (coarse aggregate)

Note: Connect pipe to outlet or daylight it at natural drainage area.

French drains move water away from foundations, walls, and over-wet planting beds.

popular means of handling runoff on site, instead of allowing it to enter storm sewer systems. This solution is ideal in geographic regions with high rainfall. Detention areas are ideal places to develop moist-soil (or even bog) gardens.

Trench drains are narrow, prefabricated devices that capture surface water and direct it elsewhere through underground pipes. Unlike catch basins, which resemble underground boxes, trench drains are linear. This makes them great for using at the base of steps or along swimming pool decks.

Drainage can be shown on the same plan as grading. Use small arrows to indicate the direction of flow. A landscape architect can help you design underground systems if your drainage cannot be handled on the surface.

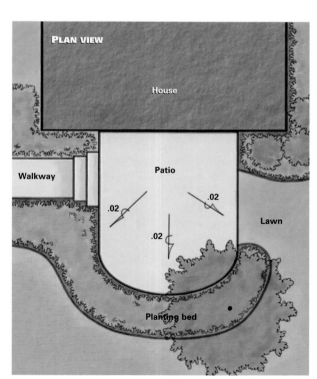

PLAN VIEW

House

Walkway

Patio

.02

.02

.02

Lawn

Planting bed

Sloping patios (as little as 2 percent) direct runoff toward beds and eliminate the need for a center drain.

PLANTS FOR MOIST PLACES

HERBACEOUS PERENNIALS
Bee balm (*Monarda didyma*)
Buttercup (*Ranunculus* spp.)
True forget-me-not (*Myosotis scorpioides*)
Canada lily (*Lilium canadense*)
Big blue lobelia (*Lobelia siphilitica*)

SHRUBS
Arrowwood (*Viburnum dentatum*)
Carolina allspice (*Calycanthus floridus*)
Red-osier dogwood (*Cornus sericea*)
Yellow-twig dogwood (*Cornus sericea* 'Flaviramea')
Inkberry (*Ilex glabra*)
Pink-shell azalea (*Rhododendron vasey*)

TREES
Birch, river (*Betula nigra*)
Bald cypress (*Taxodium distichum*)
Fringetree (*Chionanthus virginicus*)
American larch (*Larix laricina*)
London plane (*Platanus ×acerifolia*)
Red maple (*Acer rubrum*)
Swamp white oak (*Quercus bicolor*)

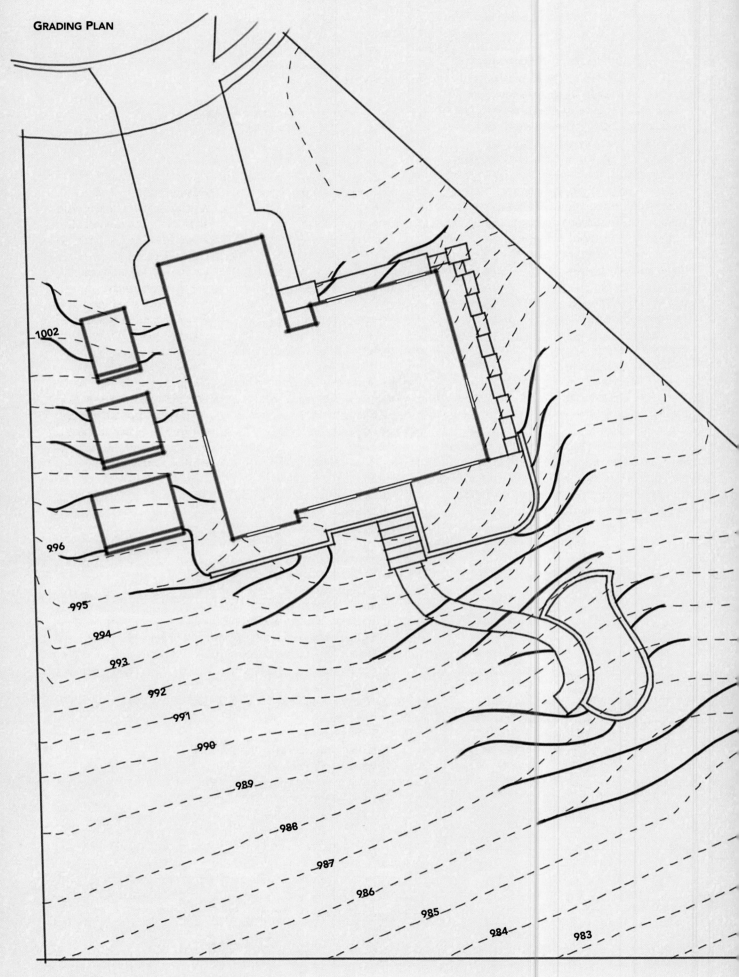

1002

996

995

994

993

992

991

990

989

988

987

986

985

984

983

Creating a Grading and Drainage Plan

A grading and drainage plan is a working drawing that shows how earth will be moved to incorporate your design ideas and to move water away from structures. Planning how you will shape the earth also helps you refine your design. If you have a steep site that needs retaining walls, steps, and earthwork to create level areas, you'll want to have a grading and drainage plan before the earth-moving equipment arrives.

Conceptual plan

If your site is fairly flat or level and grading is uncomplicated, prepare a conceptual grading and drainage plan instead of a detailed working drawing.

Place a tracing of your base map over your layout plan so you can trace new hardscape features. Make notes on this new plan, indicating which areas should be level and which areas you want to raise. Mark inclines, even very slight slopes, with arrows to show the direction storm water will flow. Make sure water is flowing away from all structures. Paved areas should be sloped to shed water.

Topography map

If you are solving tricky drainage problems or drastically changing the shape of your land, you'll need a detailed grading and drainage plan. Because it is more detailed than a conceptual plan, you will need to prepare a topography map first.

A topography map shows elevations on your existing terrain. For complex projects, hire a surveyor to shoot elevations and translate the existing form of the earth (refer to the illustration below). Ask if you can have only spot elevations measured or contours shot at 5-foot vertical intervals (instead of 1-foot intervals) to save costs. (The smaller the interval, the longer the survey will take to shoot.) You may need only a portion of the site shot to produce a grading plan that focuses on a specific area if the rest of the site will remain unaltered.

What the lines mean

On a topography map, the surface of the earth is shown in contour lines. Each line represents equal points of elevation. Contour lines are labeled with numbers to show their relationships to each other and to structures on site. The difference between numbers shows the changes in elevation. Contours that appear close together on a plan indicate a steep slope. Those that are far apart represent a level or gradually sloping area.

On a grading and drainage plan, dashed lines show existing contours. Solid lines show how the contours will change with grading. A plan as complex as the sample on the left would likely be drawn by a professional. If your plan is equally complex, it's probably a good idea to consult a landscape architect. Bring copies of your master plan and layout plan. They will be the basis for the more detailed working drawing your site requires.

WHEN TO COMMISSION A SURVEY

A topography map shows the existing surface of the earth. A grading and drainage plan shows existing topography as well as changes that will be made to the shape of the earth. A topography map prepared by a surveyor is necessary to produce a detailed grading plan and drainage plan. You won't need a topography map if grading and drainage changes are minimal. You can conceptualize your goals with arrows showing the flow of water and notes on where to add or remove small amounts of soil.

Choosing, Spacing, and Placing Your Plants

Choosing healthy plants that are suited to your climate and growing conditions is key to a beautiful landscape.

The right plants, spaced and placed properly, are the key to any great landscape. It won't pay to skimp on any part of this process. If you try to cut corners now, you'll pay twice—once to buy the plant originally and again when you have to replace it. Choose appropriate, healthy plants and plant them correctly, and you'll enjoy years of watching your landscape grow.

A GUIDE TO BUYING PLANTS

■ Avoid brittle or limp foliage as both are signs of distress.
■ Skip plants with withered new growth or puckered, discolored mature leaves—also indicators of stress or disease.
■ Healthy plants stand upright; their stems are strong and their roots hold them firmly in their pots. Plants with damaged roots will tilt or flop over, and you may be able to see their anchor roots partially exposed above the soil.
■ When buying trees or shrubs, avoid bark with splits, holes, scratches, cankers, and other damage.
■ Don't buy plants with broken branches or stems.

■ Look at the roots. Tip the plant out of the container (or check the root ball of shrubs or trees) to be sure the roots aren't tightly wound around the base of the plant. If they're tightly wound, the plant is root-bound and should be avoided.
■ Do not buy balled and burlapped plants with dry or broken root balls.
■ Plants sold bare-root should have healthy—not dried out—roots.
■ Plants should fit snugly in their containers. They shouldn't move up and down freely.
■ Buy only plants that are clearly identified.

Choosing the best plants

The process of selecting the best plants is threefold—choose the right plant for the right place, the right plant for your climate, and the best possible plant available.

As discussed in previous chapters, select the right plant for the right place. You now have an idea of what kind of plants you want and what the conditions are in certain areas of the yard, so you only have to match the plant to the space you've chosen. Pay attention to what plants will survive in what conditions. For instance, don't choose a plant that needs at least six hours of sun a day for a shady area. Read the tags on the plants or ask the nursery workers if you're not sure, but choose the right plant for the right space.

Don't try to force a plant to grow in a climate where it wasn't intended to grow. Exotic, tropical plants may grab your attention, but if they're not meant to grow in your climate, you're setting yourself up for failure. Choose plants that are native to your area and be sure they have been grown locally. Just because you can buy a plant at your local home improvement store doesn't mean you should.

Plants that are trucked in from other areas may already be suffering from climate shock, and the additional stress from replanting may do them in. Locally grown plants are already acclimated to your area, so they stand a much better chance of survival.

Take the time to choose good, healthy plants and buy the best possible plants you can for your money. Plan to spend some time looking for them—you may need to go to a few different sources to find everything you need.

Spacing

Pay attention to the planting instructions regarding the spacing of plants. For instance, if you're planting a line of shrubs and the instructions say to plant them at least 18 inches apart, make sure you plant them at least 18 inches apart. While the plants may look small now, they're going to grow. Crowding plants causes competition for sun, moisture, and nutrients in the soil, damaging the plants' ability to get all they need. Stagger plants in the planting bed to give the illusion of full coverage while giving the plants the room they need to grow.

Placing

Preparing the planting bed and following the planting instructions are equally important to a successful landscape. Follow the directions when getting the area ready to plant. If you need to dig a hole 1 foot deep to accommodate a certain tree, do it. Don't make it ½ foot deep and try to get away with it—doing so may expose roots that are too close to the soil surface, and the plant will suffer. Alternately, don't dig too deep if it's not warranted. Setting plants too low can cause them to drown. The instructions on the plants are there for a purpose—to help your plants survive and thrive.

Bed preparation

First, determine the size you want the planting beds to be, then measure and stake them before preparing the soil. When preparing the soil for the beds, use the traditional dig-and-till method.

Make sure you have good soil. A good soil for planting has topsoil that is several inches deep, is reasonably fertile, has a good balance of sand, silt, and clay particles, and the right amount of airspace between those particles to promote balanced drainage and water retention.

No matter what soil problems you start with—whether it's heavy clay that drains too slowly or light sandy soil that drains too quickly—the best thing you can do is to amend it by adding lots of organic matter. As matter decomposes, it creates humus—a soft, dark substance that improves drainage, structure, microbial activity, aeration, and other soil properties. Aged manure, ground bark, and straw are common organic amendments. Agricultural byproducts such as peanut hulls or ground corncobs are also excellent and inexpensive; check to see what is available in your area. A quick method of amending your soil is to purchase and import topsoil. If your topsoil is shallow, this may be the best solution.

Digging and tilling is a traditional option for preparing planting beds. Turning the

soil to the depth of a spade or fork (single digging) is simple but labor-intensive. First, clean off any debris from the planting area. Spread amendments and fertilizer. Then, with a shovel, spade, or fork, till them into the soil, turning the soil over to bury the weeds and grass. Dig one row at a time. Forks are effective in light soil; spades work best in clay or uncultivated soil.

To double dig a bed (see illustration page 210), dig a spade-deep trench about 2 feet wide and cart the soil to the far end of the bed. Now dig the trench another spade depth. If the soil at the bottom of the trench is reasonably good, loosen or turn it with a spade or garden fork to the full depth of the blade or tines, then mix in the amendments thoroughly. If the soil at the bottom is rocky or compacted, remove it, pick out rocks or roots, mix in amendments, and return it to the trench. Dig the next trench, but turn the topsoil into the previous trench—inverting the layers would bring poorer subsoil to the surface.

If your soil is reasonably fertile and free of rocks and tree roots, rototilling is easier. You can rent a walk-behind rotary tiller at many garden or rental shops. If the soil is hard or dry, it may be necessary to make several passes with the tiller. With each pass, till a couple of inches deeper than the one before. Make these successive passes at right angles to one another. Do corners by hand.

After tilling, use a cultivator to smooth the surface. If you need a seedbed with finely textured soil, use a garden rake.

Don't skimp on the width or depth of a hole when planting; roots need an amenable environment to get established.

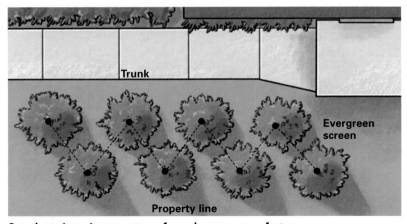

Set plants in a zigzag pattern for a denser screen faster.

Planting Trees

Take care transporting trees from the nursery; even a short ride, unprotected from wind and sun, can put a tree at risk.

The successful tree needs the right site and a healthy place for its roots. Roots grow outward and branch through the soil, absorbing water and nutrients. The reach of the root spread is usually well beyond that of its branches. New root growth is horizontal—in the top foot or two of soil. Roots need oxygen from the air, water and nutrients from the soil, and moderate temperatures.

Prepare the hole and place the tree

Plant trees first so you'll have room to maneuver without stepping on other plants. Prepare the planting hole before taking the plant to the site. Meanwhile, be sure the roots are kept moist.

For bare-root trees, first carefully prune roots of all broken, damaged, and straggling tips. Dig the planting hole wide enough to accommodate the spread of the roots. Make a mound of soil in the center of the hole to support the trunk at its nursery depth, and evenly spread the roots over it.

For balled-and-burlapped trees, dig the hole four times as wide as the root ball but no deeper at the center than the height of the ball to minimize settling. Loosening this large an area lets the roots spread to

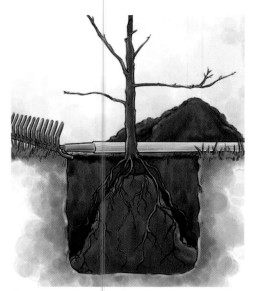

Plant a bare-root tree with roots fanned over a mound of soil and the top of the root ball just below ground level.

anchor the tree. Place the tree in the hole and untie and open the top of the burlap. Trim the excess burlap from the top of the ball and cut away any twine that was used to hold the burlap in place. If the ball is covered in anything but natural burlap, remove the covering completely before planting because it will not decompose.

Dig the hole for a container-grown tree the same size as you would for a balled-and-burlapped tree. Then remove the tree and loosen any roots that encircle the root ball. Hold the tree by the root ball—not the trunk—and lower it into the planting hole.

SOIL AMENDMENTS

Recent studies have shown that most trees establish themselves faster when no soil amendments are added at planting. A soil heavily amended with peat moss, fertilizer, or formulated soil mix becomes overly moist and fertile. Roots will tend to remain in this pocket instead of growing outward into the surrounding soil to anchor the tree.

There are, however, two exceptions. First, when the soil texture and drainage of the root ball differs markedly from that of its new surroundings, the planting hole may need amendments. A clay root ball

planted in sandy soil, for example, can act as an oasis and keep roots within its boundaries. On the other hand, a sandy root ball planted in slow-draining clay may become waterlogged and rot. In either situation, amend the soil in the planting hole with compost, peat moss, or well-rotted manure.

Second, because phosphates don't travel far when added later and watered in, it's a good idea to add superphosphate or bonemeal to the bottom half of the backfill.

Be sure the root ball top is no lower than ground level after settling.

Finishing up

Add fill soil around and over the roots of the plant, until the hole is about half full. Water gently to settle the soil and eliminate any air pockets. Let the water drain away, then fill the rest of the hole with soil. Form a ridge of soil around the edge to retain water. Fill this basin with water, let it drain, then fill it again.

Most trees benefit from a 2- to 4-inch-thick layer of mulch, at least 6 inches from the tree trunk, on the ground underneath their branches. Mulch insulates the ground and stabilizes the soil temperature. It conserves moisture by reducing evaporation from the soil surface and smothers weeds that compete for moisture. Mulch also reduces soil compaction and mechanical damage to trunks and roots by keeping lawn mowers at a distance.

WHEN TO PLANT AND TRANSPLANT

■In most parts of the country, early spring (while deciduous plants are still dormant and leafless) is the best time to plant any deciduous tree and the only time you should plant bare-root trees. Leafless trees draw less water and nutrients from the roots and recover more easily from transplant shock. For the same reason, balled-and-burlapped trees should be dug from the nursery when they're dormant in early spring, late fall, or even winter (if the ground isn't too frozen). They can usually be held in the nursery longer than bare-root trees and planted later in the spring or early summer with reasonable success. Container-grown trees, however, can be planted successfully nearly any time of year, although, cool, moist days are always best.

■Planting in the fall or winter is recommended in areas where summers are extreme and winters mild, such as the South (where summers are hot) and the West (where summers are dry).
■Trees with active late winter sap flow, such as birch and sugar maple, are risky choices for early spring planting. Wait until the sap flow ends, just as the leaf buds begin to unfold. For spring planting of fleshy-rooted trees such as magnolias, it is best to wait until the leaves have expanded slightly.
■Evergreens are best planted in early autumn, after summer heat is gone but early enough for full establishment before winter.
■Avoid hot, dry days when planting or transplanting any tree.

Place a balled-and-burlapped tree in the hole at the correct depth, then remove all twine or wire.

Pull back the edges of the natural burlap, trim off excess, then gently backfill the hole, being careful not to compact the soil. If the wrapping material is not 100-percent natural, remove it entirely from the root ball and hole.

After you backfill the hole, water thoroughly to settle the soil and get rid of air pockets. When the water drains away, fill the hole with remaining soil, make a ridge of soil around the hole to retain water, and water thoroughly once again.

Planting Shrubs

The secret to a shrub's health lies in the root system, which spreads deep and wide below the ground. These extensive roots allow established shrubs to contact moisture and nourishment beyond their immediate area of growth, where they may have competition from shallow-rooted ornamentals.

Rhododendron 'Trude Webster'

The hole

You can plant shrubs at almost any time, as long as you can work the soil with a spade. If possible, however, avoid planting shrubs in late spring, right before hot summer weather moves in, and late fall, when shrubs may not have time to establish themselves before the onset of frost. Dig the planting hole twice as wide and slightly shallower than the root ball, because plants often sink as they settle into the earth. The root mass should sit on stable, undisturbed soil. When the hole is deeper than the root ball, it creates a situation that can lead to crown and root rot.

The backfill soil

Many plants flourish in transition soil or backfill to which amendments such as compost or well-rotted manure have been added. Such organic materials help the soil hold moisture and micronutrients. Shrubs planted in amended soil tend to grow better at first than shrubs planted in native soil; however, recent research shows that shrubs often do better in the long run when planted in unamended soil, because their roots spread deeper and wider into the surrounding area. If you decide to amend the backfill, take soil from the planting soil, estimate its volume, and add either compost or rotted manure. Roughly no more than 25 percent of the final mix should be soil amendment.

Planting the shrub

Most small shrubs are sold in plastic containers. Before removing the shrub from its pot, dampen the rootball to help it stay intact. A shrub's root system may not recover from a broken or damaged root ball. Invert the pot, holding the top of the root ball, and gently tap the edge on a bench or other solid object. A simple shake may suffice, if the plant is not especially pot-bound.

With pruners or a sharp knife, make shallow vertical cuts along the side of the root ball, cutting any girdled, matted, or tangled roots so they radiate from the root ball. Matted roots do not extend into the surrounding soil.

Place the shrub in the hole and work the soil around the root ball with your hands to eliminate air pockets. Fill the hole with backfill to the level of the surrounding soil.

When planting a container shrub, dig a hole at least twice as wide as the rootball.

Remove shrub from container and loosen cramped roots by cutting through outside roots.

Place shrub in the hole, backfill, and build a shallow basin to retain water.

Water deeply to settle soil, add remaining soil, and water again.

Build a shallow basin around the shrub to concentrate irrigation water where it is needed most.

Thoroughly water the soil around the root zone. Apply the water slowly so it penetrates the root ball until the soil is loose and muddy. Gently work the soil to eliminate air pockets. Use the basin for watering until some roots have had a chance to expand into the surrounding soil (usually within six weeks). Be sure to break down the watering basin once the plant is established.

Planting balled-and-burlapped and bare-root shrubs

Handle the ball carefully, setting it in the hole with the wrap intact. Adjust the height of the root ball as you would with a shrub from a container. If the wrap is plastic or the burlap has been treated to retard rotting, remove it before planting. For natural burlapped shrubs, untie the material, pull it away from the top of the root ball, and remove the strings or wires. Cut the wrap back so that it is below the surface of the soil because exposed material wicks water out of the soil. Fill the hole and water the plant.

Bare-root shrubs, which are planted while dormant, are usually acquired by mail order in the spring. Pruning the bare roots by one-third or more results in a stronger shrub. Store bare-root shrubs in a cool place with their roots in moist sawdust or bark until ready for planting. Soak them in a bucket of water for several hours just before planting. Dig a hole large enough to accommodate the full span of the roots. Prune off broken or very long roots and plant the plant in the hole with the top root 1 inch below the level of the surrounding soil. Work the backfill soil between the roots with your hands to remove air pockets. Finish with filling the hole and water the plant.

Check containers for cleanliness, overall condition, and adequate drainage before putting plants in them.

Drainage: Every container must drain freely. If drainage is inadequate, water can collect, pooling on the surface and smothering the roots. This wetness can lead to crown or root rot and eventually kill the plant by preventing uptake of oxygen, and reducing root activity. Although most terra-cotta and plastic pots have drainage holes, pots made from other materials may have no drainage at all. The latter can be drilled: First cover the site of the proposed hole with masking tape, then drill the container at slow speed with a ¼-inch masonry bit.

Drill holes in the bottom of your container; your potted shrub needs to drain freely.

Prepare the soil: When possible, use a commercially prepared, lightweight, packaged soil mix. Commercial mixes provide excellent drainage for plants. If you're using garden soil, add soil amendments such as compost, peat moss, leaf mold, or shredded bark, along with perlite to lighten the mix and improve drainage. Typical proportions are one part garden soil, one part sand or perlite, and one part organic material. Before filling the container with the soil mixture, wet down the soil in a wheelbarrow to make it easier to handle.

Plant the shrub: Add several inches of soil mix—enough to hold the plant at the desired depth—to the planter, then add the shrub and fill the rest of the container with the mix, leaving 2 to 3 inches between the top of the soil and the

rim. This space holds water while it soaks through the soil to the bottom. Pour water on the plant until it runs out the drainage hole to make sure the plant is thoroughly watered. The water that flows through the drainage hole may contain nutrients from fertilizer applications and from the organic matter in the soil, so use a shallow drainage tray to catch excess water and keep it from staining the deck porch or patio. After planting you may wish to add a slow-release fertilizer such as Osmocote.

Plant bare-root shrubs so the top roots are at least 1 inch below the soil surface.

Creating Hedges

Shrubs are unique in that they can be grown close together to create a tightly packed hedgerow. Whether you want a hedge for privacy, a windscreen, or just looks, you can create a beautiful hedge with some simple pruning techniques.

How to batter a hedge

A formal hedge has batters, or sides, that slant outward from top to bottom. Besides looking good, this tapering allows sunlight to reach all the branches and stimulates new leaf growth, preventing lower branches from dying out. A 5-foot-tall hedge could have a base 2½ feet wide and a top 1 foot wide.

The easiest method for clipping an established hedge is to use the battered sides visible under the new growth as your guide. If you're starting to batter a hedge from scratch, create a simple wedge-shape template with three pieces of wood to define your chosen form. Don't take too much off the hedge the first time you form it—you don't want to take away all that growth you've worked so hard to achieve. If you want to further refine the shape, you can always go back and trim it again to a more desirable shape and size.

Use hedge clippers or a power trimmer to batter a formal hedge.

HOW TO MAKE A TOPIARY

To create a cone, pyramid, or obelisk, start with a naturally conical, finely textured evergreen shrub such as yew *(Taxus)* or boxwood *(Buxus).* For a pyramid, plant the shrub in its permanent location. Head the plant for a couple of growing seasons to make it bushy. In the second or third year, place a pyramidal, wire-mesh former over the shrub, making sure the former is level and upright. During the summer, cut off shoots that grow through the mesh. When the pyramid is full-grown, the mesh will be invisible.

Straight cuts can become an obsession of hedge lovers. Take the time to build and use your guidepost and string for a perfect cut every time.

How to make straight cuts

Build a wooded guidepost with a short perpendicular piece of wood at the top. Drive the post into the soil next to the hedge. Attach a weighted string (use a fishing weight or a small bag of sand) or a plumb line to the crosspiece. The string should hang a few inches above the ground. Use the vertical line to make straight vertical cuts. For a horizontal guide, site posts at either end of the hedgerow. Attach a string between the posts at the same height, pull the sting taut, and secure it to the post.

How to renovate an old hedge

If you have an old, overgrown hedge in your landscape, don't despair. Certain hedging shrubs such as yew, honeysuckle, holly, and boxwood can be renovated when too big. It may take a while, but you can bring that hedge back in line to fit your landscape plants.

To renovate, clip one side of the hedge back to the main stem or stems, cutting the other side to its usual proportions. Wait a year or two before hard pruning the remaining overgrown side. Prune evergreen shrubs in spring, deciduous shrubs late in winter.

THE PROPER TOOLS FOR PRUNING SHRUBS

The more you work with shrubs, the more you'll discover the value of good pruning tools. The best tools have steel blades that keep a sharp edge longer and are more comfortable to use than cheaper models. Although high-quality tools are more expensive, the additional cost is worthwhile because the best models have ergonomically designed handles.

It's essential to have handheld pruning shears that you can use for cutting stems up to ½ inch in diameter. A small folding saw is another useful item for pruning thicker branches. Loppers are long-handled pruners that provide extra leverage for cutting even stouter branches at the base of deciduous shrubs and thinning young branches on small, new trees. Flat hedge shears and electric hedge shears work best for creating a flat wall of foliage.

In a dense hedge, cut an intriguing peek-hole that offers an interesting view beyond.

Planting Vines and Climbers

If you select healthy plants that are appropriate to your zone and planting location, prepare your soil, and plant properly, you should have no problem establishing your vines and climbers.

Planting

Dig the planting hole as deep as the roots and at least twice as wide as the root spread. If you're planting under an established tree, dig the hole only as wide as the root spread.

For bare-root plants, build a mound of soil in the center of the hole, gently spread the roots over the mound, pack soil around the roots, and fill the hole with the remaining soil.

You don't need a mound for container-grown plants, but if their roots are tight and have begun to circle around the container, make a vertical cut in the center of the soil mass. Cut about a quarter of the way up; it will encourage the roots to grow straight.

Set the root ball in the hole to the same depth as it was planted in the container and fill the remainder of the hole with soil. Finish both kinds of planting with a 6- to 8-inch-high rim of soil at the edge of the root spread in order to direct water to the roots.

Once the plant is established, it may need help in growing toward its structure. Place a "nurse stake" between the vine and its structure; the vine will grow around the stake, then you can train it toward its structure.

Watering

Newly planted vines need daily watering for the first week. After that, and through the first year, water thoroughly whenever the soil feels dry to the touch. Watch for drooping leaves—this indicates severe stress. Touch the soil above the root area; if it's dry, water immediately. If it's wet, don't water; you may be watering too much or the plant may be injured.

Fertilizing

A slow-release organic fertilizer returns natural ingredients to the soil and insures a light but steady supply of ingredients as roots develop. Work it into the soil a week

Dig a hole twice as wide as your plant's root ball.

Plant to the same depth it grew in the pot.

If the plant is bare-root, spread roots over a mound of soil.

Gently insert a small stake to encourage vine to grow toward desired structure.

before planting, or sprinkle it and water it in. For faster action, a good general-purpose fertilizer for vines will have a 5-10-5 analysis (see page 61) on its label. If you're trying to encourage flowering, use a "tomato fertilizer" with low nitrogen. If your vines are growing healthily, you may not need to supplement with fertilizer. And if they're growing overly vigorously, fertilizer definitely is not required.

Controlling pests

Healthy, vigorous plants are more resistant to pests and diseases. It also helps to keep your garden area clean and weeded. If a plant is being attacked, first check the soil to see if it's too wet, too dry, or compacted. These conditions may be weakening the plant and making it vulnerable to pests. If you address the soil condition and your pest or disease problem continues, consult your garden center or the county extension office for the best remedy for the problem in your area. Inspect your plants regularly to catch problems early.

Tying climbers

Rambling roses and other climbers can't attach themselves to structures so they must be fastened or woven to supports such as lattice, steel arch, wrought iron, or string. Tie loosely or the vine's stem may become girdled as it grows and expands.

For solid surfaces such as walls, attach wire, twine, or string with fasteners. String or twine is easier to use, but wire is strong and long-lasting. It can hang horizontally or be made into a design. On wood walls, use a screw hook or eye. Special fasteners are sold for use on masonry walls and are either inserted into the wall or are attached with adhesive. Choose tying materials such as flexible gardening fabric, green twine, or "twisties" that will blend in and be hidden by the climber.

You can attach climbers to lattice with flexible fabric. Wire and fasteners are necessary for attaching to a wall.

GROWING VINES IN CONTAINERS

Plants growing in containers require more care than those in the ground; specifically, they need more watering and fertilizing because the container doesn't hold enough soil for proper moisture and nutrient support for the plant. The soil needs to be relatively light and to drain well. The container needs to be big enough to allow for long-term growth and must have holes in the bottom for drainage.

Fill the container with a commercial soil mix that's fortified with a small amount of slow-release fertilizer and moistened but not soggy. Plant the vine as described on page 204. If the support on which the vine will grow is going to be in the container itself, put it in at the time of planting. If the vine will be grown on a support outside the pot, use a nurse stake to make a temporary bridge from the pot to the support. Mulch will keep the weeds down and reduce the need for frequent watering.

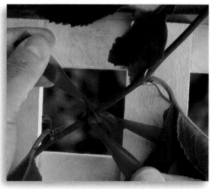

Planting Lawns

You can start a new lawn from seed, sod, sprigs, or plugs. Sod is best for lawns if you're in a hurry; seed is cheaper, less labor-intensive, and offers the greatest choice of turfgrass varieties. Sprigs and plugs—small tufts of established grasses—are the only choice for some turfgrasses. No matter how you plant, lawns won't grow unless the soil beneath them is reasonably healthy.

Soil preparation

Improving the soil for lawn growth is as important as it is for any other planting. Take time to test the soil, and be sure to specify that the test is for a lawn. Amend the soil as needed; if your soil doesn't need amending, broadcast a starter fertilizer over the area at the rate recommended on the fertilizer label.

If your soil is more than 60 percent clay or 70 percent sand, work in at least a 2-inch layer of organic matter or a 3-inch layer of topsoil that is high in organic matter.

Till to a depth of 6 inches, or for larger lawns, make one or two passes with a tractor-mounted disk. Then broadcast starter fertilizer and rake the surface smooth.

The soil will be soft after this procedure; rent a roller and fill it one-third to one-half with water and roll the soil. Don't wait long to plant after rolling.

If you are working in an area where an old, undesirable lawn must be removed, rent a sod-stripper—a machine about the size of a lawn mower—to take off the existing vegetation (consider hiring someone to complete this step). Expect to lose some of your topsoil along with the sod. Then prepare the soil as outlined.

Starting from seed

Calculate the amount of seed you will need to cover the space you've prepared. Use either a drop or broadcast spreader to sow the seed. Divide the recommended amount of seed into two equal portions. Sow the first portion across the lawn in rows, then sow the second portion in rows at right angles to the first until you have crisscrossed the whole lawn.

After seeding, ensure good contact between seed and soil by lightly raking the entire area. Then go over it with a water-filled roller. Don't rake too roughly. Doing so could redistribute the seed, ruin the final grade, and bury the seed too deeply.

Mulch after seeding to keep the soil moist and hasten germination. Use finely shredded compost or dried manure, topsoil, straw, or even a thin layer of sawdust. Apply the mulch no more than ½ inch thick and as evenly as possible.

You must thoroughly soak the soil to a 6-inch depth after sowing, then lightly water with a sprinkler as often as three to four times daily until the grass is established. Use a fine spray or nozzle with a mist setting to avoid washing away soil and seed.

Sod, sprigs, and plugs

Lay sod as soon as it's delivered so the roots won't dry out. Begin laying sod against a straight edge, such as a sidewalk or driveway. If you have an irregularly shaped lawn, create a straight line by drawing one on the soil with spray paint or by stringing a line across it. Carefully unroll a piece of sod and set it next to your straight line. Set each roll tightly against the previous one, staggering the end joints at each row. Roll a water-filled roller across it to ensure good contact between sod and soil. Water thoroughly after installation, then water daily, soaking the soil beneath for at least two weeks.

The fastest planting method for sprigs is broadcast sprigging. Strew them over the

If your lawn is thin but not too weedy and you're otherwise happy with the looks of your existing lawn, it's probably a good candidate for overseeding. This technique allows new grass plants to fill in bare patches.

This lawn was overseeded with a new variety of grass over the existing lawn to eliminate weak spots and bare patches.

soil by hand, then cover them with a light layer of soil and roll lightly with a water-filled roller.

For plugs, use a steel plugger to dig holes of the proper size in the soil, spacing them 6 to 12 inches apart, depending on the type of grass. To help the lawn take hold evenly, offset the rows of plugs in a checkerboard pattern.

Lightly moisten the soil and place the plugs in the holes. After planting, roll them as with sod and sprigs.

Water sprigs and plugs daily for the first two weeks after planting. It is vitally important to keep the soil between them free of weeds until they have filled in the lawn.

Overseeding

If your lawn is thin but not too weedy and the existing grass is attractive and healthy, you may not need to start a new lawn from scratch. Rather than replace the entire lawn, you can repair it by overseeding.

The success of overseeding depends on the seed contacting the soil. To ensure this happens, prepare the old lawn by mowing it as closely as possible. Rake up the clippings, then mow and rake

again. This helps expose the soil. Next, scratch the soil vigorously with a metal garden rake to rough it up and create a good seedbed.

Because you're not sowing into bare ground, you'll need to sow seed at two to three times the amount recommended on the seed package. After sowing, firm the seed into the soil with a weighted roller. Then cover the seed with a thin ¼- to ½-inch layer of topsoil or finely ground compost. Water daily until the seed germinates.

Mowing helps the new lawn fill in. When the new seedlings emerge, allow them to grow to maximum cutting height. Don't let the seedlings grow so tall that you're taking off more than one-third of their height.

When overplanting an existing lawn, evenly seed with a spreader at two to three times the amount recommended on the package of seed. You need more seed so it can find its way to the soil amidst existing grass.

To prepare for overseeding, scratch the soil vigorously with a metal rake to rough it up and create a good seedbed.

Planting Groundcovers

Early spring is an ideal time to plant most herbaceous groundcovers. The soil is easier to work then, especially in cold climates where the ground freezes in winter. And early spring planting allows the groundcovers to become established before the next winter arrives.Wait to plant in spring until any threat of a frost is past, the soil is fairly dry, and its temperature has reached at least 60°F.

Early fall is also another good time to plant, especially in areas where the soil is typically too wet to work in spring. Dormant woody shrubs can be planted in the winter if the soil isn't frozen. Avoid planting in summer unless you live in a mild climate. Heat and dry weather stress plants, making it difficult for them to become established. If you must plant groundcovers in summer, take care to keep them adequately watered.

Whichever season you plant, the groundcovers need plenty of time to become established before the onset of harsh, cold weather or extremely hot, dry weather.

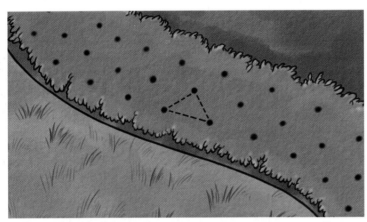

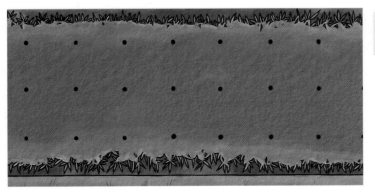

The two basic planting patterns—staggered spacing (top) and planting in rows (bottom)—make for fast, uniform ground coverage. Staggered spacing is best on slopes.

Laying out the bed

When planting a large area exclusively with groundcovers, it's a good idea to plant them in a uniform pattern for more attractive coverage. Plant with staggered spacing or rows (illustrated below), making sure that the plants are spaced at the distance specified on the plant label or by your garden center.

Container plants

Holes should be deep enough that the plant's crown is right at or just above the soil level and wide enough to allow room to work as you set the plants in the hole. An inch on all sides should be enough for plants in small pots. For groundcovers in 1- or 2-gallon containers, allow 2 inches on each side of the plant.

The hole for larger container plants should also be at a depth that keeps the top of the root ball at or slightly above the soil surface. If the container soil holds together, simply dig the hole and set the plant in place. If the soil around these larger plants breaks up, form the soil in the middle of the bottom of the hole into a cone. Set the plant on this cone of soil and spread out its roots.

Handle plants with care when removing them from containers. Squeeze or press the bottom of the pot to push the plant out; do not pull by the stem.

Carefully tease the outer roots of the root ball by hand or with a gently spray of water. If the root ball is tightly matted, lightly massage it to loosen the roots. Place the plant in the hole and spread the roots in the hole. Refill the hole with soil and pack it firmly around the plant—but not so tightly that the soil becomes compacted.

Balled-and-burlapped groundcovers

Dig the hole for balled-and-burlapped plants as you would for container grown plants. Leave natural burlap around the root ball—it will decompose in the soil—but loosen it slightly to give the roots some room. If the covering is made from plastic or coated burlap, remove it completely before placing the plant in the hole.

Remove any twine that was binding the burlap—it can strangle roots and stems.

Place the plant in the hole, so the uppermost roots sit at or just above the soil surface. Refill the hole with soil and pack it firmly around the plant.

Bare-root groundcovers

Dig a hole deep enough that the topmost roots will sit at or above the soil line. The hole should be as wide as the roots' spread. Taper the soil in the hole to form a cone and spread the roots over the cone. Set the plant upright in the hole, then scoop backfill soil around its roots, tamping lightly to pack the soil around them.

Planting on slopes

You'll want to modify a steep slope so water reaches plant roots and does not run off. To do this, create a basin around each plant, much as you do when planting a tree. Instead of building the basin around each groundcover plant, though, simply mound soil higher on the downhill side the catch the water as it runs down the hill. You can also terrace the slope or install retaining walls made from lumber or cross ties.

After care

When all plants are in place, water the area gently and thoroughly so it settles the soil and seeps into the root zone. Then mulch the bed to secure the soil and retain moisture. Mulching is especially important on slopes because it helps prevent soil from eroding as plants establish.

Groundcovers need plenty of moisture to get them off to a good start and alleviate transplanting stress. Water plants at least weekly for the first three to four weeks after planting, or whenever they show signs of wilting. Once they are established, most groundcovers can be irrigated less frequently.

Groundcover plants are sold as seedlings in flats, bare-root, and potted in containers of all sizes.

Choose robust, healthy-looking plants, such as the one on the left, for the best chance of success in the landscape; puny, less vigorous plants, like the one on the right, will struggle to become established.

Young plants placed in a staggered pattern are the best bet for quick, even coverage.

Planting Beds and Borders

Placement and planting go hand in hand—they are the keys to a healthy and handsome garden. Before you plant, consider the relative vigor and ultimate size of each plant. In a well-filled border, neighboring plants barely touch; they weave a tapestry that looks unbroken but allows air to freely circulate. To create a more generous look, start young plants close and move them as they mature. You may find it useful to stake the location of your plants before setting them in.

Prepare the soil

Good garden soil is a balance of drainage and retention; it allows air and water to pass freely, yet retains enough nutrients to support active plant growth. Most soil needs to be loosened to prepare for planting because it's dense or compacted. Plants grow best in beds of loose soil to 18 inches deep, but you only need to dig as deep as necessary to break up compaction according to the condition of your soil. Soil is loose enough when you can easily dig in it. If you have to hack at it with a pickax or a shovel, it needs to be broken up. You can do it by hand or with a tiller.

To loosen by hand, use a spade or spading fork. Single-dig to loosen well-drained loam (see instructions left). Double-dig to break up densely packed soil or when significant soil amendment is required (see instructions below, right.)

To dig a bed, use a spade or spading fork to loosen the top 8 to 10 inches if the soil is loamy, drains well, and there's no compacted layer within the top 18 inches of soil. Loosen the soil by inserting the fork to its full depth, then pulling back on the handle to lever the tines. You can compost any sod stripped from the area.

Tillers are useful for loosening topsoil or deeply mixing in amendments. Rear-tine, self-propelled tillers are the easiest to operate.

Double digging is a labor-intensive but very thorough method of digging a bed deeply. Dig a 9-inch-deep trench across the bed, stockpiling soil on a tarp. With a fork, loosen the trench bottom to 9 inches deep; top with compost. Dig a second trench, tossing its soil into the first. Loosen, add compost, and continue to the end of the bed. Fill the last trench with the soil you set aside. Rake to the level of the soil; soil will settle but will be higher than before.

STAKING

Even if you've selected sturdy, self-supporting plants, some of them will need unobtrusive staking to stand tall. Where heavy summer rains are common, staking will prevent or minimize the collapse of prized blooms. In exposed, windy gardens, many plants will be better off with staking. There are dozens of ways to keep plants upright, from simple webs of sticks and string to expensive hoops and linking systems. The goal is always the same: effective but nearly invisible supports. Install them in early spring, long before the need is obvious.

One simple approach is to drive a bamboo pole or rebar into the ground. Use a stake a foot longer than the expected stem height; place it 5 or 6 inches out from the plant crown to avoid damaging roots. Sink it a foot into the ground. Secure the stem to the stake with string, fabric, or a plant tie, tying every 12 to 18 inches of new growth. Another method requires grow-through supports that are positioned over a plant while it is young; stems and leaves grow through it, hiding the support.

Above: Grow-through supports can be positioned over young plants; stems and leaves will grow right into it, hiding the support.

Left: Traditional staking calls for tying a single-stem plant to a pole with string, soft fabric, or a plant tie.

Loosen with a rototiller when you have large, mostly weed-free areas to prepare. Avoid overtilling or working in wet soil. Soil cut too much by tilling loses its substance. Tilling time is also an opportune chance to add amendments to the soil. Before manual turning or tilling, spread a 2- to 3-inch layer of your material over the area. Then mix it to the depth that is being loosened. Compost, composted pine bark, and gypsum are excellent additives because bits of clay and sand attach themselves to the additive, making airy little crumbs of soil that help prevent compaction.

Planting

Wait a few days before planting your new purchases—especially annual and perennial seedlings—which are often fresh from a steam greenhouse. Put them in a protected location in the garden for a few days so they can become accustomed to the "real world." This process, called hardening off, is an important step to remember, especially in spring.

When your plants are ready to move into the garden, avoid transplanting when it's warm and sunny. Cool, overcast weather gives tender transplants a better start because it inflicts less stress on the plants.

Planting Beds and Borders
(continued)

If your soil quality is poor, consider building a raised bed. As little as 4 inches of rich soil will support many kinds of plants. Mound soil slightly so water will drain toward the sides. Frame beds with material appropriate to the shape of your bed in order to contain the soil.

To plant, dig a hole slightly larger than the root ball of the seedling. Loosen the roots a bit with your hand and place the plant in the hole at the same depth it was growing in the nursery pot. Backfill with an improved soil mix and tamp down thoroughly to eliminate air pockets in the soil. Then use a watering can or a garden hose to soak the area around the plant. Moisture is vital during and after transplanting, so water every day for the first week or two until the plants become established.

For bare-root plants, fill the hole halfway, making a conical mound in the center. Loosen the roots with your fingers, cut off any dead, damaged, or diseased roots, and fan them over the mound. Sprinkle soil over them and firm it with your hands, making sure the crown stays at soil level. If your plant has a taproot, a single long root, you won't need to make as big a hole or mound. Use a trowel to make a narrow hole as deep as the root,

plant it with its crown at soil level, and tamp the soil firmly.

After you plant and water, mulch the bed with several inches of shredded bark, pine needles, or compost. This will eliminate weed competition and maintain soil moisture.

Feeding

Plants, especially annuals and roses, need to be fed during the growing season. If you've added compost and/or rotted manure in early spring, you probably don't have to begin feeding your plants until early summer. You can choose from either liquid or dry plant foods. Time-release dry fertilizers can be sprinkled around the base of your plants where they will provide a slow but steady supply of nutrients over the course of the summer. Liquid fertilizers are a good choice for plants that need a quick boost of energy. You can apply liquid fertilizers in two ways: by mixing them into the water when you irrigate or by spraying them directly onto the leaves of your plants. This process, called foliar feeding, is probably the fastest way to see results.

Grooming

Grooming is a constant chore, but the more often performed, the lighter the task. Removing spent flowers and damaged or browning foliage daily or weekly keeps the garden pleasantly tidy and the gardener aware of the garden's subtle changes. There are four grooming practices for perennials, two of which should be performed on annuals as well.

Thinning (perennials) involves spring removal at ground level of some of the stems of bushy plants. Thinning lets the light in and the air circulate and helps prevent mildew.

Pinching (perennials and annuals) at the tips of stems makes leggy plants more compact because side branches with new blooms will grow where you've pinched it back. Begin in late spring or early summer, pinching back a third of the stems by two-thirds of their length about every week or so.

Disbudding (perennials)—or pinching out smaller buds—will give plants such as peonies and roses larger blooms.

Deadheading (perennials and annuals) involves removing faded flowers, which prevents seed from setting. The plant will attempt to set seed with new blossoms and you will have fresh crops of buds all summer. In general, cut the flower stems back to the next set of leaves; that's where the side shoots and buds are waiting to make new blooms.

Remove spent blossoms to prolong the blooming season.

Index

Note: Page references in *italic type* refer to photographs, illustrations, and information in captions.

Ortho Complete Guide to Landscaping
Editor: Michael McKinley
Contributing Editor: Veronica Lorson Fowler
Photo Researcher: Harijs Priekulis
Copy Chief: Terri Fredrickson
Publishing Operations Manager: Karen Schirm
Edit and Design Production Coordinator: Mary Lee Gavin
Editorial and Design Assistants: Kathleen Stevens,
  Kairee Windsor
Marketing Product Managers: Aparna Pande, Isaac Petersen,
  Gina Rickert, Stephen Rogers, Brent Wiersma,
  Tyler Woods
Book Production Managers: Pam Kvitne,
  Marjorie J. Schenkelberg, Rick von Holdt, Mark Weaver
Contributing Copy Editor: Jane Schorer Meisner
Contributing Proofreaders: Thomas E. Blackett, Kim Catanzarite
Contributing Map Illustrator: Jana Fothergill
Indexer: Ellen Davenport

Additional Editorial Contributions from
  Lark Productions
Designers: Oxygen Design
Photo Editor: Ilene Bellovin
Editorial: Rachel Cagney, Karen Watts, Lisa DiMona,
  Robin Dellabough

Meredith® Books
Executive Director, Editorial: Gregory H. Kayko
Executive Director, Design: Matt Strelecki
Executive Editor/Group Manager: Benjamin W. Allen
Senior Associate Design Director: Tom Wegner

Publisher and Editor in Chief: James D. Blume
Editorial Director: Linda Raglan Cunningham
Executive Director, Marketing: Jeffrey B. Myers
Executive Director, New Business Development:
  Todd M. Davis
Executive Director, Sales: Ken Zagor
Director, Operations: George A. Susral
Director, Production: Douglas M. Johnston
Business Director: Jim Leonard

Vice President and General Manager: Douglas J. Guendel

Meredith Publishing Group
President: Jack Griffin
Senior Vice President: Bob Mate

Meredith Corporation
Chairman and Chief Executive Officer: William T. Kerr
President and Chief Operating Officer: Stephen M. Lacy

In Memoriam: E.T. Meredith III (1933–2003)

Note to the Readers: Due to differing conditions, tools,
and individual skills, Meredith Corporation assumes no
responsibility for any damages, injuries suffered, or losses
incurred as a result of following the information published
in this book. Before beginning any project, review the
instructions carefully, and if any doubts or questions remain,
consult local experts or authorities. Because codes and
regulations vary greatly, you always should check with
authorities to ensure that your project complies with all
applicable local codes and regulations. Always read and
observe all of the safety precautions provided by
manufacturers of any tools, equipment, or supplies,
and follow all accepted safety procedures.

All of us at Meredith® Books are dedicated to providing
you with the information and ideas you need to enhance
your home and garden. We welcome your comments and
suggestions about this book. Write to us at:
  Meredith Corporation
  Meredith Gardening Books
  1716 Locust St.
  Des Moines, IA 50309–3023

Thanks to: Janet Anderson, Staci Bailey, Brenda
Witherspoon

Photographers
(Photographers credited may retain copyright ©
to the listed photographs.)
L = Left, R = Right, C = Center, B = Bottom, T = Top
John Bertrand/Positive Images: 137B; **Richard Bloom/Bloom
Pictures:** 8B, 8T, 48B, 62, 63B; **Patricia Bruno/Positive Images:**
2B, 2C, 52T, 139R, 159T,197T; **Gay Bumgarner/Positive Images:** 5,
12B, 21T, 42T, 43B, 46B, 49BL, 49TR, 76TL, 84R, 88B, 89B, 94, 96T,
98, 138B, 146T, 169B, 182B; **Philip Busey:** 147B; **Karen Bussolini/
Positive Images:** 51T, 90T, 130B; **Robert Cardillo:** 209C; **Walter
Chandoha:** 85L; **Jennifer Cheung/Getty Images:** 12T; **Crandall &
Crandall:** 205CL, 206; **Todd Davis:** 122T; **Catriona Tudor Erler:**
163C; **Peter Estersohn/Getty:** 95T; **Derek Fell:** 87T; **Fernlea.com:**
97T; **Charles M. Fitch:** 131BR; **Jean Fogle:** 120B, 121TL, 121B,
122B, 135B, 136B, 156B, 157, 167TL, 168BL, 168BR, 171T, 172T,
176BL, 180T, 181TL, 181B, 184TR, 185B,; **John Glover:** 9T, 14B, 17T,
19T, 44, 64T, 87B, 102TR, 173T, 176TR, 176BR; **John Glover/
Positive Images:** 15T, 17T, 18T, 18B, 19B, 20B, 20T, 25, 41, 42B, 45,
52B, 74B, 91, 99B, 103L, 104BL, 115L, 123T, 135T, 170T, 177T; **David
Goldberg:** 58B, 58T, 199R, 204T, 204TC, 204B, 205BL, 205BR, 205T,
211R, 211L, 213; **Jeff Greenburg/AgeFotostock:** 13B; **Peter
Gridley/Getty Images:** 3C, 10B; **Tom Grill/AgeFotostock:** 1;
Darrell Gulin/Getty Images: 23B; **Harry Haralambou/Positive
Images:** 71B, 96B; **Jerry Harpur:** 133T; **Meredith Hebden/
Positive Images:** 155TR; **Margaret Hensel/Positive Images:** 55L,
69T, 90BR, 185T; **Jerry Howard/ Positive Images:** 22BL, 40, 47T,
49TL, 50, 68T, 70, 72T, 82L, 84TL, 86B, 100, 115R,128BL, 168T,
176TC; **Irene Jeruss/Positive Images:** 121C; **Susan Jones/
AgeFotostock:** 48T; **Larry Kassal:** 149L; **Scott Leonhart/Positive
Images:** 121TR; **David Liebman:** 152B; **Lee Lockwood/Positive
Images:** 126CR; **Allen Mandell:** 101B; **Charles Mann:** 148T, 148CL;
Ivan Massar/Positive Images: 133T; **Bryan McCay:** 6T, 7T, 26B,
26T, 27, 30B, 30T, 31BL, 31BR, 31T, 32T, 33BL, 33BR, 35T, 36T, 37B,
37T, 65B, 65T, 191T, 198, 205CR, 207BL, 207BR; **Allison Miksch/
Brand X/Getty Images:** 2T, 64B; **Steven Nikkila:** 210T; **Maggie
Oster:** 207T; **Jerry Pavia:** 131BL; **Barbara Peacock/Getty:** 3B;
Diane Pratt/Positive Images: 126B, 144B, 158B; **Anne Reilly/
Positive Images:** 127BC, 153B, 154B; **Graham Rice/
GardenPhotos:** 22BR, 117B, 118B, 138T, 145C, 172C, 176BC, 181TR;
John Rizzo/Getty Images: 55LC; **Susan A. Roth:** 150; **Eric
Salmon:** 188, 189T, 189BR, 189BL; **Jeremy Samuelson/ Getty
Images:** 11, 134; **Richard Shiell:** 85BR; **Ann/Rob Simpson:** 155TL;
Evan Sklar/Getty Images: 3T, 14T; **Evan Sklar/Positive Images:**
15B; **Pam Spaulding/Positive Images:** 104BR, 107B, 131T, 141R,
156T, 158T, 162; **Albert Squillace/Positive Images:** 105T, 163T,
166C,; **Steve Struse:** 209T, 209B; **Peter Symcox/Positive Images:**
73; **Thinkstock/Getty:** 23C; **Nancy Trueworthy/Positive Images:**
93T; **judywhite/GardenPhotos:** 4, 9B, 10T, 13T, 16, 21B, 22TL,
22TR, 23T, 24L, 24R, 43T, 43C, 46T, 47B, 49CR, 51B, 51C, 53B, 53T,
55CR, 55R, 59, 60, 68B, 69B, 71T, 72B, 74T, 76BL, 77R, 78T, 78B, 79,
80, 81B, 81T, 82R, 86T, 88T, 89T, 90BL, 92T, 92B, 93B, 95C, 95B,
97B, 99T, 101T, 102TL, 102B, 103R, 104T, 105B, 106T, 106B, 110,
112, 113, 114, 116B, 116T, 117TL, 117TR, 117C, 118TL, 118TR,
119TR, 119TL, 120T, 123B, 124, 125, 126T, 126LC, 126C, 127TL,
127BR, 127TR, 127BL, 128TL, 128TR, 128BR, 129T, 129B, 130T, 132T,
132B, 136T, 137T, 139L, 140T, 140B, 141L, 142, 143B, 143T, 144T,
145B, 145T, 146B, 147T, 149T, 148BL, 153T, 153C, 154L, 154B,
155BR, 155BL, 159B, 166TL, 166B, 167TR, 167BL, 167BR, 169T,
169TC, 169BC, 170B, 171B, 172B, 173B, 176TL, 177CL, 177CR, 177B,
180B, 181CL, 182T, 183T, 183BC, 183BL, 183BR, 184TL, 184BL, 187T,
187BL, 187BR, 191B, 197T.

If you would like to purchase any of our gardening,
home improvement, cooking, crafts, or home
decorating and design books, check wherever
quality books are sold.
Or visit us at: meredithbooks.com

If you would like more information on other Ortho
products, call 800/225-2883 or visit us at:
www.ortho.com

Scotts
Sprinklers
& Watering Systems
Complete

ORTHO'S All About Building
Waterfalls,
Pools, and Streams
■ Complete guide to building materials and construction techniques
■ Thorough advice on choosing and installing the equipment
■ Ideas and plans for the ultimate water feature

ORTHO BOOKS

THE COMPLETE
Perennials
BOOK

ORTHO

...WING ■ HOW-TO ■ GARDEN DESIGNS

Miracle-Gro
Beautiful
GARDENS
MADE EASY
39 quick projects
Simple Techniques to Make Your Home Sensational
By Elvin McDonald
Foreword and tips by Peter Strauss

Scotts
Lawns
YOUR GUIDE TO A BEAUTIFUL YARD
by NICK CHRISTIANS
with Ashton Ritchie

Get dramatic results

Pick up these exciting titles from the brands you trust
for gardening expertise—wherever books are sold.